Bangkok

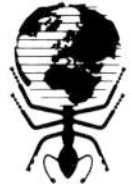

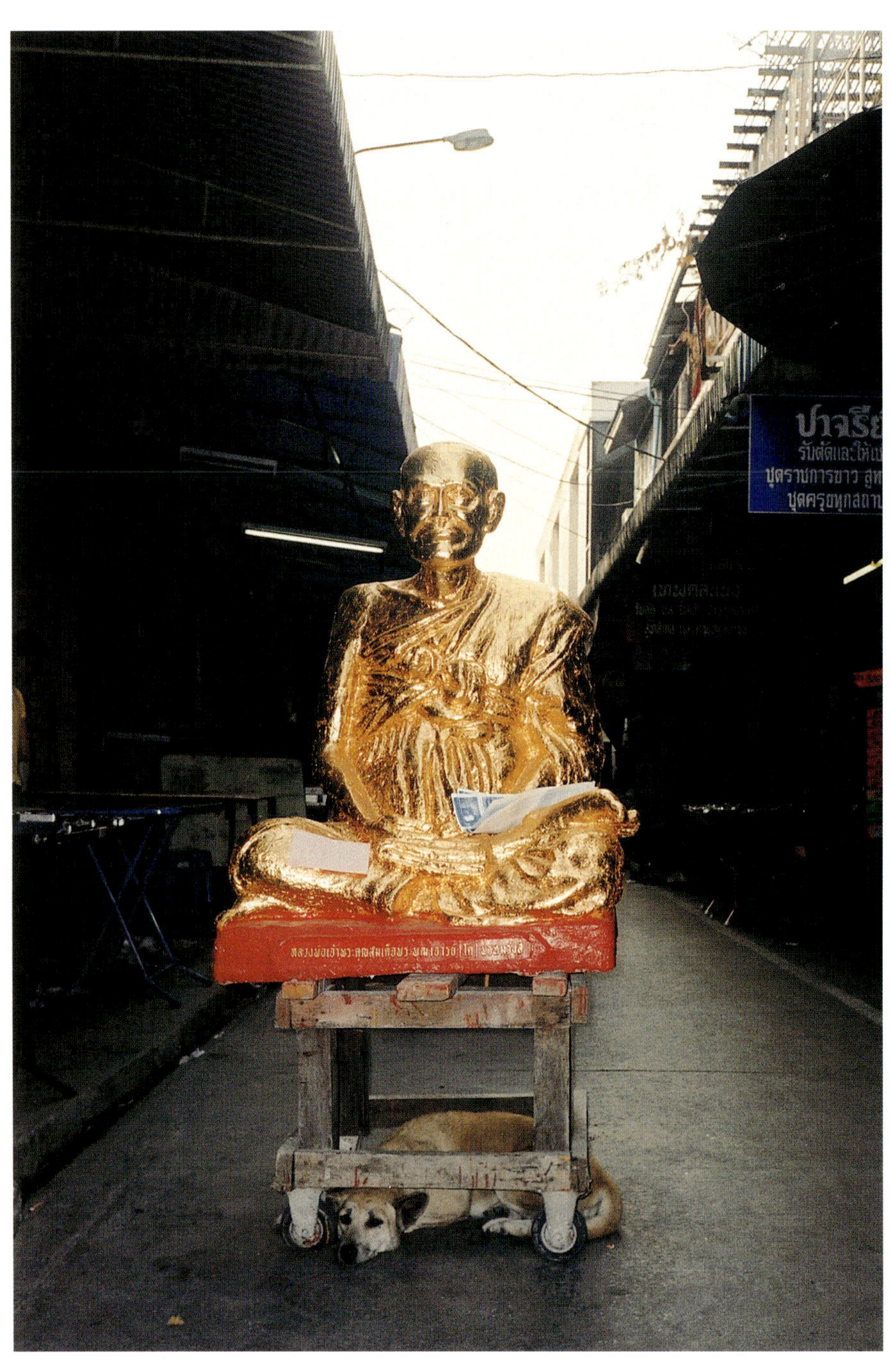

ปาจรีย์
รับตัดและให้เช่า
ชุดราชการขาว สูท
ชุดครุฑทุกสถาน
หลวงพ่อเข้าพระคุณสมเด็จพระพุฒาจารย์ (โต) พรหมรังสี

Bangkok

Angelic Allusions

Barry Bell

REAKTION BOOKS

Published by Reaktion Books Ltd
79 Farringdon Road
London EC1M 3JU, UK

www.reaktionbooks.co.uk

First published 2003

Printed in China

British Library Cataloging in Publication Data

Bell, Barry
     Bangkok: angelic allusions
     1. Bangkok (Thailand) – Pictorial works
     I. Title
     959.3'00222

ISBN 1 86189 157 1

Contents

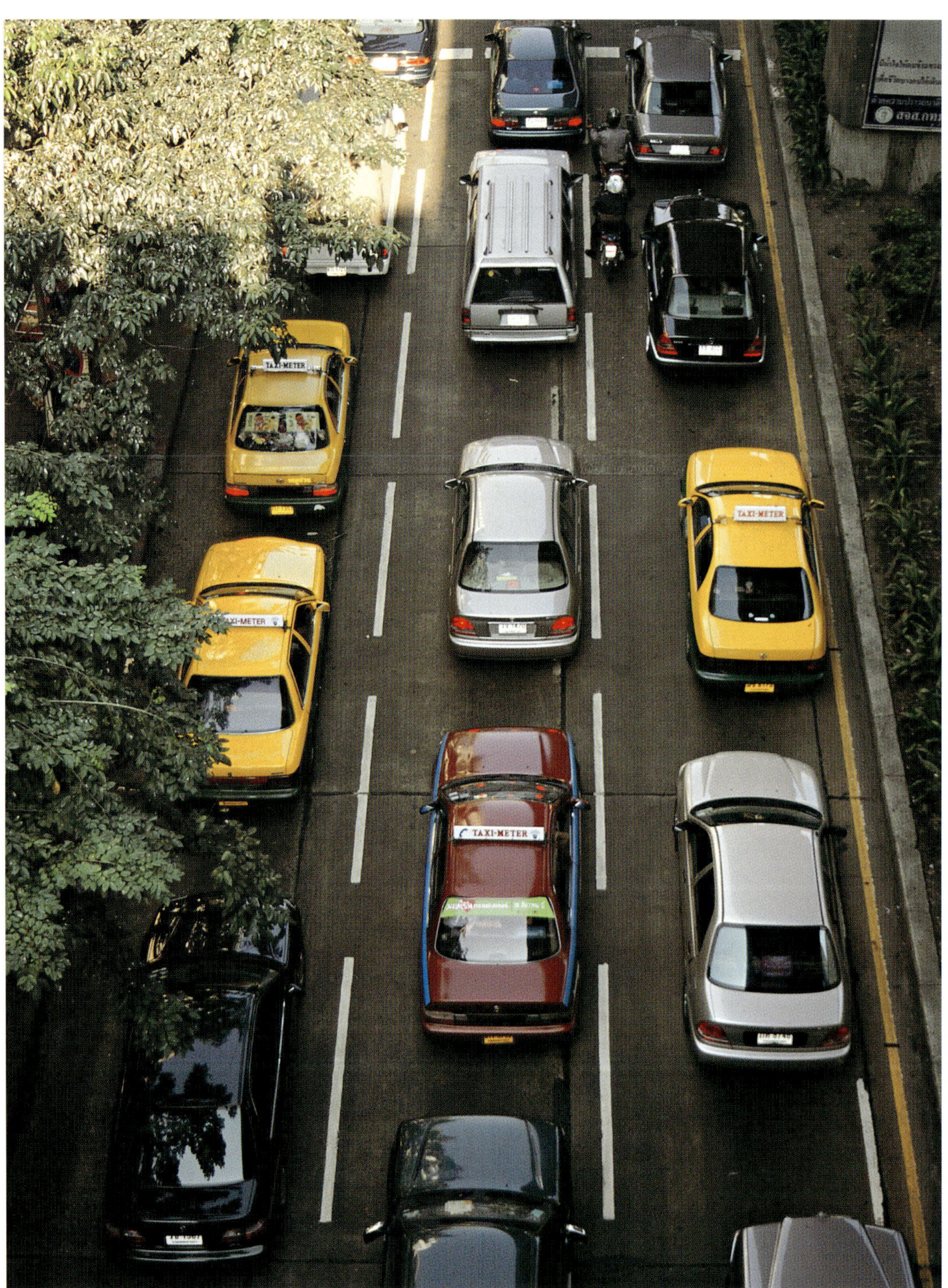

ONE

Bangkok: Formless City?

PART ONE

*A chaotic city: formless, disorganized
and polluted. A city without order.
A city with moments of remarkable beauty
and social vitality. A setting to challenge the
search for urban coherence, and the
understanding of the city in general.*

Formless City?

Traffic. Traffic at speed. Traffic stopped. Exhaust spilling out in dense clouds, obscuring the relentless sun. Machines of all kinds, fighting for space. Traffic; crazy traffic. A flat landscape crisscrossed with roads, lacking a natural topography sufficiently robust to interrupt the vehicular flow. Yet the shortest path between two points is rarely straight. One-way streets are set in perplexing geometries. They extend distance, exponentially multiplying the volume of traffic and exacerbating its effects.

First impressions of Bangkok are coloured by its traffic, exaggerating the immediate perceptions of density and confusion. The lengthy route from the airport crosses a featureless landscape of low industrial buildings and residential blocks. Distance passes in a surreal blur. Racing (or stalled) along roads of all scales, the journey is composed of a veritable taxonomy of driving possibilities. Raised highways randomly traverse the terrain, carving the land into sunken and oddly configured fragments of edge city. Clusters of tall buildings, possible centred moments in a centre-less range, are seemingly discarded in the barren wastes and pass with a limited sense of geographic purpose. All is lost in the horizontal sprawl. Roads at grade, smaller in scale and more local in quality, gradually divert the oozing stream towards invisible neighbourhoods and

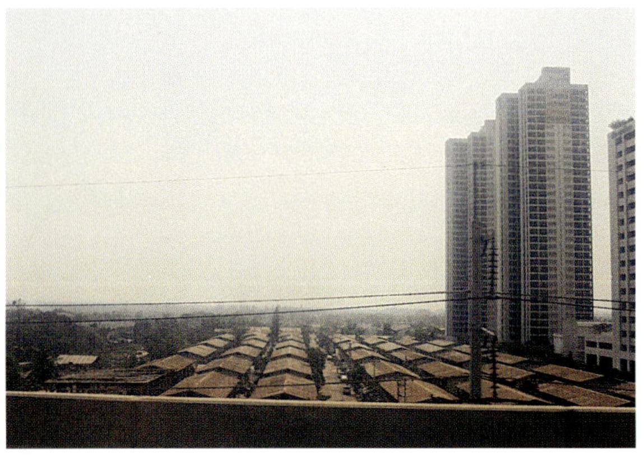

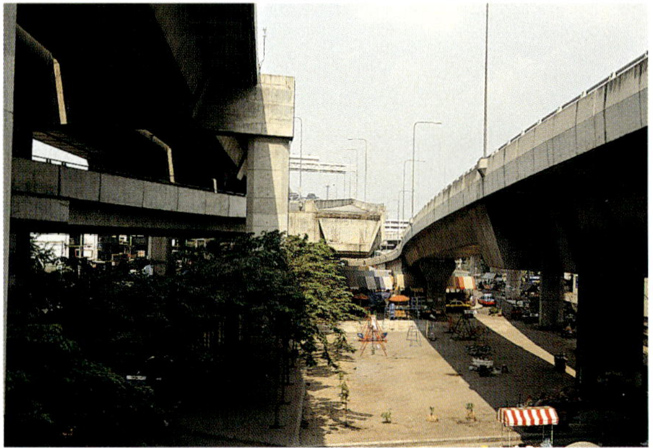

obscure destinations. Home to approximately twelve million people, one quarter of Thailand's population, Bangkok gradually appears as a curious mirage, viewed through the filter of its traffic.

Within the city, on grand avenues and more humble streets, all is mechanized motion. The pedestrian is the anomaly – pushed away, unwanted. Sanam Luang, the National Parade Ground fronting the Grand Palace, identifies Bangkok's symbolic heart. Place of festivals, royal coronations and funerals, it is the city's pre-eminent piece of public terrain. Yet the tour buses have taken over, diminishing any relaxed appreciation of the space and its adjoining buildings. Great hulking objects,

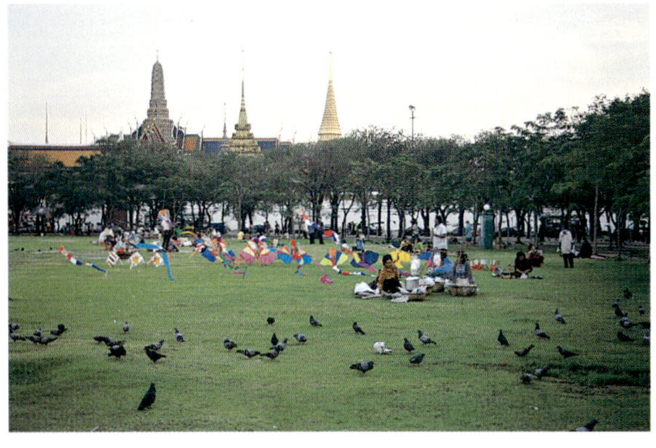

engines running even when parked to preserve their sacred air-conditioning, they subvert the public realm in favour of an interior world of cool plastic and insulated travel.

The National Museum, housing a significant collection of historic sculptures, and the National Gallery, dedicated to more recent Thai paintings and touring exhibitions, are both key figures within this royal ceremonial zone. The distance between them is perhaps 300 metres; a short stroll between major destinations. Yet to traverse this distance is a foolish, if heroic, undertaking, for it requires crossing the Phrapinklao Bridge Road. The patient suffer a pointless wait for a safe break in the relentless flow of traffic; the brave offer their lives in a mad dash through the multiple lanes of charging vehicles. In the urban battle between machine and pedestrian, Bangkok's cars have emerged clearly victorious. But it is a Pyrrhic victory. The sheer numbers of congested cars disqualify any efficient movement.

Studies on Bangkok's traffic have estimated its dire impact on the city's social, economic and human health. Excessive carbon monoxide levels cause stunted growth, learning disabilities and reduced life expectancy in young children. Time lost in traffic

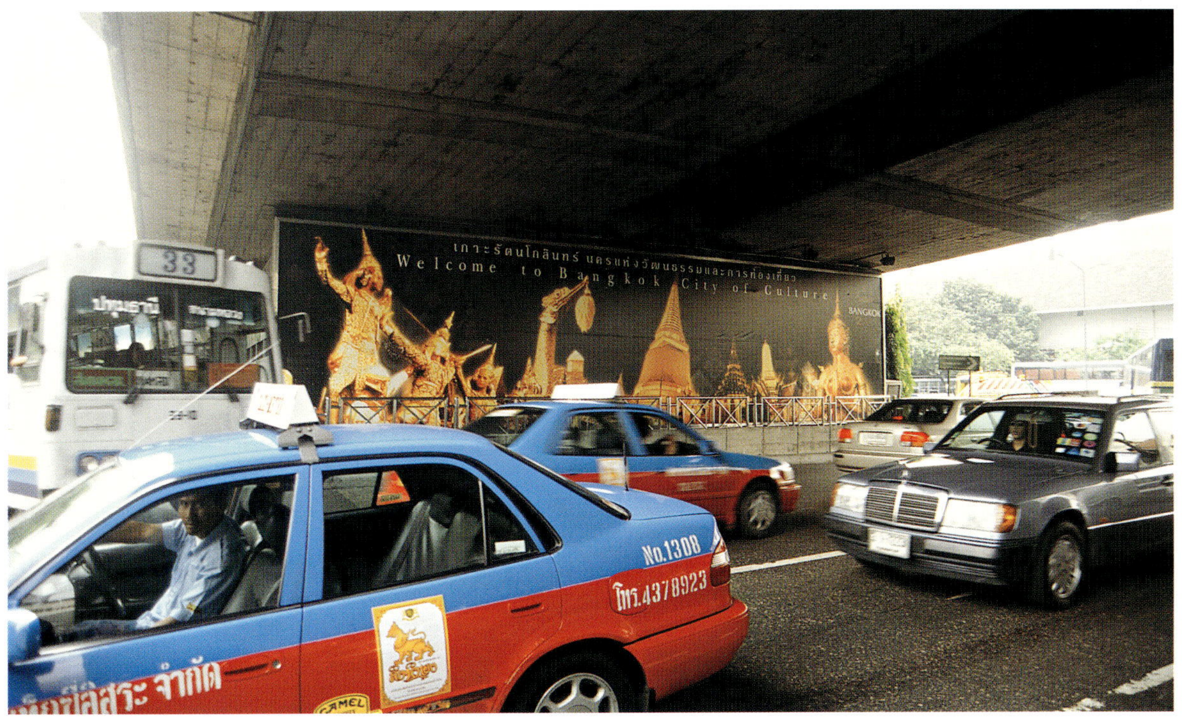

costs the economy a large portion of its efficiency, just as an inability to circulate threatens business development and foreign investment. Frustrations with accessibility hinder tourism, diminishing a major source of foreign income. Rather than securely representing Thailand as its iconic cultural focus, Bangkok risks becoming a temporary port of call for the southern beaches and northern hills, those 'real' Thailands less impinged on by modern life.

Traffic City

Not surprisingly, this traffic is emblematic of Bangkok's greater reality. Seemingly chaotic, the city is messy, noisy and hot. It lacks perceptible order. Indeed Bangkok's assault on urban assumptions is relentless. Part of its challenge lies in the unfulfilled expectations of centre and grounding. While a taste for centralized form may be a historic and cultural bias, founded on the experience of the post-Renaissance European city, its absence here is especially provocative. A place of multiple centres, Bangkok doesn't present any singular focus. Its fabric flows freely, dispersed amongst a myriad of special moments and distinct activities. This lack of an accepted centre is paralleled with a remarkable temporal variety. A young city, Bangkok expresses its short history through a wild spectrum of building types and styles, all intermingled with little regard for historical hierarchy. The city is a dedicated consumer of architectural fads and fashions, and their combined effect, while visually energetic, does little to form any coherent stylistic order. Bangkok is not a Florence or a Prague, presenting and protecting

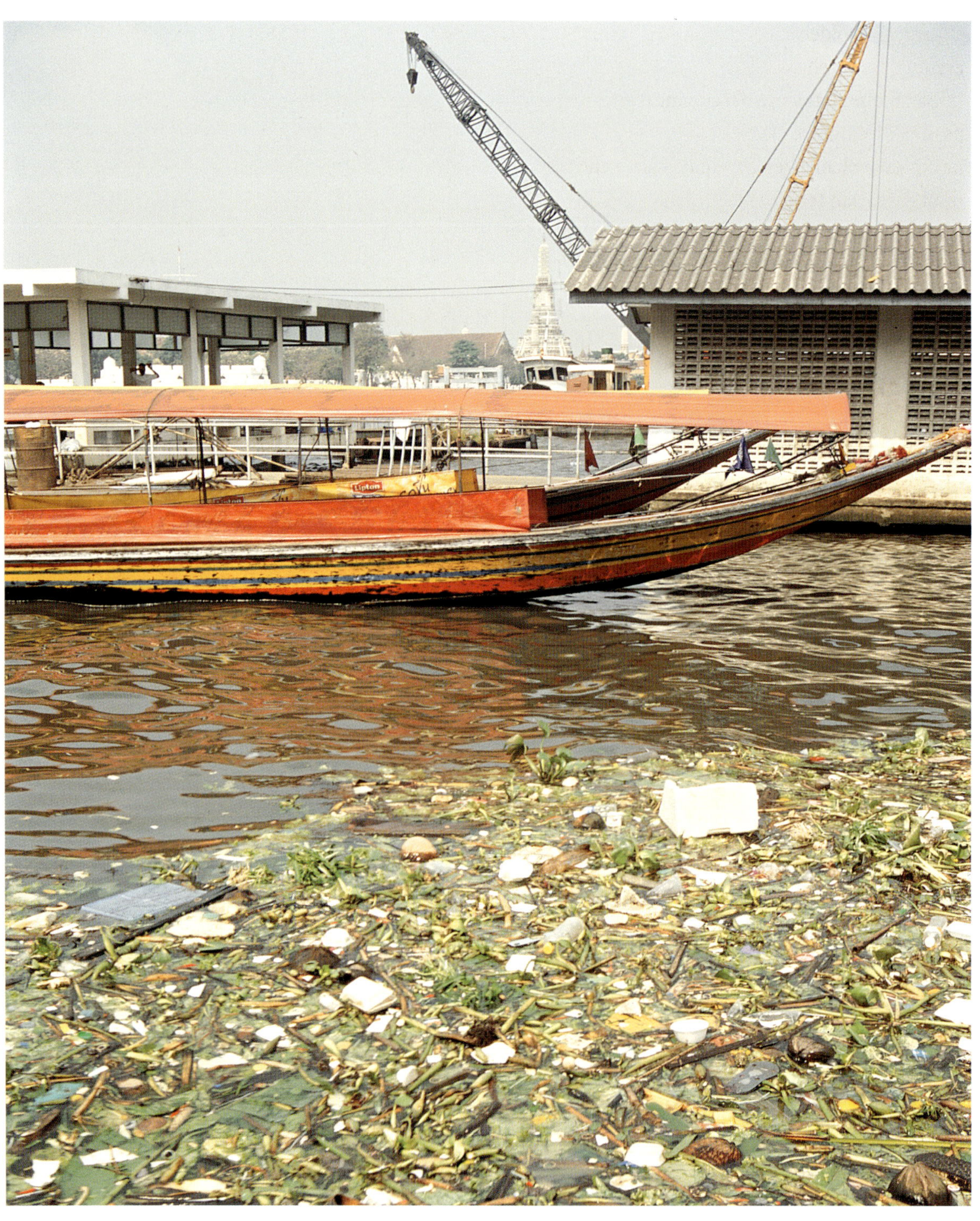

a privileged golden artistic age for reflection and eventual comprehension.

Bangkok's status as a developing city, in the passionate embrace of modernity, creates further interpretive challenges. Its rapid growth and resulting urban transformation, manifest through generic forms of international development, crowd out the few remaining indigenous survivors. The city of traditional experience has arguably been sacrificed to an abstraction of macro-economic planning, collapsing on itself through the manifest desire for a brave new future. This dedication to progress, deemed valuable for its own sake, has left behind a strange and denatured landscape. Bangkok's legendary canals are polluted; the water table has been damaged by excessive building; and the air is often toxic. Subject to regular flooding, the land is further corrupted with the casual accumulation of garbage. Bangkok's very hold on physical stability is fragile.

The city's modest topography doesn't help. With the exception of the Chao Phraya River, Bangkok does not have any significant natural features. Nature does not assist to define its form, or to maintain an indigenous image in the face of sprawling development. In Hong Kong or Rio de Janeiro one can squint away the more squalid aspects of the modern world to appreciate the striking settings still present beneath. Bangkok's landscape is more visually reticent. The city's image, such as it is, is entirely of its own making: a creation of mysteriously directed or casual artifice alone. Its cryptic rules of self-generation have created a remarkable state: a city seemingly without form, nor bothered by its absence. Architectural and urban design appear to be circumstantial at best, a condition

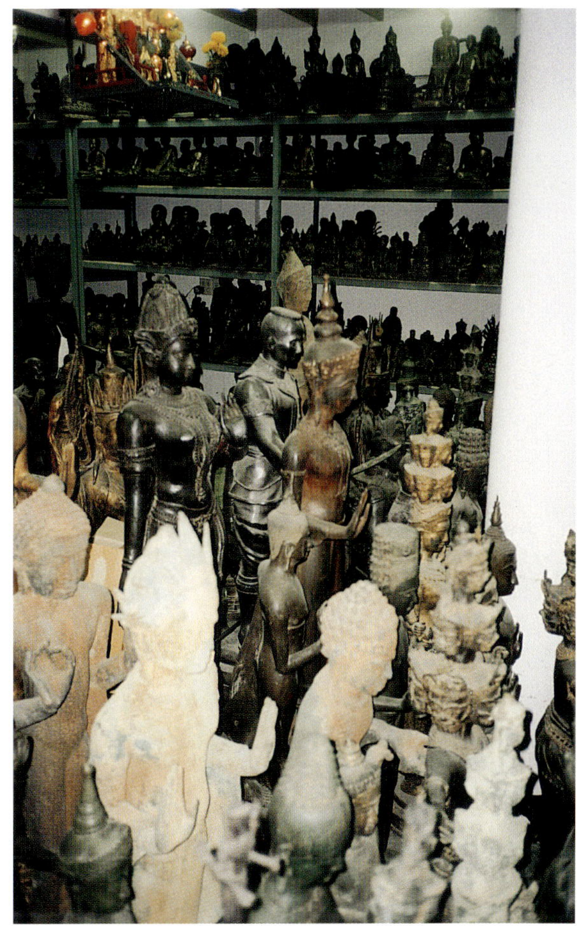

that challenges any significant interpretation of urban form whatsoever.

A negative reaction to these conditions has led many to reject Bangkok as a lost cause, a rapidly self-destructing urban mistake. Its form is confusing; its patterns of use perplexing. The city's effects, both physically and mentally, are dangerous. It is a place in which to lose one's wits.

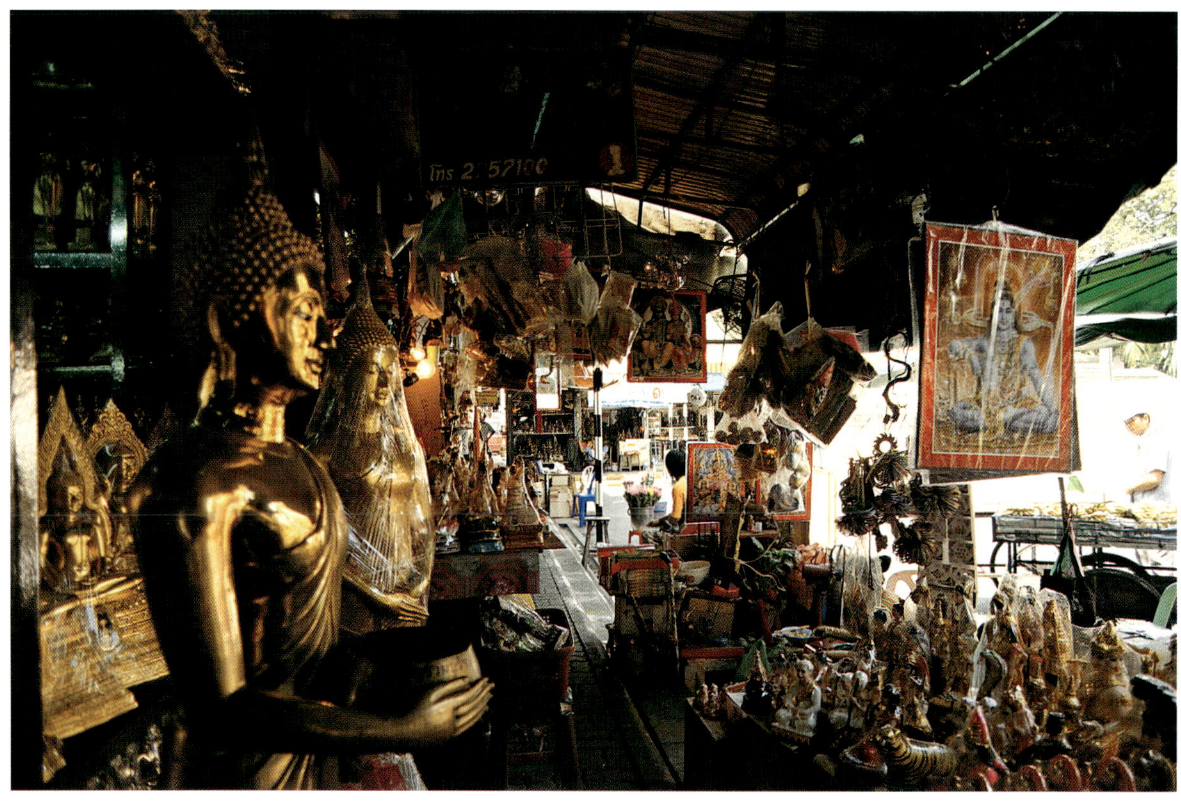

City of Beauty

And yet. In the midst of these disreputable conditions Bangkok presents moments of striking beauty and social vitality. Young saffron-clad monks clamber on to river ferries, dispensing colour, calm and barely hidden youthful mirth in their wake. The celebration of daily prayer is so essential as to appear casual. The shy smiles of uniformed school-girls paying respect to their teachers; brilliant temple roofs, flickering in the day, to be transformed to a warm glow by the setting sun. Spirit houses animate secular streets with mysterious colour and form, the miniature temples housing unnamed domestic guardians. Unsuspecting trees become shrines through the application of multicoloured garlands and flowers. The Wat Phra Kaeo at night, floating above its darkened grounds, as an ethereal vision. Bangkok is a city of exquisite food, manners and fashions, housing its beautiful people and their idiosyncratic creations in a perplexing urban setting.

Such expressive beauty, remarkable as it is, instils further confusion. How can a tolerance for urban blight coexist with a taste for luxury and experiential indulgence? Without such revelatory moments it would be easy to dismiss Bangkok as yet another casualty to rapid development conjoined with relative poverty. Yet the value of heightened

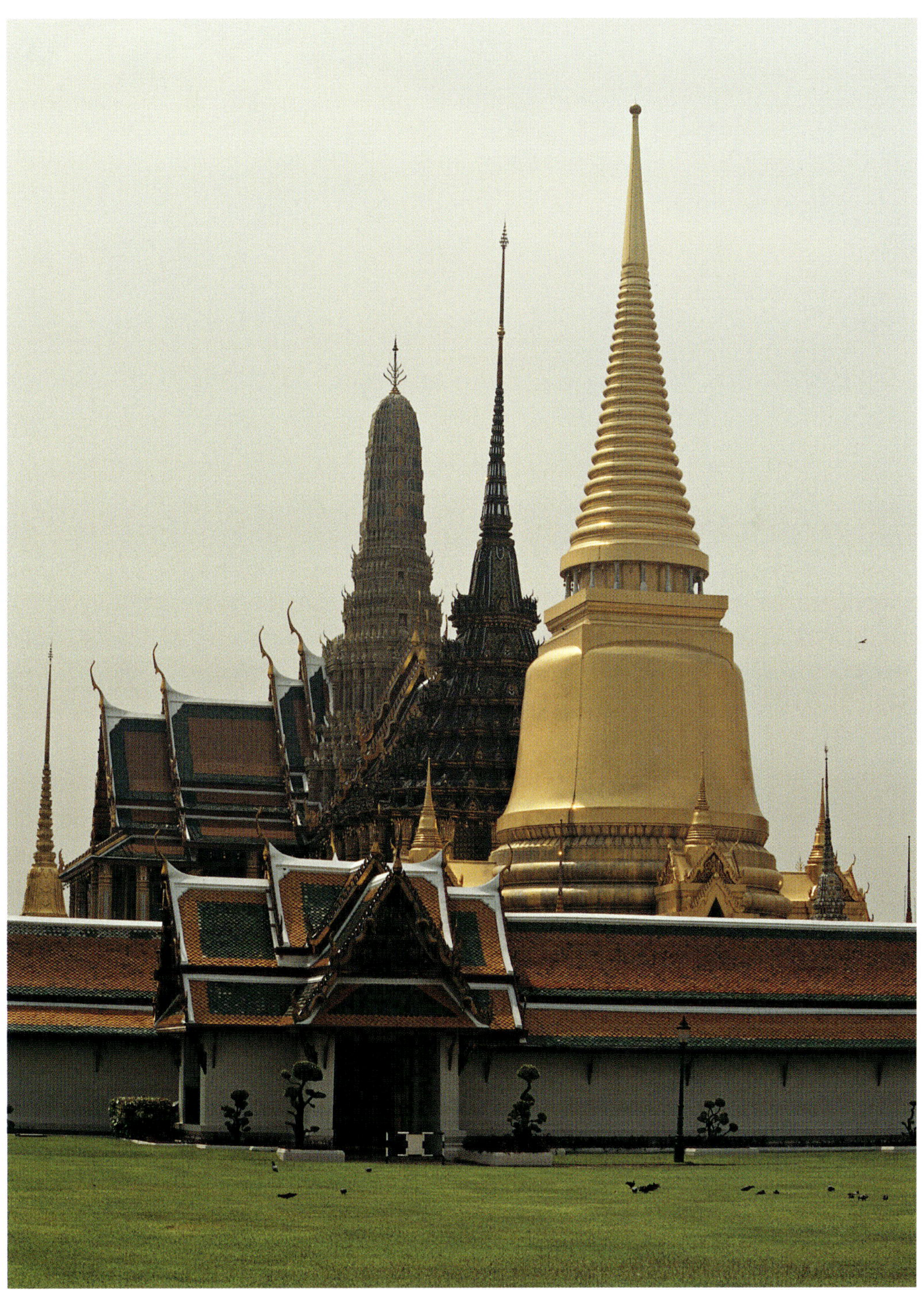

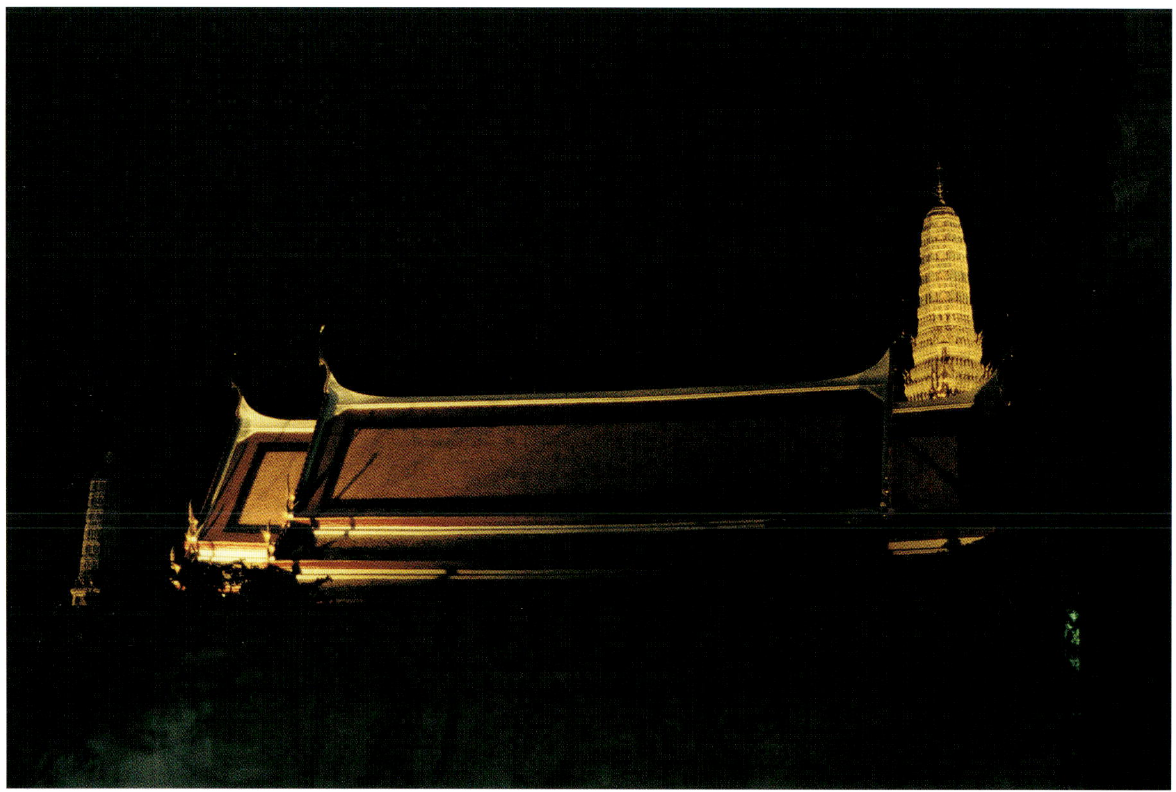

experience, manifest in so many aspects of Bangkok's daily life, does not allow for such easy assumptions. Its reality is far more perplexing.

What kind of city is this, and what is its urban purpose? How can this apparent civic duality of simultaneous charm and disrepair be acceptable? Are there forms of differently configured urban order that exist independently from this dialectical conundrum? What is the bonding spirit of the place?

Traffic? In Bangkok one alternates between the frustrations of daily travel and the mad, life-threatening exhilaration of a high-speed tuk-tuk ride at night. Hair flows, crazy in the wind, neon blurred. Despair of the chaotic or exult in its crazy freedom? The manic-depressive nature of contemporary urban life is here rendered extreme. The challenge of Bangkok is the challenge of the city today.

A city like all the rest; a city like no other?

Distinct history, self-conscious creation.

A city caught between.

Why Bangkok? Every City or Fallen Angel?

The dynamic collisions of growth and tradition (or good food amid civic disorder) are hardly limited to Bangkok. Fragments of beauty within urban chaos may be discovered almost anywhere. The sunlight filtered and reflected by the saffron clouds of Old Delhi's spice markets, just a short distance from the lepers begging outside. The glint of gold beneath the melted crimson wax of Katmandu's altars; the sunset on the Bosphorus. The world's developing cities, with their intense contrasts of poverty and wealth, proud histories and current, often envious malaise, create surprising moments of visual delight (and pathos). Visual, social and cultural frictions, generally submerged within the more sedate environments of Europe or North America, here flourish. In this respect Bangkok, manifesting the realities of rapid development, urban crowding and historic mis-management overlaying a rich artistic and cultural heritage, may be considered as one member of a global club. It is the perfect developing city, exemplary of similar conditions faced elsewhere. Like the others, it faces the challenges of modernization and globalization while attempting to maintain its own indigenous culture.

More specifically, Bangkok may represent a South-East Asia confronted by the West. Local culture, with its semi-tropical flora and the trappings of imported modernity, juxtapose to create intriguing and occasionally shocking panoramas. Heavily scented gardens rest aside air-conditioned office buildings, BMWs parked next to small markets serving idiosyncratic food. Collisions of temples and commerce. The crowded, ubiquitous McDonald'ses, jazz bars in Bali, French cafés in Phnom Penh: the 'mysterious East' is conjoined with the modern West in curious ways. Indigenous moments appear in visual fragments and fleeting sensations, hidden under illusions of familiarity. Bangkok presents a striking version of this state. Dense and sensual while so outwardly international, it remembers an idealized Asia, mysteriously present within its contemporary disguise.

A City In Between?

But Bangkok is also different. In spite of its many parallels with international others, Bangkok presents an intriguing and distinct reality. Its particularities exempt it from the generalized historical readings that often summarize the region or the developing city in general. It has a provocative individuality.

Bangkok is unique in its region as a non-colonial capital. Thailand's nineteenth- and early twentieth-century political history was circumscribed by its buffer status between the British (Burma, Malaysia) and French Indochina (Laos, Cambodia and Vietnam). While the Portuguese, Dutch and Japanese were locally influential at times, the two major Western powers posed the greatest threat to Siam's independence. Both sought greater influence within the kingdom, occasionally attempted outright control, and were otherwise occupied in challenging its borders. Yet ultimately the 'green zone' of Thailand served both colonial powers well, keeping their fractious forces at a safe distance. Bangkok maintained this geographic balance through careful diplomacy, and thus avoided being subjected to any foreign overlord, an accomplishment that no other regional power could match. Also striking, especially with regards to the French efforts, was the lack of success achieved by Western missionaries. The Jesuits, in particular, were unable to convert more than a handful of Thais to Christianity, a fact that perplexed Western commentators throughout the period. An urban footnote perhaps, though clearly significant to Bangkok's cultural and political survival.

Thailand was born amid previous East–West challenges. Struggles with the Burmese of Pagan and the Khmers of Angkor, both more established empires, defined its earlier history. Centuries of negotiating between, and adapting to, the changing fortunes of these two major nations cultured the gradual development of a Thai sensibility. It was one always aware of (and occasionally subject to) the power of its larger neighbours. Siam's survival depended on a careful balancing of these external forces, a principle that remains active in its dominant city. Bangkok, like its country, is used to being in-between.

Bangkok maintains limited historical links to place, or at least to its own place. The city was created in 1782 as a refuge from the Burmese destruction of Ayutthaya, the former capital to the north. Ayutthaya itself was a late power, appearing after the flowering of Sukhothai, arguably the first real Thai capital. Unlike cities based on sacred foundations, in singular and blessed landscapes (Rome, Athens), Bangkok is a city remade, a city on the move. It manifests an attitude of flexible and sequential creation rather than any fixed relationship to a historic location.

With its cultural and historic foundations elsewhere, Bangkok places limited value on its terrain. The physical earth maintains modest significance in the city's self-definition. Bangkok rests between the mountains and the sea, between a murky history and an uncertain future. A city built on water, its only explicit founding mythology derives from the northern forest. the *Ramakien*, a Thai transposition of an ancient Indian epic, the *Ramayana*, tells of the God / hero Rama's struggles to cleanse the world from demons. He battles on the earth and in the sky, within the forested mountains. Yet Rama's name is borrowed by the ruling Chakri dynasty, the founders of the aqueous city, as the honorific title for their kings. Rama's city, Ayodhya, is referenced in Ayutthaya, the Thai city to the north that provided Bangkok's predecessor and model.

Bangkok was the capital of a Buddhist kingdom, and Bangkok's royal structures reference mythical Hindu foundations. These Brahmanic traditions appear in royal rituals, are carved on temple reliefs and painted on temple walls. They percolate within Bangkok's literary foundations to celebrate the relation between Thai royalty and its Indic foundations. Yet the city's countless temples and the majority of its population are reverently Buddhist, dedicated to the rejection of earthly seduction.

Both Hinduism and Buddhism originated in India, reaching Thailand via a lengthy voyage through South-East Asia, most notably Sri Lanka (Ceylon). With its water-based neighbours to the south, such as Bali and Java, Thailand forms part of a transformed Indic diaspora. Yet ethnographically the 'Tai' people descended from southern China, initiating a pattern of north–south migration often to be repeated. Artistic influences from China are

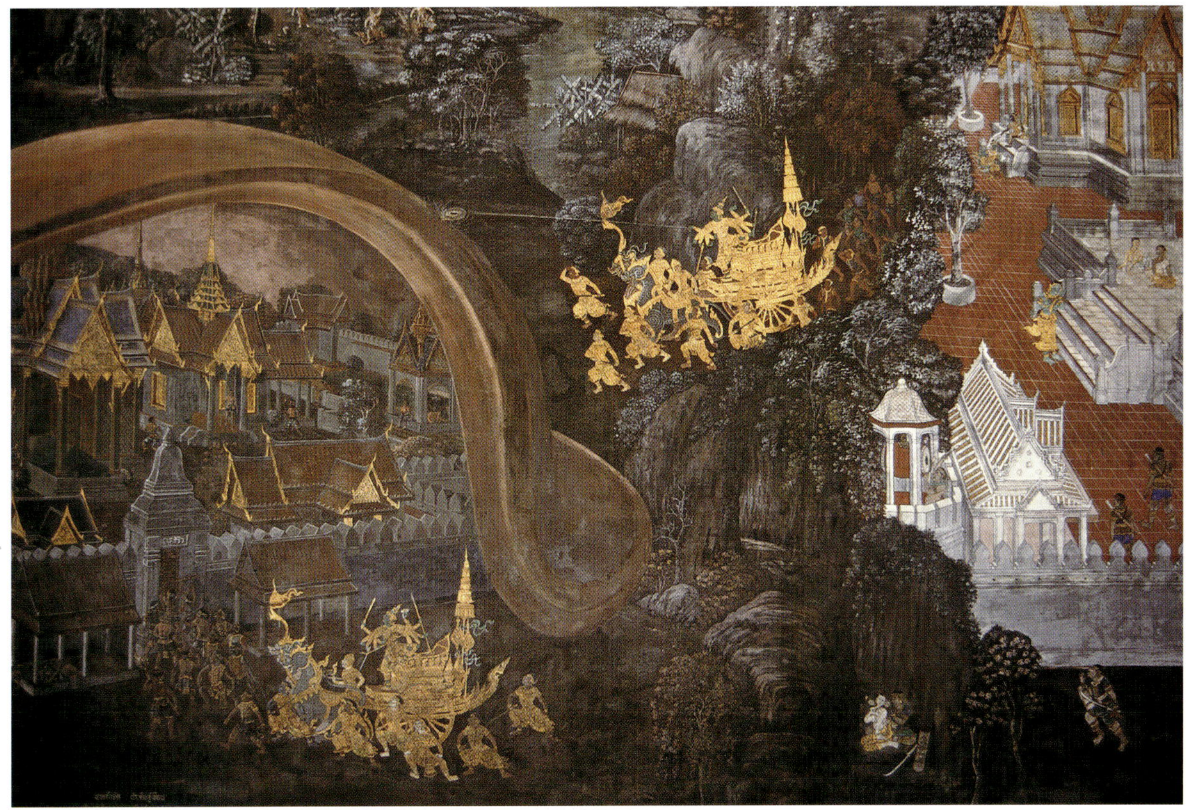

evident in temples throughout Bangkok, just as Chinese commercial authority is predominant within the city. Bangkok combines these diverse Indian and Chinese influences within a salad of references and interconnections, challenging any easy notions of historical, racial or religious purity. The final result, however, is all its own.

A Brahmanic city in a Buddhist kingdom, dedicated to its own culture but accepting of external influences. A major metropolis in a largely agrarian land. Bangkok represents Thailand, but is not of it directly. It is a unique construction, enigmatic in its referential lineaments and their underlying significance.

The Enigmatic Smile

The absence of a simple colonial or historical dialectic is central to Bangkok's reality. The city doesn't (or could not) define (or excuse) its problems through any singular historical blame. Its history is too varied to support the simple seductions of post-colonial revenge. Perhaps due to this lack of a colonial past, Bangkok has traditionally retained a remarkable sense of openness to the outside world. Its nineteenth- and twentieth-century governments employed many foreign advisors, with different nationalities judiciously spread among opposing ministries. Equally, the city's relationship to modernity is an open and flexible one. Bangkok bears little grudge against the idea of progress; it enters the future at breakneck speed. International development, travel, infrastructure, growth are all accepted with few outspoken reservations. Nostalgia appears a relatively alien conception.

This easy acceptance of modernity and foreign influence is remarkable. Yet it does not imply any submersion of a local character, nor is the culture necessarily appreciative of external criticism. The film versions of *The King and I* (Anna Leonowens and the King), recounting the self-described adventures of a late nineteenth-century English governess to the royal children, have been routinely banned, even though the book is readily available in Bangkok.[1] More recently, an issue of *The Economist* (2 March 2002) containing a profile on Thailand was withdrawn from distribution in the kingdom. Some blamed its suppression, like *The King and I*, on its presumptuous and disrespectful treatment of the monarchy, others on the increasingly prickly nature of the current government.

A city with an uncertain future and a quasi-mythical past, Bangkok retains an enigmatic relation to these historical conditions. The country has always been subject to a series of influences and counter-influences, without being directly controlled by any. New hybrids are created, linked by an intriguing sensibility of creative integration. Yet an awareness of, and desire to maintain, a Thai distinctiveness is ever-present. Arguably the in-between nature of Bangkok's history manifests this spirit, still persistent, if perhaps difficult to perceive, amid the noise of the city's conflicting images. Any first sense of existential negligence is illusory. Bangkok is a self-conscious place, responsible for its own curious state. The city

of Bangkok, *The Village of Wild Plums* (The Village of the Plum Olive?), or more properly Krung Thep, *The City of Angels*, presents an interpretive challenge. Fully named, the

> Great city of angels, the supreme repository of divine jewels, the great land unconquerable, the grand and prominent realm, the royal and delightful capital city full of nine noble gems, the highest royal dwelling and grand palace, the divine shelter and living place of the reincarnated spirits,

Bangkok is a compelling artefact whose rules remain obscure to those with eyes trained elsewhere.

A city where angels fear to tread; a city where they laugh. Fragments as clue, paradoxical form revealing urban intent?

Bangkok: Angelic Apathy or Mischievous Delight?

The Bangkok Post, Friday 12 April 2002. A brief perusal of the main headlines. 'Songkran Extravaganza' describes the traditions of the upcoming Songkran Festival, and its celebratory rituals (traditional dance, beauty contests, music . . .). Songkran marks the Thai New Year, the start of summer and the impending rainy season. Known colloquially as the Water Festival, its tradition of respectfully sprinkling a few drops of scented water on the hands of one's elders has been largely replaced by a riotous water fight. This year, marking Bangkok's 220th birthday, the festivities were extended for a full nine days. The national tourism authority plans to market Bangkok's Songkran to the larger world as a kind of exotic Asian Mardi Gras.

Related to the festival was a general concern for safety. Also from the *Post*'s reporters: 'Songkran Festival: Ban on police using water-guns as road-safety drive begins':

Police have been banned from using water-guns to shoot at passers-by during the Songkran celebrations. Police chief Sant Sarutanont was concerned they might get confused and use their real firearms by mistake, spokesman Pol Gen

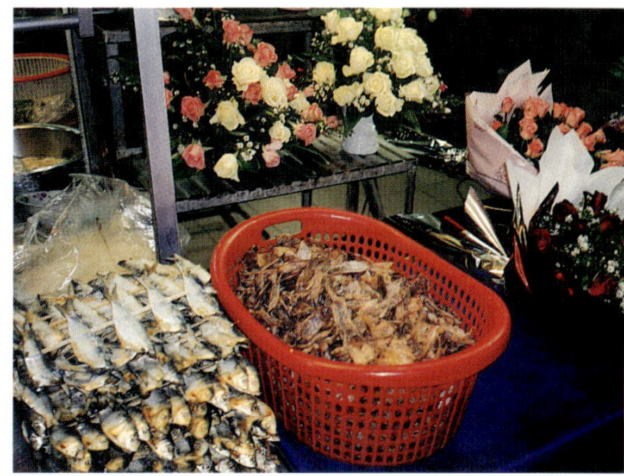

Pongsapas Pongcharoen said. 'So carrying water guns is deemed inappropriate, and especially those who are on duty', he said. If they wanted to join the fun, police would have to use the traditional bowl of water.

There was more good news in the business pages. Commenting on a survey conducted by Abac Poll, a local marketing company, the article 'Foreign businessman generally favourable' reported that Thailand was voted the 'most friendly' country in South-East Asia (including China). 'Moreover the quality of Thai labour is also the best, says the survey of 571 foreign investors . . . On the negative side, besides the traffic and pollution problems, Thailand was listed as having the second worst corruption problem and a slow bureaucracy.' The news on the foreign reserves front was also generally positive. A *Bangkok Post* exclusive described the efforts of a local monk in assisting with the recent economic crisis:

Luangta Maha Bua made another gift of 40 gold bars, raised through public donations, to the

Bank of Thailand yesterday. Governor M. R. Pridiyathorn Devakula said it was the final contribution the central bank would accept from the revered monk, who has campaigned since 1997 to shore up foreign reserves. 'Last year he asked me whether the country's foreign reserves were adequate', M. R. Pridiyathorn said. 'I told him that they had been much strengthened, and there was no need to seek additional funds. But he said that the public's faith was strong, and that people still wanted to make donations.' M. R. Pridiyathorn said that the country's finances were now well on the road to recovery with foreign reserves of US $36.6 billion. Luangta Maha Bua had collected gold and foreign currency valued at 2.4 billion baht over the past four years.

Luckily the money was there, because the politicians wanted new cars. In another *Bangkok Post* exclusive, 'Uthai eyes B5.7m Jag':

> Taxpayers' money is being used to buy a Jaguar car worth 5.7 million baht for House Speaker Uthai Pimchaichon, a Democrat party MP revealed yesterday. According to Suvaroat Palang, vice-chairman of the House Committee on parliamentary affairs, the procurement of the luxury sedan was 'very costly and unprecedented'. Mr. Uthai's predecessors used cheaper Mercedes-Benz automobiles.

The issue of corruption was addressed at a larger scale in 'Expressway Compensation: 19 held culpable, face charges'. The latest phase of a lengthy investigation into costover runs and corruption in the construction of Bang Na-Chon Buri expressway

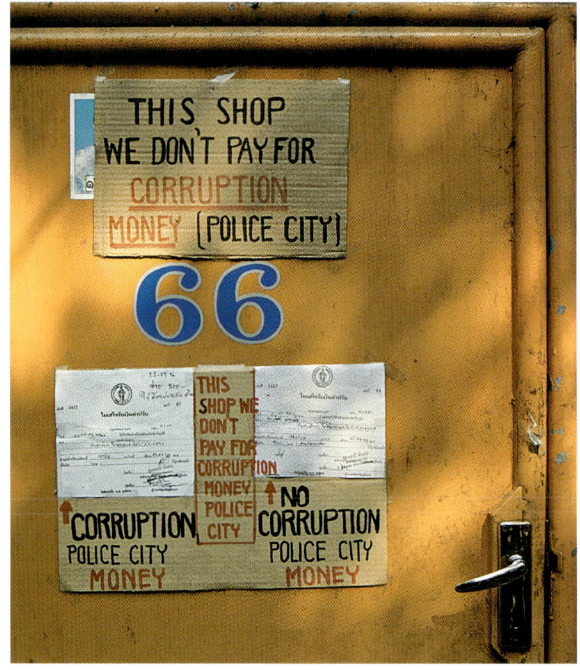

was addressed. In what seemed an expression of surprise, the article reported that no politicians identified were named in the judgement. 'Interior Minister Purachai Piumsombun admitted not one politician was included on yesterday's list, attributing it to limited evidence. "These people are smart enough to give orders verbally. As a result, the investigation could not reach them." he said.'

Amid the heat, noise and pollution, Bangkok contains clear signs of social vitality, tolerance and humour. To an outsider, the city should be a social nightmare, but somehow its citizens survive, mostly rather well. In the shapeless city, urban life is constructed, one perplexing or engaging fragment at a time. If Bangkok makes any sense, it does so as an attitude rather than as a form. A consistent approach may underlie its physical diversity, and perhaps establish its own version of civic order. But how to

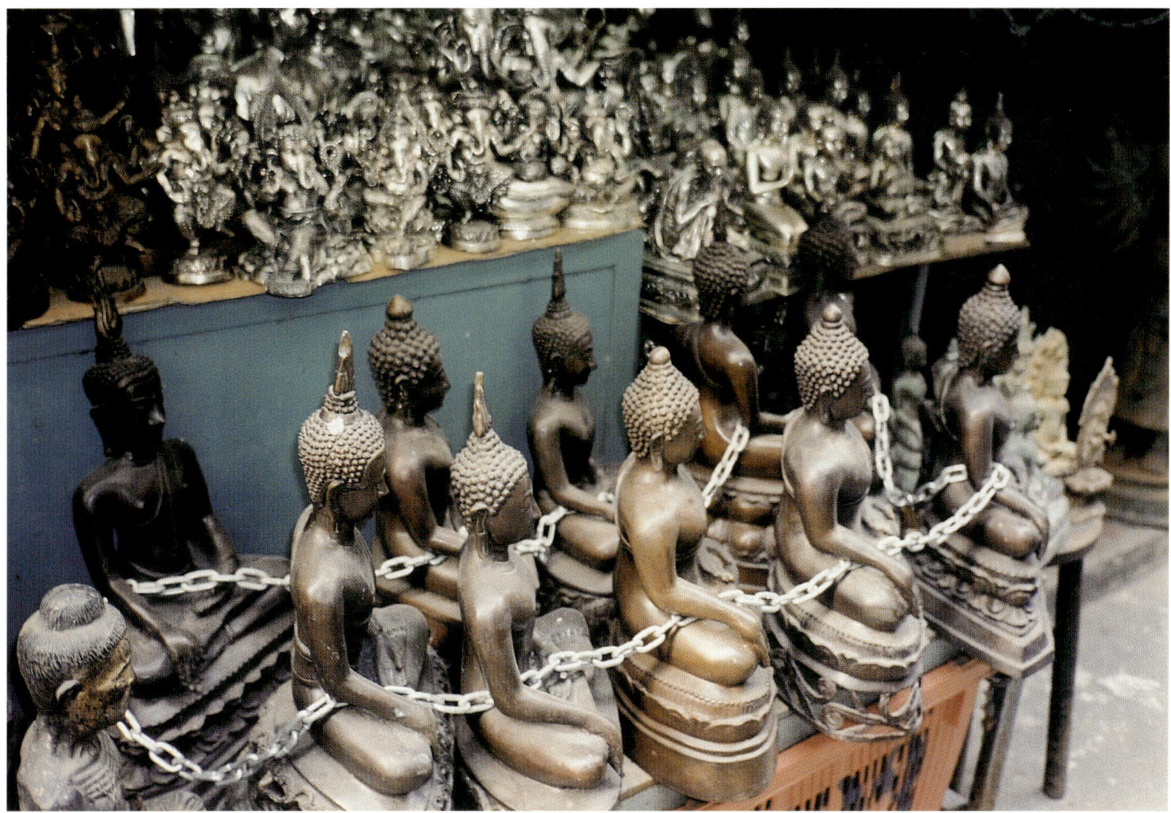

discover and articulate this attitude? What are the urban clues?

Mirror City: Dream City

As a manifested attitude, or perhaps more accurately an intangible dream, Bangkok is a slippery phenomenon. To ascribe a central mythology or collective dream to such a city is a different matter from simply ascertaining its personality. The issues of essential desire and a subconscious sublimation of parts to a possible future resolution imply a high degree of shared intent. Yet such an underlying sensibility might begin to articulate Bangkok's urban consciousness. A possible mythical city carried in the very bones of the real city, a city of patient angels obscured within the regional metropolis.

It is a strange urban condition: a city of angels where angels fear to tread. Or perhaps their angelic message simply takes form in strange ways. Its enigmatic surface reflects back on its viewers, providing each with what they seek, but only in fragments. The whole remains intangible. Even the fragments eventually slip away, like temporary flashes of light in a darkened mirror. Yet captured in these flickering reflections lie possible messages, ones that may, paradoxically, be found in the city's ambiguous physical expression.

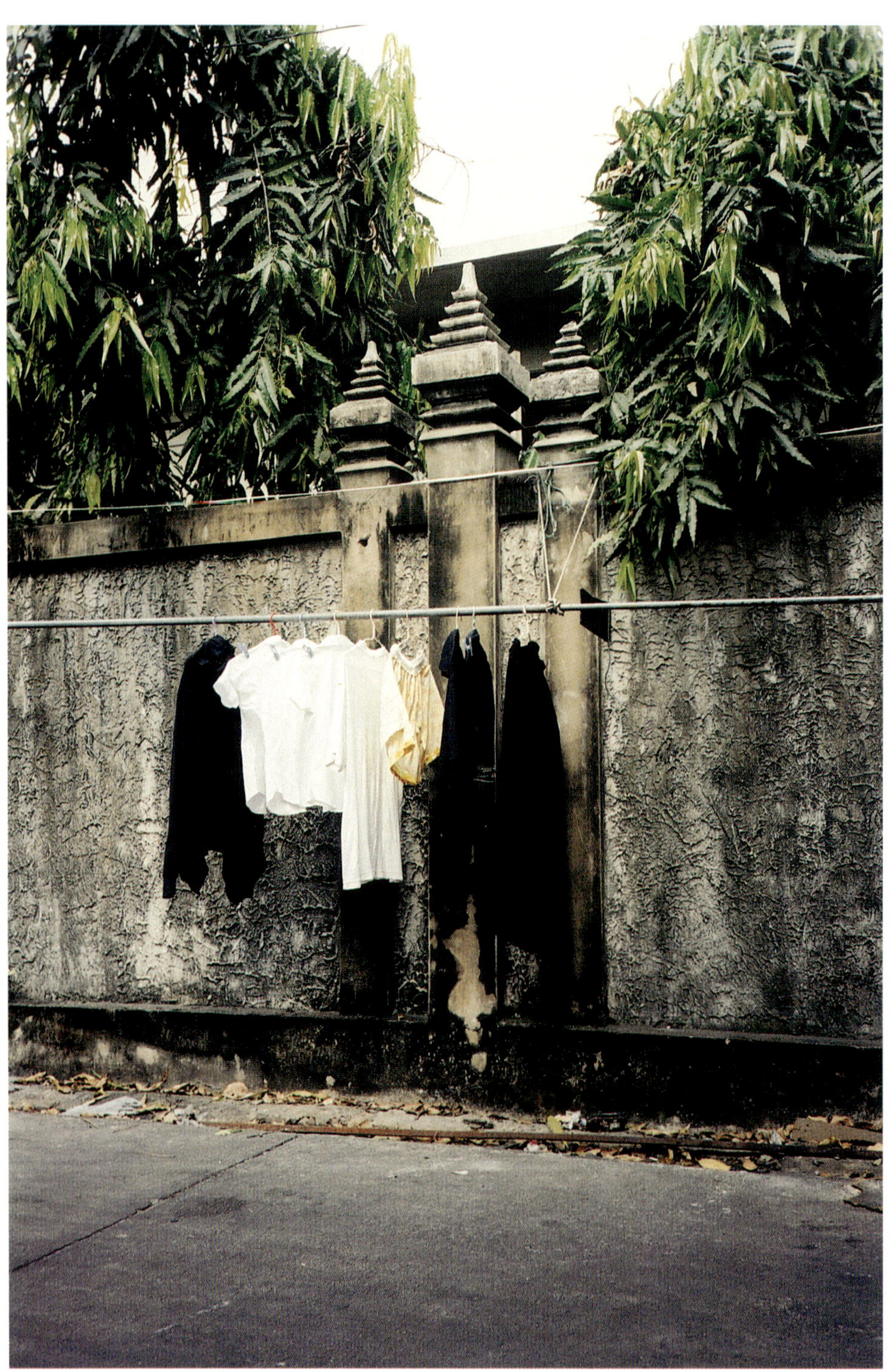

Paradoxical Form: Angelic Allusions?

The central paradox of Bangkok's essential order centres on the issue of form. The city appears to manifest little formal control, nor to be overly concerned with its absence. Chaos abounds. Yet if an angelic city does exist, it should arguably find at least partial physical expression, a tantalizing revelation of presence and communicative intent. There are enough striking provocations to imply that this might be possible. Form is clearly significant in the development of Thai architecture, even if its function is ambiguous. The shapes and their meanings may be symbolically cryptic, but they clearly betray value, along with a highly developed capacity for refined expression. In the city of angels, the formal power of these fragments challenges their context through contrast.

Perhaps more powerfully, an overt concern for form and earthly pleasure would appear to contradict a Buddhist sensibility. Any concentration on worldly values distracts one from the transcendent path towards earthly replacement. Indeed, the issue of art is potentially problematic for a Buddhist city such as Bangkok. Yet the role of form in Buddhist culture is far more nuanced. The very texts that describe the pointlessness of earthly value do so in remarkably poignant ways, the beauty of the verbal images belying the stated 'content' of formal rejection. 'He who knows that this body is the foam of a wave, the shadow of a mirage, he breaks the sharp arrows of MARA, concealed in the flowers of sensuous passions and, unseen by the King of death, he goes on and follows his path.'[2] The use of vivid metaphor is directed to diminishing the merits of bodily or sensual experience, a complex and potentially

contradictory task. One requires symbols and images to explain the importance of their rejection, a condition that hypothetically underlies the experience of the city too.

Can a concentration on formal moments provide the path to interpret a place seemingly free from formal preoccupations? Will identifying a function for symbol and experience assist in clarifying the ideals of the formless city? Bangkok may manifest an attitude rather than form, but the fragments of the city supposedly provide the path tangibly to elucidate this quality. Its elements and their arrangement offer glimpses into its cryptic message. Formal moments may present a murky path for understanding a city that seems to delight in its own formal dissolution. Yet the presence of these angelic emissaries illuminates the city, revealing its mirrored shadow resting latent within.

The hypothetical assumption of a critical wholeness underlies the effort, a belief in Bangkok's narrative coherence. The paradox of form centres the attempt to discover the spirit of a seemingly formless city, a city that defies formal interpretation.

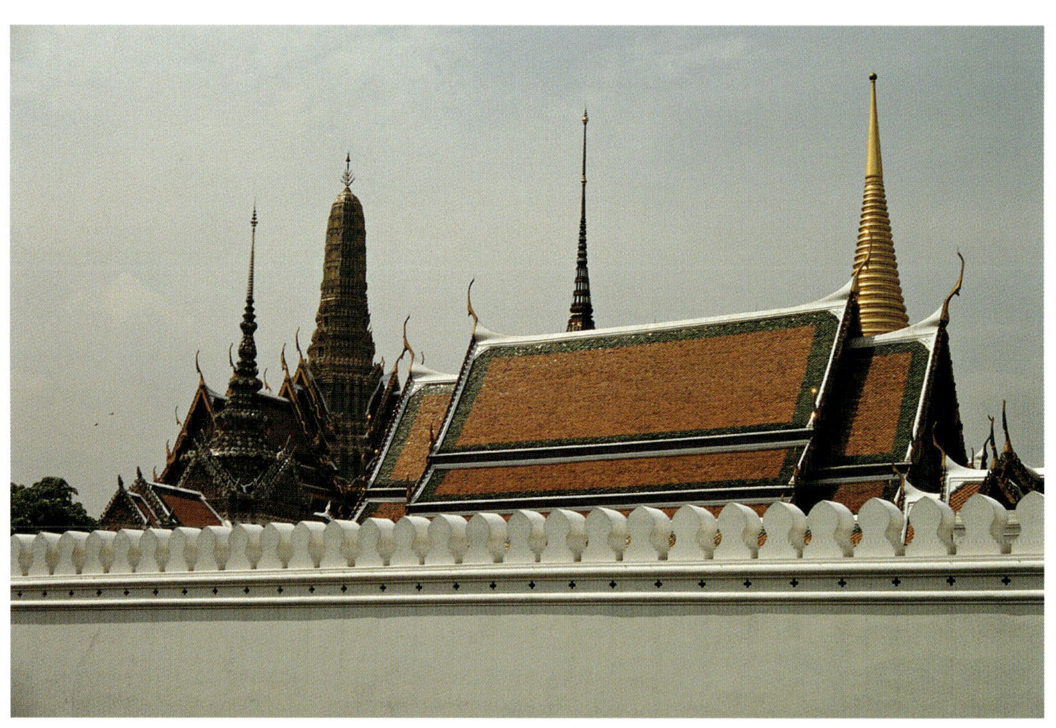

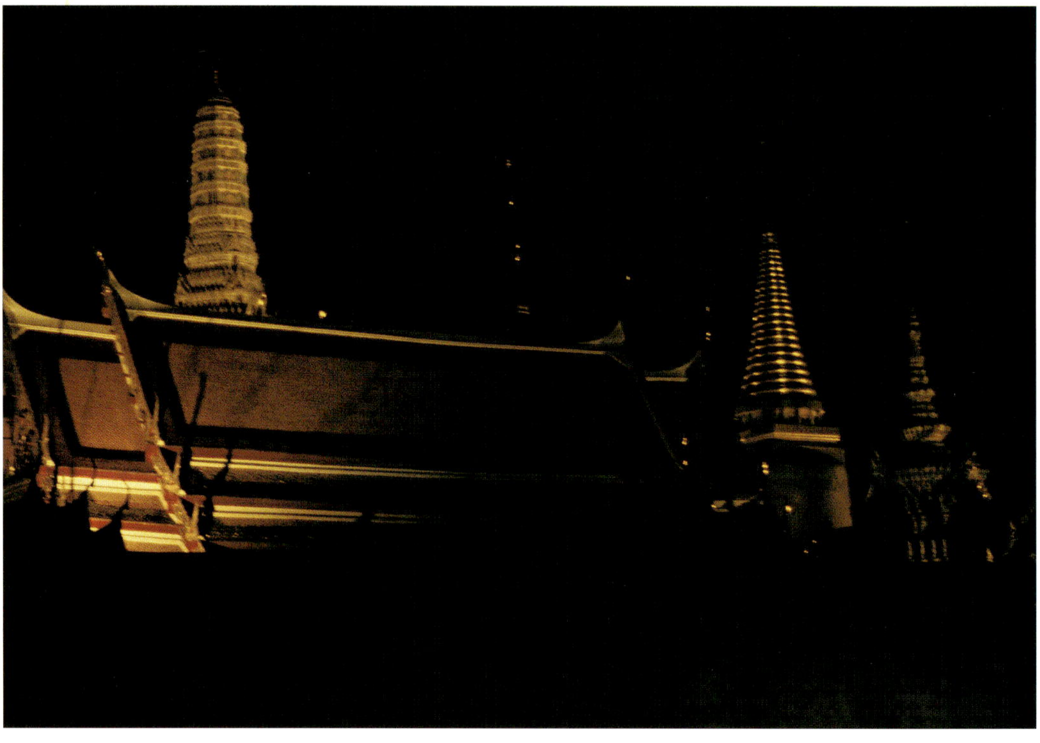

TWO

Roofs

PART ONE

Roofs of gold, geometrically pure. Images of order. Urban conscience and architectural provocation. A city whose figures of the imagination float above terrestrial reality, and ignore its concerns. A perfect architecture unattainable by the earthly.

Pictorial Order

Bangkok is a city whose angels appear most clearly at night. Like the fickle moon occasionally visible within the cloudy nocturnal sky, its vivid ethereal figures surface as intermittent visions. Elusive traces cautiously emerge from the sensory overload of the frantic day. The chaotic city of commerce and consumption is replaced by a luminous dream, whose protagonists enliven the sensual backdrop of humid and silky darkness.

Bangkok's roofs are the most striking of these visions. Mysteriously powerful in their disengaged reality, they float above the darkened streets to offer beacons of hope in the quest for symbolic order. An abstract and compelling, if enigmatic, urban vision is revealed. The shimmering roofs construct a different, more enticing city than its terrestrial counterpart.

This visionary roofscape takes precedence in Bangkok's visual representation, a fact quickly recognized in the city's tourist posters and brochures. Indeed, Bangkok's roofs define its visual appeal. A city of images: photographically potent, if functionally cryptic. A city whose architectural angels await the revelatory power of darkness, or the editing authority of the camera lens to appear in their full and independent glory. Contrasting first impressions of overwhelming confusion, this parallel city of form awaits interpretation.

The general experience of Bangkok is horizontal. The city spreads out along the great avenues of royal authority, following spines of passage across the flat landscape. Aside from a few moments of commercial intensity (speculative excess?), the majority of the city remains low. Two- or three-storey shops, houses and apartments bleed over the even terrain, amorphous in their collected form. Historically, Bangkok's temple roofs were the only figures capable of disrupting this horizontal sprawl. Vivid blazes of colour, in complex figural confections, they continue to float above the smaller-scale fabric, creating an independent and dynamic terrain.

In the shapeless city, strong forms attract attention; its notable moments are created most simply by difference. One significant means is colour. Bangkok's fabric is generally monochromatic. Its buildings, streets and canals all manifest subtle variations on a fairly dirty brown. Flashes of unexpected colour accordingly take on special significance. In the social realm: neon, brilliant flowers, remarkable domestic shrines, the vibrant colours of

Thai silk. Architecturally and urbanistically: the temple roofs. Rich fields of glazed ceramic tiles, in deep greens, ochres and blues, are framed as great geometric figures. Their modulated surfaces reflect the sun, capturing and retransmitting its celestial energy to the earthly city. This flickering presence is a unique one, demanding attention within the more muted settings of domestic life.

Contextual contrast is established more fundamentally through form. Bangkok's roofs present the city's most striking architectural figures. While the temples provide the most extreme examples,

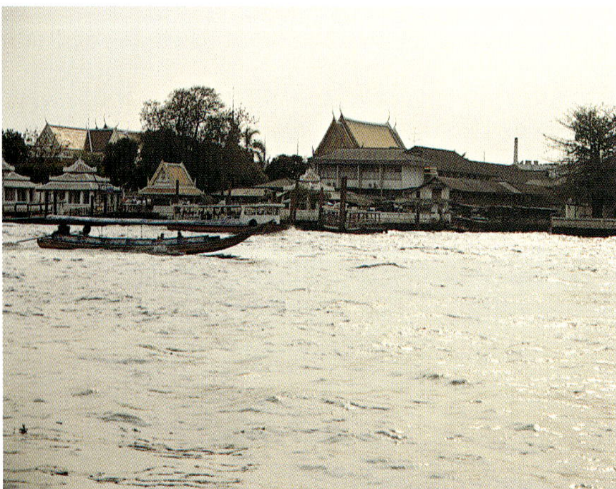

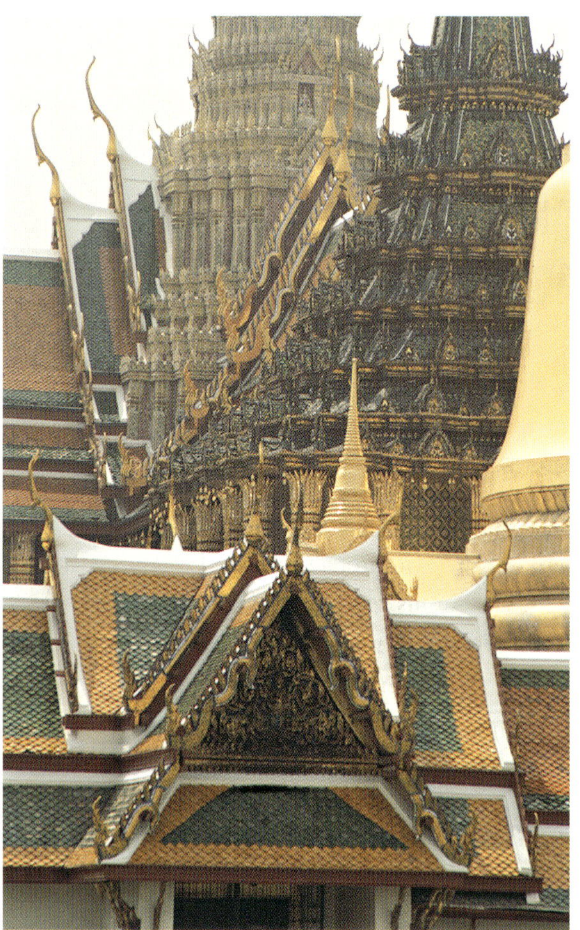

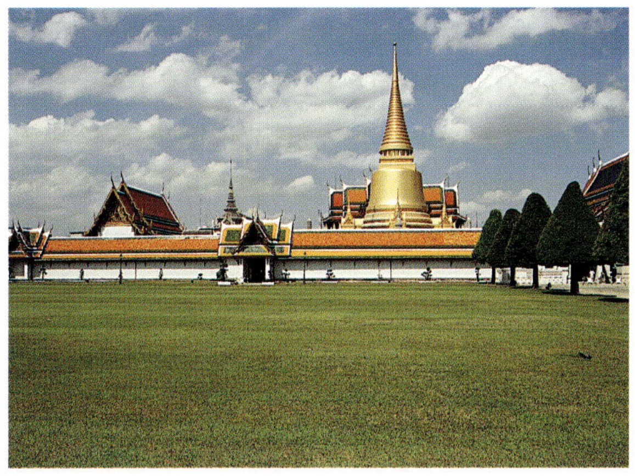

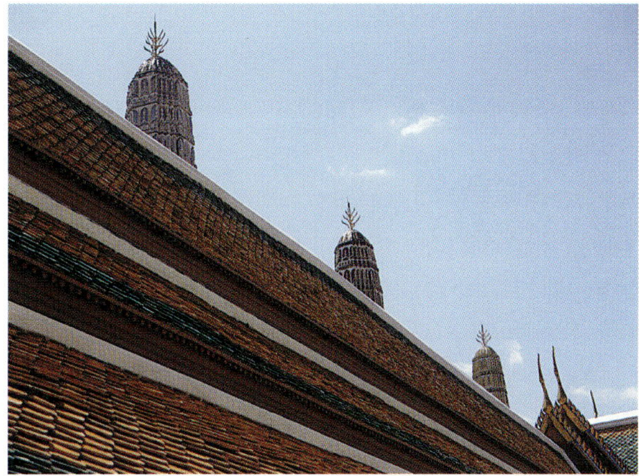

domestic buildings also manifest similar tendencies at a smaller scale. Houses and shops figurally transform as they progress vertically. The lower storeys of Bangkok's buildings are generally casual. Opening directly to their streets and alleys, their architectural treatment is modestly configured, even practical in its expression. The roofs on the other hand are more carefully crafted, more celebrated. Domestic structures, so modest on the ground, are surmounted by precise geometrically ordered creations. The sky is met with greater respect than the earth: an intentional architecture replacing the circumstantial.

This separation of the roofs from their contexts is rendered explicit through the use of framing devices: clerestorys, walls, extended eaves. New horizons are established, preparing a proper ground for the appreciation of these vertical moments within the horizontal city. These events create distinct breaks in Bangkok's experience. Undifferentiated urban flow is stopped, the plane of daily life disturbed. If the ground defines the city's daily life, Bangkok's roofs comprise its idealized topography. Moments of order and value are presented for appreciation, and

regular life is held at bay.[1] A city of new horizons is juxtaposed against the sky.

Uninhabited Perfection

The curious realization is that these remarkable urban figures remain uninhabited. Bangkok's most striking architectural forms occur where no physical activity exists to corrupt their independence. Distinct from life on the ground, a perfect architecture is created. A city constructed for visual and symbolic impact alone. A city occupied by superior beings? A city that shares Bangkok's site but remains untouched by its practical responsibilities.

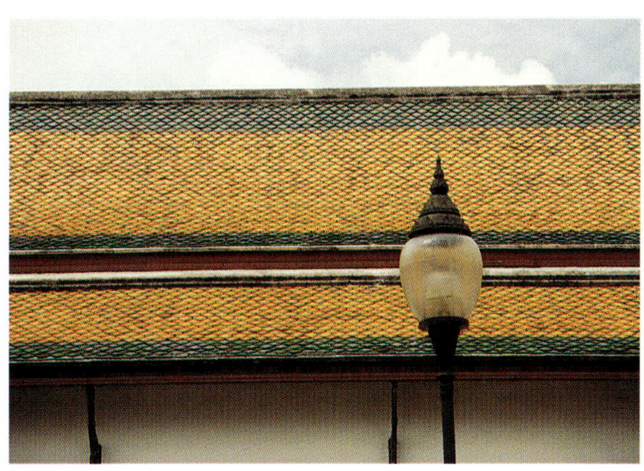

Why is the city's architecture most coherent where it least engages with physical necessity? What are the roofs' relationships to the messy realm of contingent reality? The urban role of these aloof figures remains ambiguous. Visually dynamic, they float above the city and ignore its concerns. Bangkok's roofs attract attention to themselves, but in themselves they interact directly with a distant sky.

An ideal city? The real Bangkok so easily misplaced during hectic daily experience? Constructing a city of images, Bangkok's roofs manifest a world of perfect form, inhabited by mysterious others. A world normally obscured by the noise of our material preoccupations. Yet it isn't only a lack of attention that divorces the roofs from a direct interaction with urban life. Their appreciation is further hindered by contemporary, and Western, expectations of perspectival order.

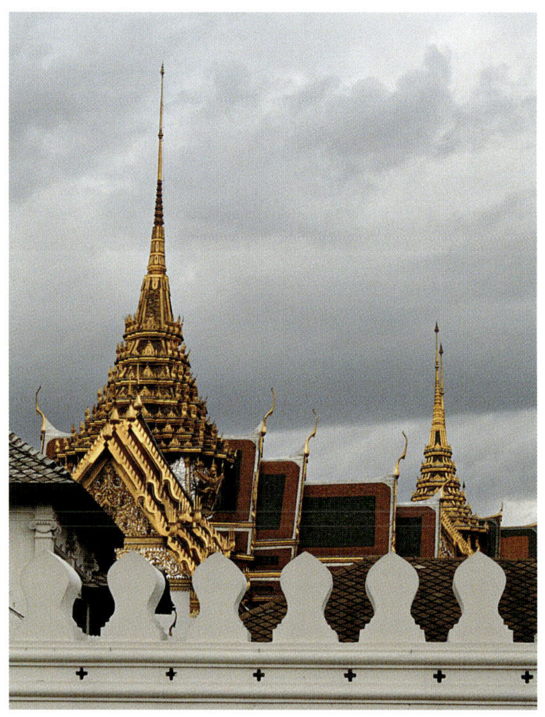

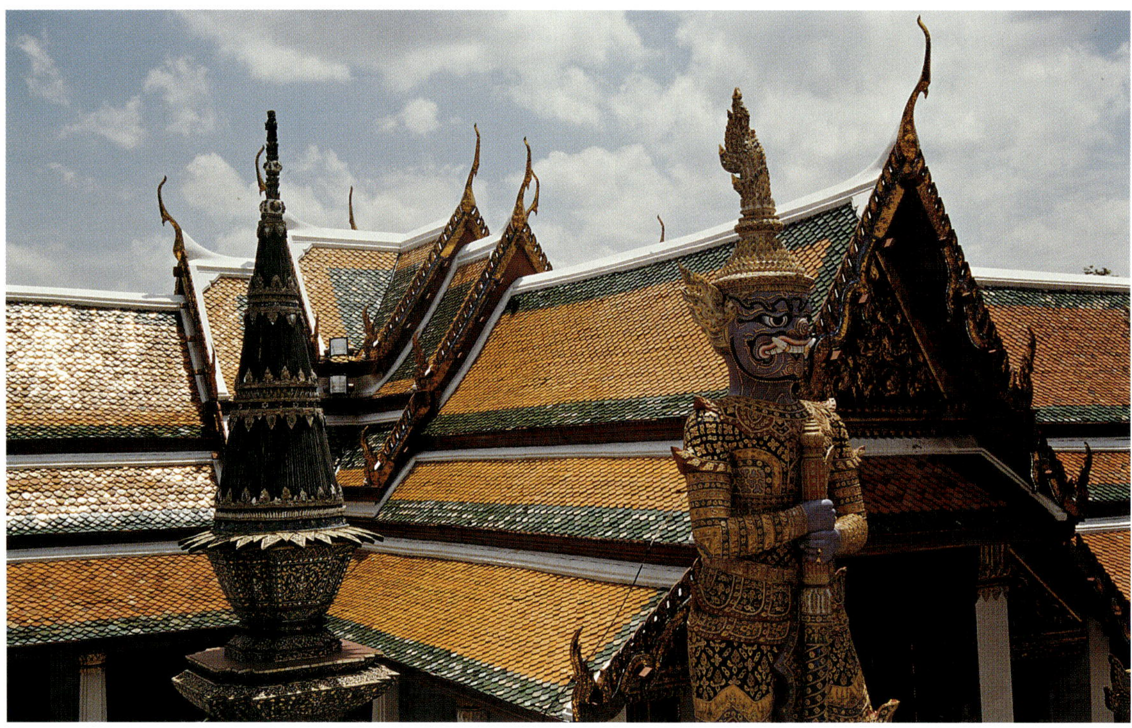

PART TWO

*Fragments of hidden worlds, signs of
obscure life. Foreshadowed realities,
separated from the city of the street.
A possibly perfect world; tantalizing,
distant. A place of stories.*

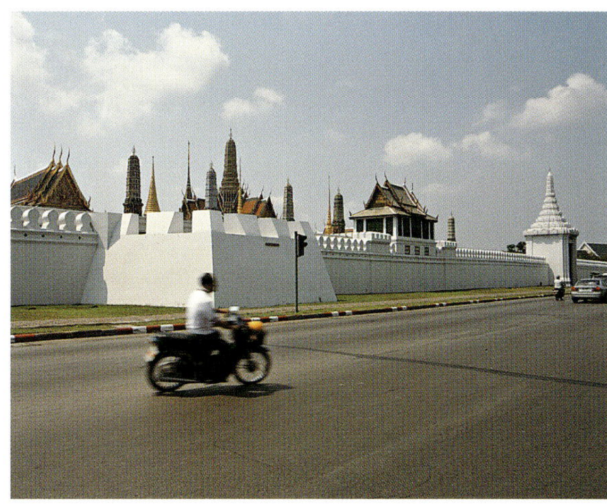

The Visual City

Bangkok's roofs play photographic tricks. The
images extracted from its dense reality portray a city
more coherent, more designed than any memory of
its experience. Bangkok, a paradoxical city, is
clearest at a distance. The city's roofs, formally
powerful, beckon the viewer with visions of purity
and strength. In experience, relative confusion
reigns. These visions of perfection are perceptible
but unattainable, distantly active within the
distractions of urban reality.

No doubt Bangkok is a visual city, but with a
different notion of what constitutes vision's purpose.
Vision is rewarded in fragments, by oblique glances.
A strange, yet clearly intentional condition. Reaction
to this urban state depends on unacknowledged,
though prevalent, notions of perspective, and the
expectation of its urban necessity. An accustomed
requirement largely rejected in Bangkok's experience
and structure.

Perspective, applied as a means for clarifying
urban order, was central to the theory and design of
the post-Renaissance European city. Straight streets
and constructed views identified significant events

for appreciation. Indeed, location along or within
clearly defined view corridors was a guarantee of
value for buildings and spaces alike. In its most
extreme versions, the Rome of Sixtus v or the Paris of
Louis xiv, visual axes were cut across entire cities and
their surrounding landscapes, subordinating
immediate realities to the presentation of significant
destinations. Visual and spatial orders co-supported
ideals of urban authority. Distinct objects,
experienced through this perspectival extension, constructed urban form. Travel and view were integrated
in a tapestry of urban lineaments of symbolic intent.

Bangkok's roofs function differently. While these
ambiguous figures may act as beacons for urban life,
they do so independently from the experience of
urban circulation. Neither the roofs, nor their
surrounding streets, act perspectively. A more mysterious visual operation takes place: an oscillation of
presentation and removal. Figures reside inside
precincts, separated from the ground. Direct access,
both visually and physically, is dislocated. Most
evident at a distance, their visual authority
diminishes in proximity. Even the most modest

domestic roofs are separated from focused appreciation, becoming less visible on approach. Beacons are celebrated, and then hidden; offered, and then taken away. Celebrating disembodied objects in the visual city, this notion of oscillating interaction is a curious one. How is the purpose of the striking roofs registered within the city of experience? Bangkok is indeed a strange city of image, where most of its imagistic activity remains inaccessible to earthly contact.

The Foreshadowed Image

The role of image in urban understanding is a broad one. Destinations may be identified and significant locations marked. Pre-established orders clarified or contrasting possibilities presented as foils. One avenue into this wide field of urban perception is provided by painting. Articulating different modes of vision, the painted representation of cities and their landscapes present symbolic analogues that may shed light on urban biases and values.

In a perspective the viewer is located within a constructed extension of visual space, whose lineaments support an expression of political and social order. It constructs a theatre of vision. As explained by Leon Battista Alberti's notion of *istoria*, these paintings presented intentional moral lessons.[2] Lines of communication, created through the perspectival bond, link actor and viewer within a shared perceptual realm. This extension is usually clarified by the spatial structure of the painted context. Streets, gardens and interiors are arranged to direct the perspectival message. And if spaces, cities and landscapes could be constructed in paint to facilitate communication, could not actual cities follow the same principle? Perspective, whose ideals were first articulated in paintings, became significant for the creation of legible civic order.

Bangkok's paintings also provide clues to its urban values. Here, however, the images present inverse indicators of spatial realities. They celebrate views that are impossible to realize in physical experience. Unlike the reinforcing aspect of Renaissance perspective, Thai landscape painting presents conflicting messages simultaneously. Painting and city demand different forms of participation than those provided by directed sight alone.

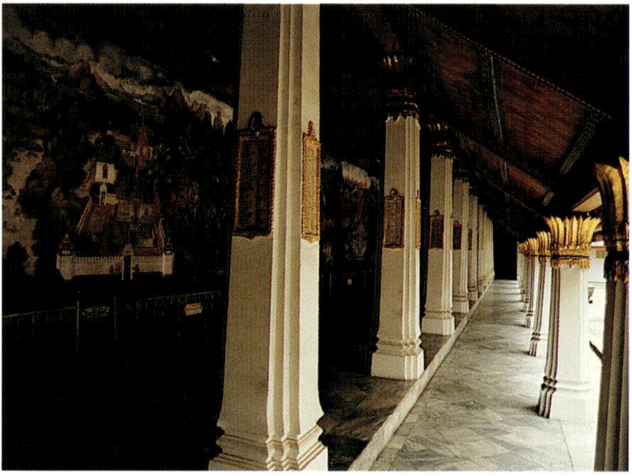

The fresco cycle of Wat Phra Kaeo, located within its principal arcade, narrates the events of the *Ramakien*. The story, its episodes and the many digressions are recounted in striking images, stretched over 1,000 metres of continuous painting. These events are portrayed in remarkable landscapes, cities and country villas. Violent action generally takes place in nature – the wild forests that Rama first sets out to pacify. Yet significant parts of the narrative also occur within architectural compositions, articulated as walled compounds set within the mysterious landscapes.

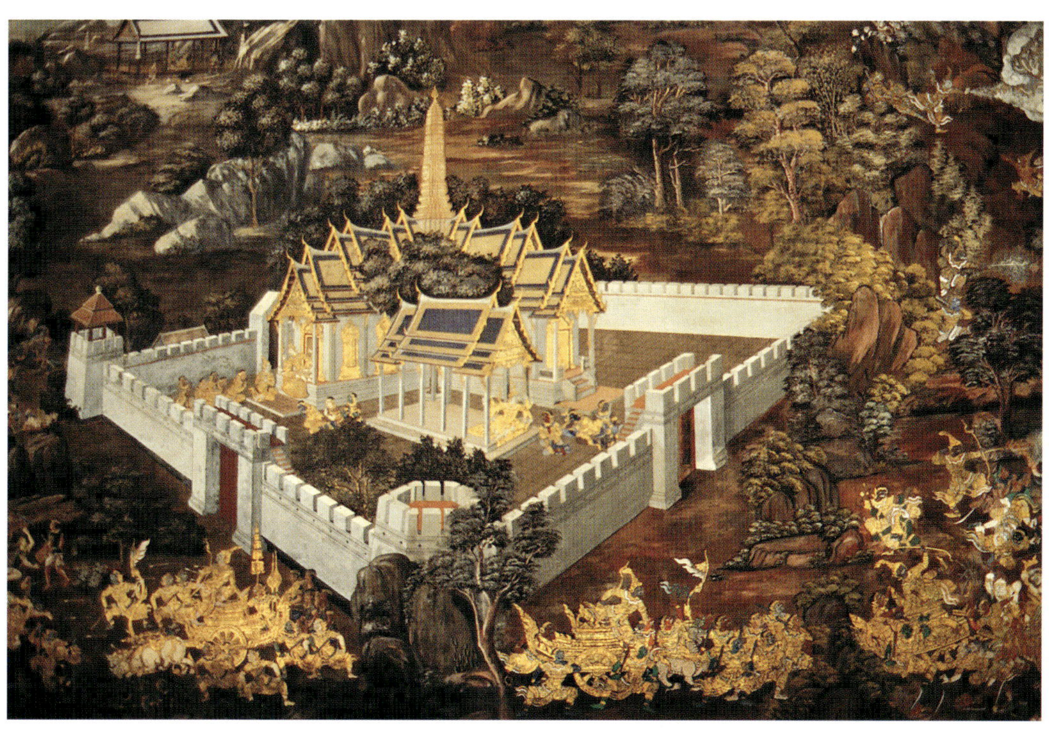

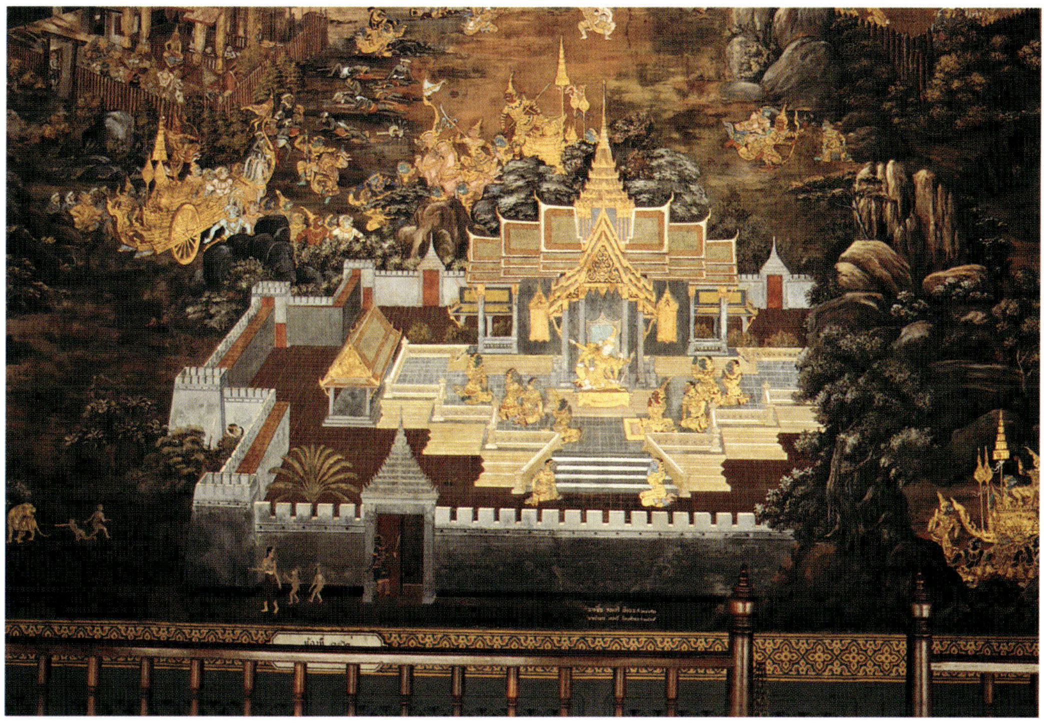

The paintings consistently present this landscape as if it rests on a great tilted tableau. The viewer is allowed a privileged, though non-perspectival, view from above. We look down on the landscape, floating safely in the sky. Technically called an axonometric projection, this view creates a consistent field for the lengthy sequence of images, arrayed without any optical break in the narrative flow. A continuous world is unveiled for our perambulatory appreciation, its elements independent from any single fixed view.

Axonometrics allow a simultaneous appreciation of object and event, evenly displayed. The image communicates more like a text than a photograph, with no explicitly defined optical axis. Activities occupy their own narrative realm. As a result the stories are made safer and more approachable in a way, more fluid, less singular. But they are also more abstract and distant. There is no direct line allied with vision to connect the viewer to the painted events. Nor does this view organize the represented space. Here one remains a disembodied observer, whose line of sight is distinct from those of the characters. The scenes of the painting, recounting Rama's mythical struggles, are clearly visible, but spatially distinct from our own reality. There is no illusion of any direct link between his realm and ours, or of our ability to participate within it. Ultimately the narrative space created by the paintings is an imaginary one.

In a flat landscape this is the only way to see inside the architectural precincts. We observe their interiors as privileged voyeurs. Elevated into the sky, liberated from our earthly limitations, the narrative becomes available. Along the horizontal fresco, vision maintains a vicarious and fragile connection to the painted action 'below'.

An imaginary and temporary omnipresence is artistically granted.

These interior spaces, so crucial to revealing the story, would remain otherwise invisible. Grounded perspectival views would reveal little beyond the precinct walls and their roofs floating above. In the paintings the roofs establish an architectural or urban context, identifying complex and highly articulated interior worlds. They effectively present the precinct's facades. We look down and past them towards the framed action. Within Bangkok, similar interior worlds are flagged by remarkable roofs. In physical experience, however, we are divorced from this intimate relationship, left outside. Rather than facades, the roofs in the world are viewed as disembodied signs. Perceptually they still identify a narrative space, but it is divorced from the reality of the exterior landscape, and hidden from sight. No comprehensive view, analogous to the one provided in the paintings, reveals their internal activities. The roof's communicative merits are therefore more ambiguous. They present striking figures for appreciation, while reminding us of what will always remain out of reach, in powerful ways.

Bangkok's roofs may be understood as flags, marking hidden worlds of heroic activity. Yet in earthly life, especially for a Buddhist, the true space of heroic activity, the site of one's most significant battles, is personal. It remains hidden: an interior space that is present only in a conscious imagination. The remembrance of the stories, however, offers assistance. The events of the *Ramakien*, and *The Lives of the Buddha* too, both painted in countless cycles throughout the city, remind the viewer of exemplary existential struggles. They provide lessons that may act as models for balancing one's own more fractious realities.

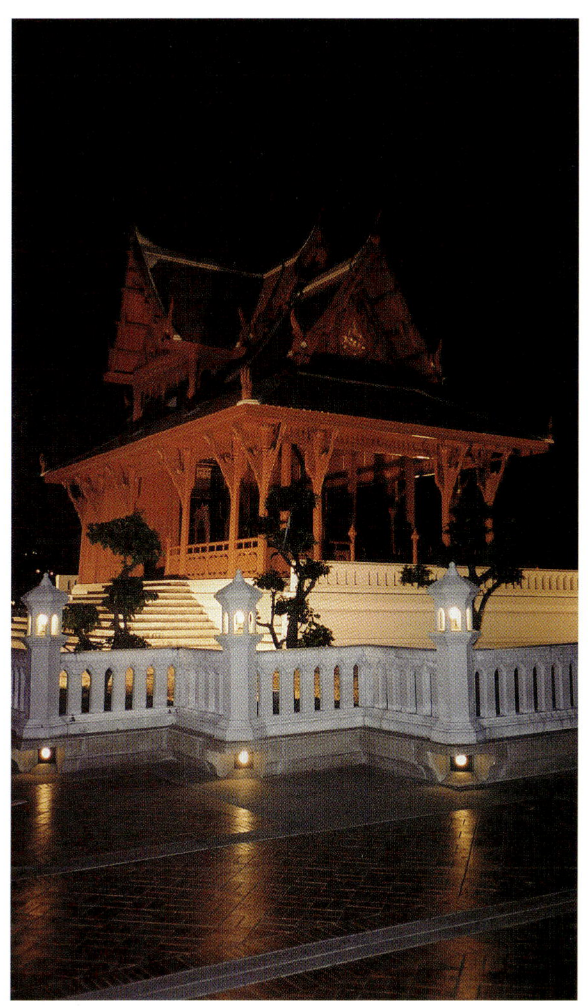

The roofs are potent reminders of the potential for different civic spaces and activities. Indeed they powerfully demonstrate the importance of distinct values within the daily flow of urban life. Yet they remain as fragments, disconnected from a literal interaction with this more messy city. Uninhabited, they stand aloof from any direct engagement with urban form: safely, and sagely, separate from a corrupted, less heroic reality.

The perfect fragment of a more idealized order, the roofs present their allusive messages, intact yet disengaged. Or more accurately, ambiguously engaged with a different kind of urban lesson. Angelic emissaries, they delight in their Delphic complexity. Any lesson worth learning requires effort, and their concessions to the simple, if forceful, clarity of a perspectival view are slight. So visually striking, so tantalizing within the city. Yet these roofs perceptually slip away, floating above Bangkok's more immediate distractions. They don't control views or order surrounding neighbourhoods. They exist rather subtly to challenge the viewer. Bangkok's roofs are provocations to interpretation, so clearly intentional, so perplexing in their intended meaning.

Pointers and boundaries; the inhabited world separated from the mysterious ether above. Summits of gold, markers of intangible journeys. Roofs: guides or barriers, outlining spiritual truth or circumscribing the limits of visual understanding?

Image and Icon

The impact of verticality in a flat landscape verges on the power of nature. Points of distinction are created, possible links with a different world presented. Do Bangkok's roofs point to missing mythical worlds, or manifest these symbolic realms in their very form? An architectural cosmology, symbolic journey, or a reminder of its impossibility?

Articulating a mimetic cosmology is a consistent theme within sacred architecture. The dome of the Pantheon in Rome, for example, creates a miniature universe, mapping the movements of the sun through the planetary spheres. Architectural experience clarifies a more distant celestial original. The Gothic cathedrals reconstruct the complexities of the heavens for a symbolic purpose, revealing their structure through analogous geometries and numerical relations. The architectural mountains of Angkor Wat or Borobudur construct symbolic landscapes to link the earth with the heavens. The pedagogic function of Bangkok's roofs is less clear. Rarely perceived as self-contained interiors or clear figures, their sculptural forms are viewed in a more fragmented way, within the disconnected context of the city.

The roof forms brought to the flat city remind one perhaps of a missing landscape, the hills of Rama's mythical north re-created architecturally. This hypothetical landscape could refer also to the actual north, the mountainous regions from which earlier migrations descended. Collective memories of either topography might be sublimated into the built forms of the new capital. More specifically, like the paintings of *The Ramakien*, the roofs potentially reference Bangkok's embedded Brahmanic inheritance, as seen through its royal rituals.

Royal cremations are held in specially constructed pavilions, that are mostly roof. Fantastic confections, they create elaborate landscapes within the city. Named after Mount Meru (or Phra Sumeru), the celestial mountain of Hindu and Buddhist cosmology, the symbolic landscape is rendered explicit through title. The architectural mountain assists the departing soul in its passage to heaven.

The cremation pavilions are temporary constructions. Built mountains create a brief link between the earth and the heavens to facilitate the journey of the cremated soul back to its rightful

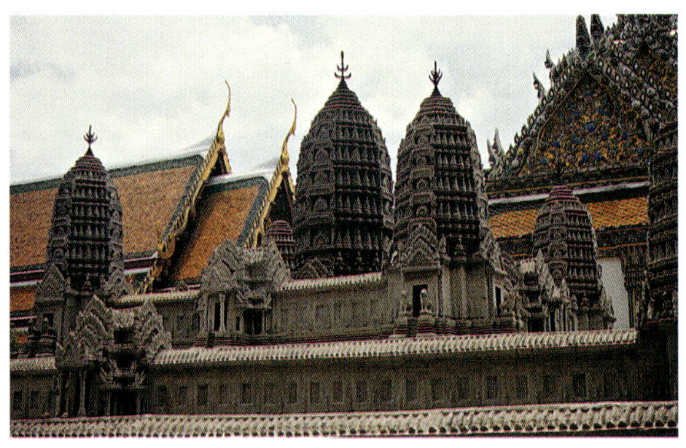

place. The coexistence of an explicit architectural metaphor with programmatic specificity is conjoined for a special symbolic purpose – an event. While radical in scale, their form is fleeting. Karl Dohring, a German architect and archaeologist working for the Thai government in the early part of the twentieth century, described the cremation construction for a prince during the reign of King Chulalongkorn:

> These edifices, which are destined for the cremation of the royal family, are of the most splendid ever invented by human imagination. They are usually more beautiful and daring in their conception than the temple architecture built to last. Built to be used only for a very short time they disappear like dream images.[3]

The Meru reference is central to earlier royal temple constructions, most notable at Angkor Wat and its successors still visible at Ayutthaya and Sukhothai. In Bangkok their clearest descendant is Wat Rachanaddaram. A centralized roof on the exterior, covering a labyrinthine passage within, the temple is a rare example of the traditional reference. Yet Bangkok's temples do not generally follow this model. While this symbolic landscape may be generally implicit within their form, they tend to avoid direct Meru analogies. Though still active in the cremation pavilions and the dramatic example of Angkor Wat, faithfully represented by a large stone model at Wat Phra Kaeo in the Grand Palace, Bangkok's temples reference other sources. It is as if the symbolic clarity of the earlier constructions is now deemed appropriate only for brief moments, whereas the living city demands a more general or subtle set of references.

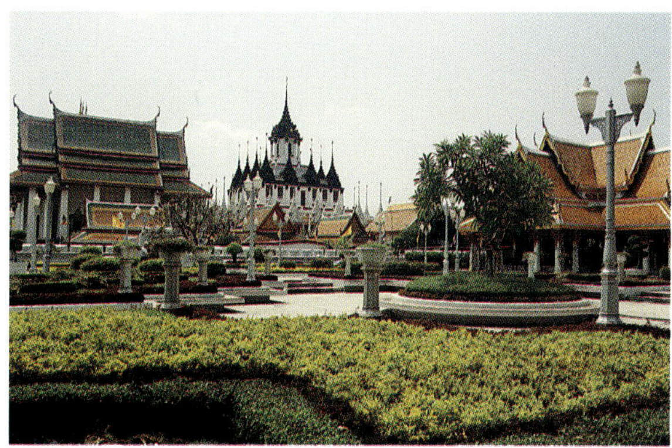

Passage and Value

The Mount Meru cremation figures represent a referential image and journey simultaneously. The notion of passage implied in their stepped profiles is rendered explicit in the major staircases that summit at the burial urn, or the long route inside Wat Rachanaddaram. While most of Bangkok's roof structures might omit the specific formal reference to mountains, it is less clear that the theme of passage has been equally sacrificed.

The notion of vertical passage is most explicit in the *chedis*, the pyramid-like structures that accompany Bangkok's principal temple buildings. Often related to funerary rites, and hence connected to Meru symbolism, the *chedis* summit at a point, which is only visible from the exterior. Articulated layers define steps towards a barely tangible completion. This gradual disappearance creates an inverse relationship to the immensity of the heavens, a foil rather than a mirror. They direct vision towards the sky rather than present its image.

Both pointers and boundaries, Bangkok's roofs articulate a passage away from the world of daily life. Guides or barriers, the roofs play an ambiguous role. Do they present a form of spiritual truth, a passage

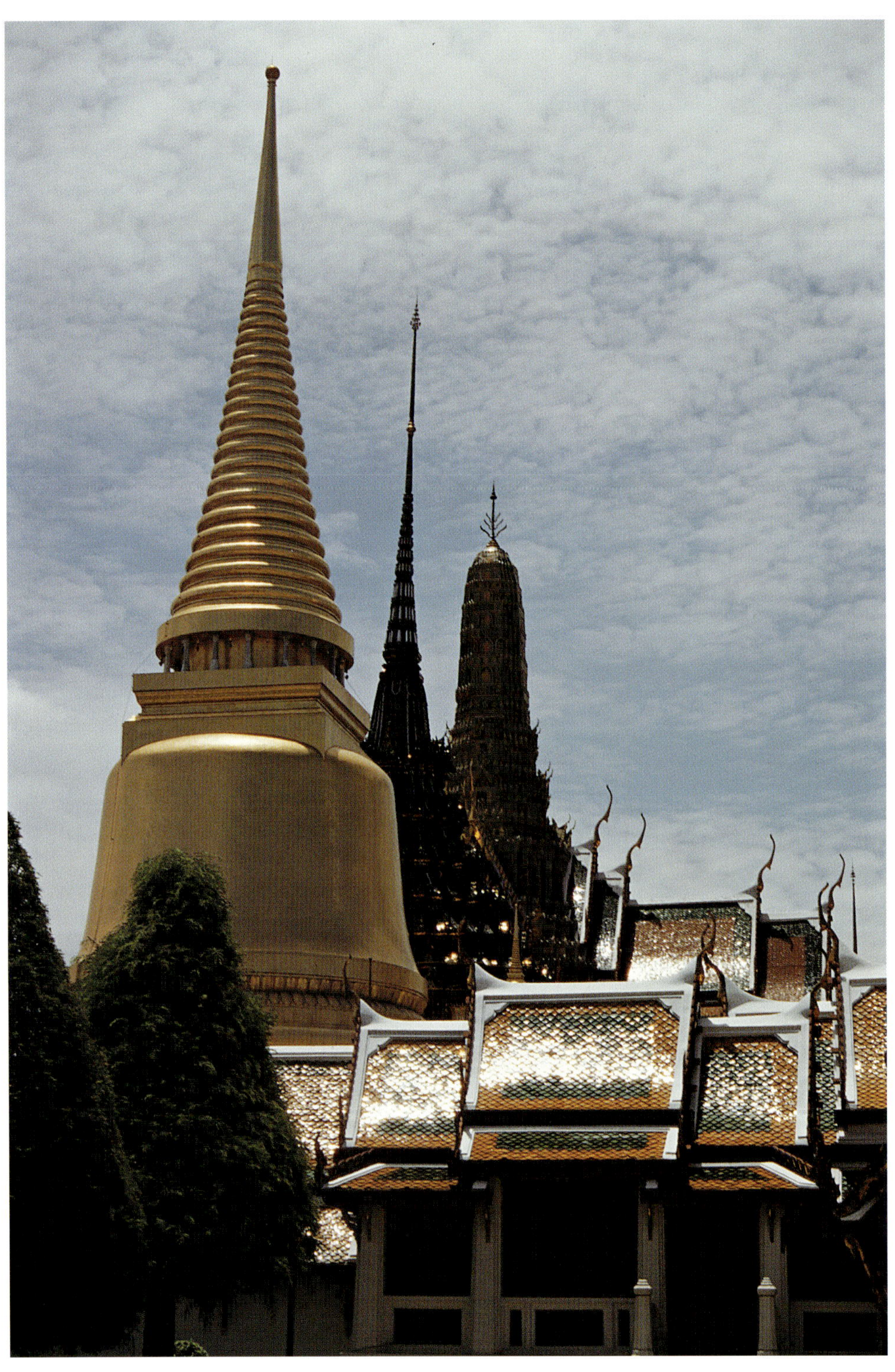

towards a more ethereal destination, or circumscribe the limits of visual understanding? Cryptic beacons, they demand attention, and then lead it away to mysterious destinations.

Elevated Orders: City of Reflection

Ultimately, Bangkok's roofs present a special city, a city of reflection. It is a city created for our visual appreciation, a different city from the chaotic plane of terrestrial activity. A curious ideal, it floats above real life and provides its conscience. An ideal attached to the real, yet pointing away from it too. But a journey to what? What are the benefits of leaving the horizontal?

There is a general value to verticality in Thai culture. It is considered rude to touch someone on the head, the most sacred part of the body. Equally anything related to the ground is debased. Shoes are removed prior to entering any place of significance (house, temple), and one must be careful never to point one's feet at an image of the Buddha. Stepping on money is highly frowned on, as it shows disrespect to the monarch's portrait. Yet Thai massage, steeped in traditional medical lore, begins with the feet, finding a summary of the body's forces in their complex structures. Base, yet worthy of attention, they provide the starting-point for the eventual progression to the head, the body's controlling summit.

In Buddhism one searches for the way, the path towards eventual enlightenment. The passage through human consciousness is a metaphoric progression towards Nirvana. Perhaps paradoxically,

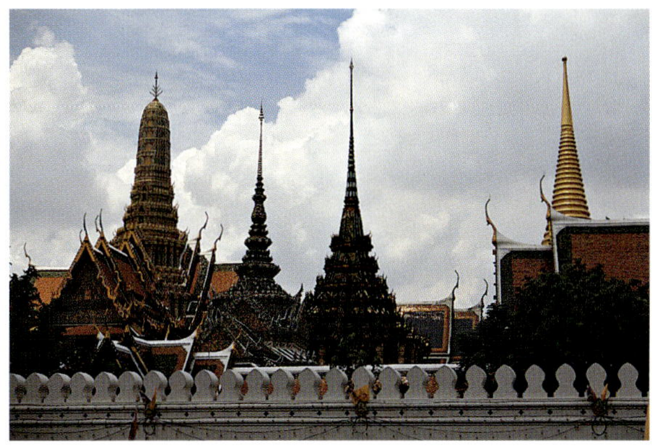

the destination is one of ultimate immobility. One engages in a journey that leads to the end of movement. Perhaps the roofs mark the end of an earthly passage, and the beginning of a more mysterious Other. The idea of passage is of virtue in itself, from earthly to abstract, from base to ethereal. The temple roofs as vertical destinations manifest the metaphoric journey most clearly. Travelling towards an ultimate stasis, they present metaphors of stability and commencement, vehicles on the journey towards invisibility.

Bangkok's roofs articulate a potential for order, present yet distant from the space of inhabitation. Both ideal and real, they are physically and visually vivid, yet also disconnected from practical life. The roofs reveal an enigmatic urban consciousness: a city of desire. Perfection is valuable, but only visually or imaginarily possible. Real life is chaotic and messy, but an imaginary world floats above as its model and conscience. The roofs demonstrate the ideals of perfection and tolerance simultaneously. One strives for perfect form, without ever succumbing to the conceit that it is possible in real life.

THREE

Streets

Streets: linear boundaries masquerading as places of travel. A dysfunctional circulation system of gridlocked avenues; referential passage to a new world. Illusions of movement; horizontal society. Rama conquers the newly created nature.

Official City: Passage and Avenue

The Grand Palace identifies Bangkok's historic centre. Resting on Rattanakosin Island, constructed as the focus of a series of concentric canals, the palace symbolizes political and religious authority within the city. Yet the functioning cities of government and commerce reside at a considerable distance from this iconic core. The new parliament and its governmental precinct, along with the current royal palace, are situated to the north, constructed as early modern buildings set in their own parks. The city of corporate towers stretches to the east, abandoning the historic centre (and its river) for the flat landscape beyond.

Bangkok is a city of many centres, in seeming competition. Or perhaps the notion of a physical centre is here meaningless, a historical bias unfulfilled in the expanse of the city's sprawl. The experience of centre has always been problematic in Bangkok's experience. The Grand Palace was an ambiguous urban focus, for official life remained hidden behind its high walls. Only in the relatively recent past has the palace and its temple, Wat Phra Kaeo, been generally accessible. Cartographically clear, this centre was historically an experiential void. A socially distinct urban mystery.

The absence of a single centre is key to Bangkok's reality. The resulting mobile focus calls attention to the connections between the city's parts rather than

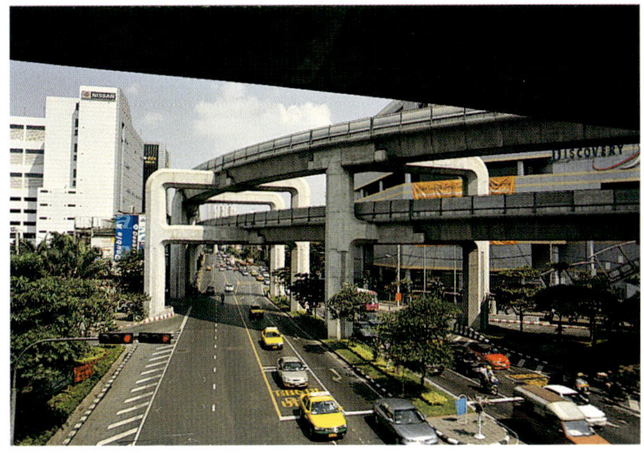

the specific qualities of the parts themselves. Bangkok is a city on the move, the ideals of reconstitution implicit in its historical travels rediscovered through its various forms of terrestrial passage. Bangkok's many partial centres are only brief pauses in this ceaseless movement. Or they would be, if the traffic wasn't so appalling.

Bangkok's major roads establish the lineaments of this city of travel, manifesting a cryptic skeleton of curious routes and vague destinations. These roads, having now mostly replaced the city's legendary canals, provide the principal settings for contemporary life. Indeed, the ideals of movement, and its difficulties, characterize Bangkok's modern existence. Extensive travel is a given, its experience a perplexing frustration. Manifesting an ambiguous order, the major avenues follow little apparent structure, or seemingly support any specific destinations. Horizontal movement may define urban form, but actual travel seems often pointless. Yet these same streets actively participate in the city's development, and measure its historical trajectory.

Arguably Bangkok's most significant road, the clearest example of a historic urban route, and the most indicative of the city's sequential transformation, begins (ends?) at the Grand Palace. Travelling east from the Palace wall, though not aligned with any entrance, the road cartographically orders the space of the official city. While assuming a variety of names on its journey. From the Palace it starts as Thanon Kalayang Matri, to become Thanon Bamrung Muang after passing the canal aligned with Bangkok's original walled periphery. In this urban phase the road links the Grand Palace to Wat Suthat and the Buddhist Swing monument, the great arch that acts as a city gate, framing views both in and out of the historic core. Leaving this traditional centre the road flanks Wat Saket and the Golden Mount, an artificially constructed hill overlooking the city. Crossing the outer canal it transforms into Thanon Rama I, named after Bangkok's founder, Phra Phuttha Yotfa (Rama I), to connect the National Stadium with Siam Square, a major shopping area. This expression of royal authority then becomes Thanon Ploenchit, and, finally, as the road veers to the south, Thanon Sukhumvit, the focus of the contemporary commercial wilderness beyond.

A clear line in plan, a confusing sequence of transforming spaces in reality. Partly due to the quirks of one-way travel, its linear nature is vehicularly sacrificed to a series of detours and realignments. Yet for brief moments the road constructs Bangkok's clearest avenue, establishing an approach to the Grand Palace and providing the outward extension of its east–west orientation. Linking the historic city to its landscape, it establishes a major ordering spine

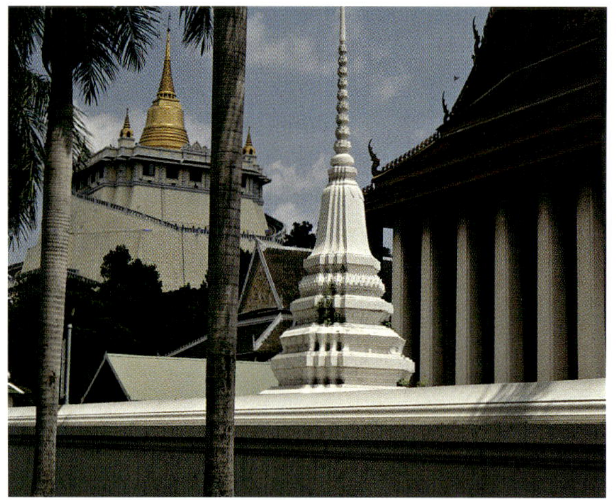

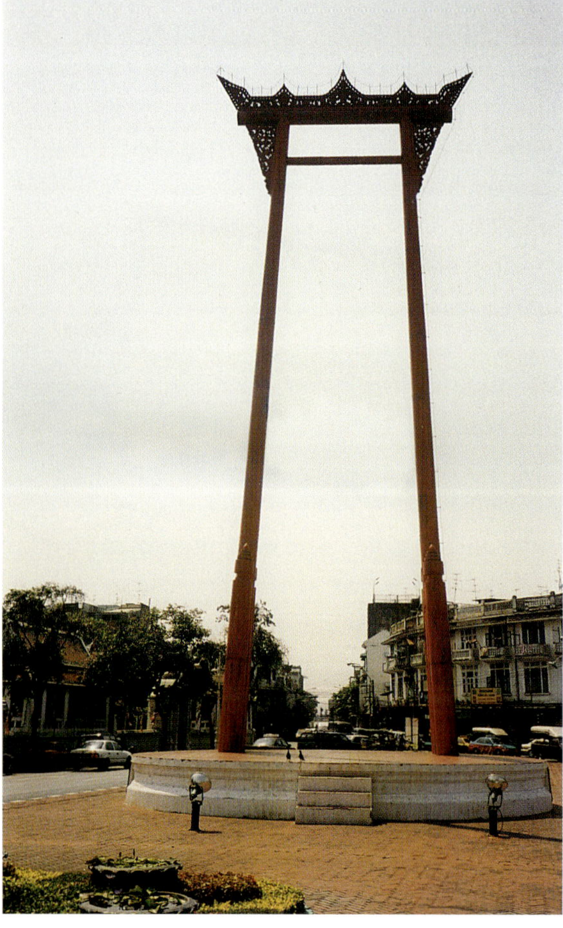

within Bangkok's fabric, while simultaneously doing its best to obscure this significant urban function.

Other avenues locate more recent monuments. The Democracy Monument, built in 1939 to commemorate the abolition of the absolute monarchy and the new constitution of 1932, is centred on Thanon Ratchadamnoenklang, the major avenue to the north of Rattanakosin Island. This road, grander in scale, is used for major parades and celebrations. Flanking the top of Sanam Luang, the royal parade-ground, it leads towards Wat Rachanadaram, the temple figure most easily associated with the Mount Meru cremation constructions. Roughly parallel, Thanon Rama IV creates a third major east–west avenue further to the south, connecting the centre to Lumphini Park. The city of official monuments is laid out along these principal boulevards, in ways that begin to match perspectival expectations, though the context clearly does not.

While connected to the historic city, with its fine grain of traditional buildings, the great avenues develop their own qualities. Indeed, Bangkok's two great commercial streets, Silom Road and the aforementioned Thanon Sukhumvit, define the city's modern face. Projecting out from the river, past its earlier boundaries, they forcefully establish the Bangkok of the modern world. Silom, architecturally the older of the two, is related to the city's earlier commercial developments. Spanning between the river and the entry to Lumphini Park (though from a different direction than Rama IV), and centred on the statue of King Mongut (Rama IV), Silom is a classic modern avenue. It is dense and international, home to banks and embassies, and still arguably pedestrian despite its traffic. Sukhumvit presents a more extreme new world, a truly contemporary

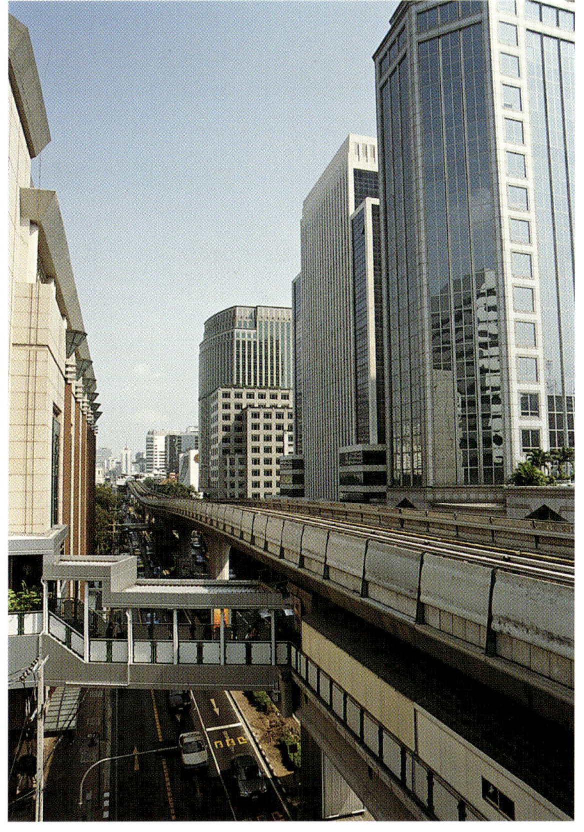

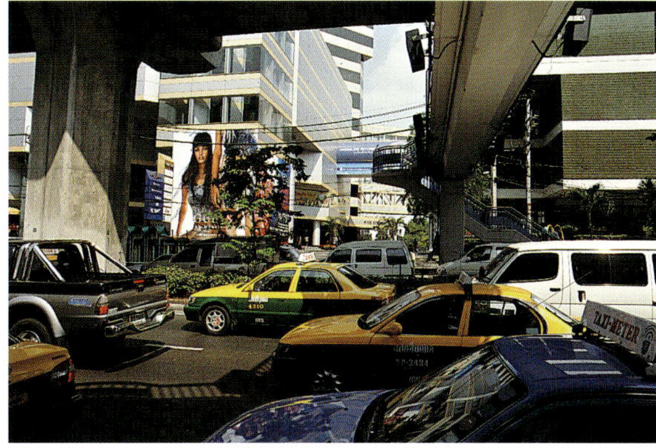

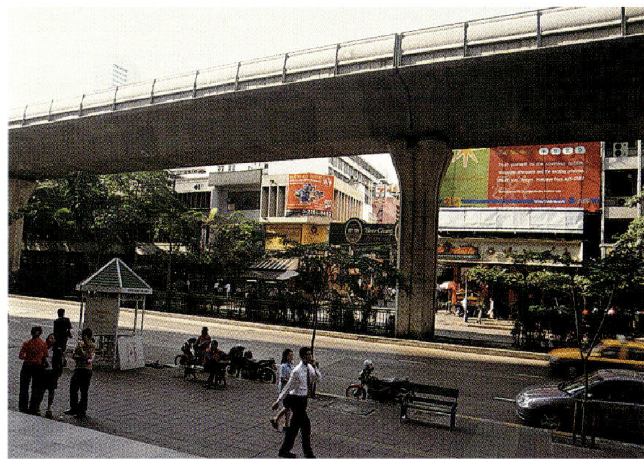

construction like no other. It locates the city of programmatic hybrids, the Bangkok that extends to the hyperactive shopping malls and cinema complexes of the idiosyncratic metropolis beyond.

Tall buildings line these principal streets, and visually support their significance. This figural weight is further reinforced by recent infrastructural developments. Bangkok's Sky Train follows the lines of both Silom and Sukhumvit roads, celebrating their importance while floating above their earthly concerns. The focus of the new city: passage at speed. Significantly, both major avenues and their high-density development avoid the historic core. They project out, in a voracious consumption of the landscape. Although this might indicate respect for the symbolic centre, it also guarantees a separation between the city of history and the locus of modern life. The city of the future, created on the outer reaches of Bangkok's denatured landscape, is divorced from its past, and each set of forms is increasingly exclusive. Indeed these avenues, remarkable for their intense traffic and manic development, are the modern city. A city known by its roads, with streets named after Rama, the mythical figure of the forest. Rama, whose name only adorns the major avenues once they leave the original city behind, never within. Rama, abandoning historic or sheltered comfort for a heroic life in the urban wilderness.

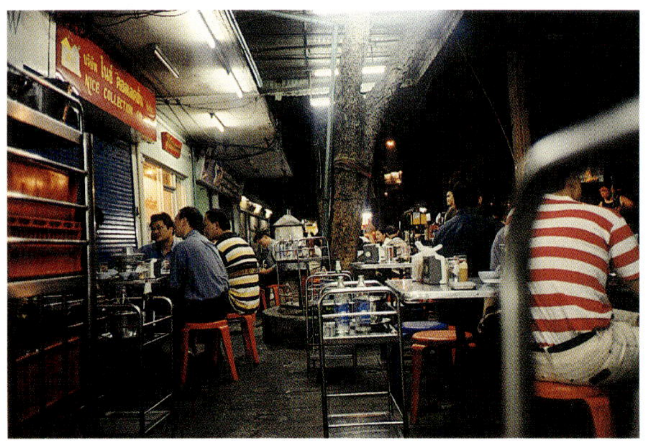

Street Culture

The noise, pollution and density of the main avenues would seem to present an anti-city: an urban dystopia of machine and asphalt. Yet Bangkok and its citizens demonstrate a remarkable urban tolerance. Both make maximum use of the city's infrastructure to animate their daily activities. The golf-course that winds between Bangkok's airport runways is perhaps the most extreme example, but more regular life manifests similar desires. River ports become markets, the city's historic fortifications support parks. Streets, even major ones, are appropriated as extended living-rooms. Building interiors open directly to the sidewalks, with little formal separation established between. Boundary zones of semi-private activity animate the public realm. Night markets, food-stalls, beer-bars – all bring an intense vitality to Bangkok's street life. Shopping, drinking and dining: the progenitors of urban activity.

The roads' social vitality is viewed in contrast to Bangkok's other spatial figures. The royal gardens of Lumphini Park and the smaller Saranrom Palace Park are urban-scale spaces awaiting inhabitation.

Examples of nineteenth-century landscape design, pleasant escapes from the city's heat, the parks create romantic settings popular with evening joggers and young couples. Yet they are generally quiet, especially in relation to the streets. Sanam Luang, the royal parade ground, is more central: a popular terrain for kite-flying and soccer. Though extremely significant as a place of festival, its daily occupation is modest. Other major urban oases, such as Chulalongkorn University and the Royal Bangkok Sports Club, remain as slightly alien figures. Programmatically distinct from daily concerns, they clarify the energy of the streets by contrast.

Bangkok doesn't really have any public squares, though the recent renovation of the ferry terminals and the City Hall plaza / parking garage may provide the exception. Siam Square, a leading contender for a contemporary downtown, is not a square at all but rather a densely packed collection of shopping alleys. Fronting Thanon Rama I, it acts as a hinge between the new city and the old: a hub of commercial activity rather than public expression. Indeed, Bangkok is a street city by choice. These streets provide its principal public spaces, its own urban nature. The city's latent desire for density is

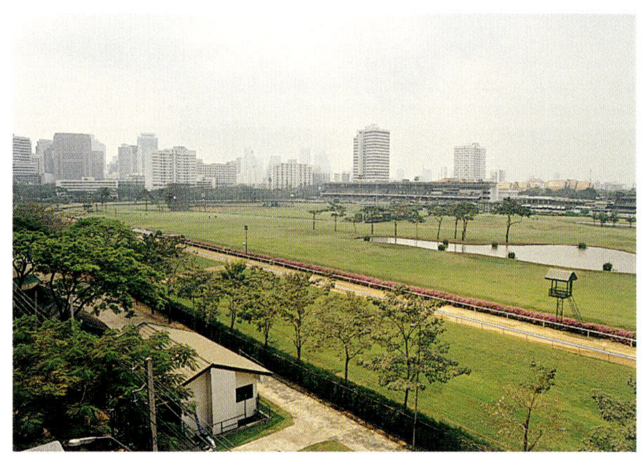

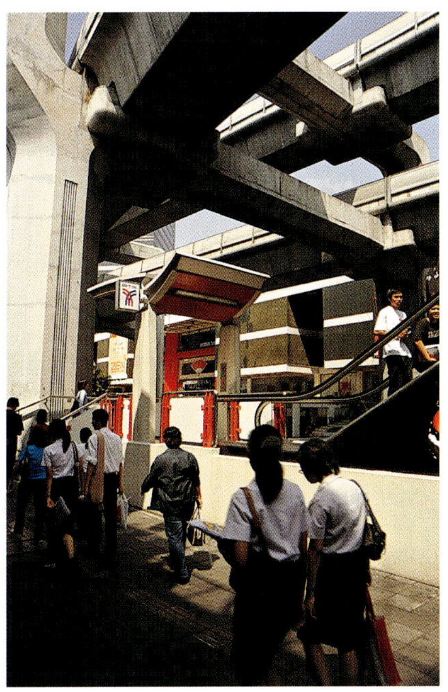

clarified by the contrast between these streets and the royal parks, the quiet foils that remind us of the process of active selection in place. The vitality of the city's streets, with their varied occupation, eliminate perhaps the need for other urban spaces at all. Rama, god of the forest, takes responsibility for these new worlds and renders them safe for habitation.

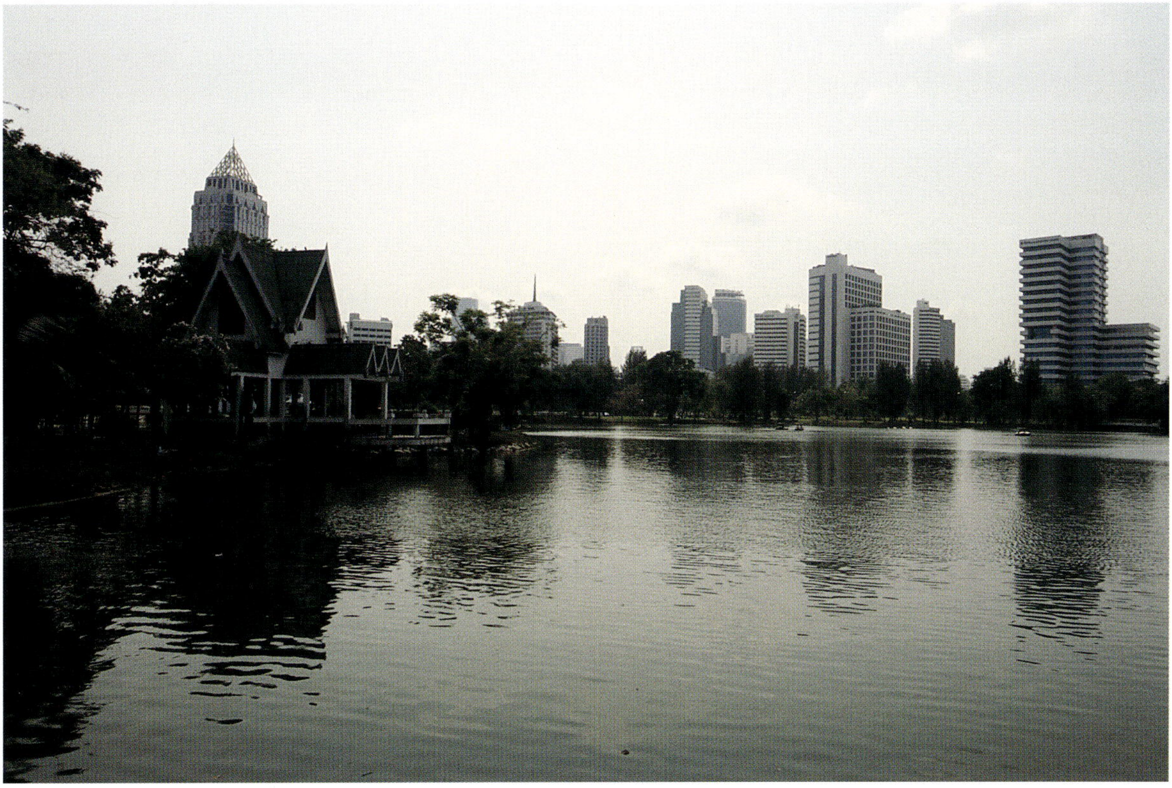

Bangkok, however, is not only a city of streets and avenues. There is an additional structural aspect to its circulation system that satisfies the implicit desires for spatial distinction. For Bangkok is also a city of alleys. This city, barely visible from the world of official passages, shelters its secret life.

Small alleys, hidden worlds.

Self-contained neighbourhoods of introspective dead-end passages.

The official city of flawed boulevards validates private anti-cities of social vitality.

Soi Life: Structure as Means

Bangkok has relatively few major streets. It is reported that the city's proportion of paved roads to occupied space is 8.1 per cent, compared with London's 16.6 per cent and New York's 23.2 per cent.[1] These principal roads circumscribe large swathes of urban fabric that remain independent from the experience of the avenues themselves. Yet this fabric is interwoven with numerous small alleys, called *sois*. Contrasted to the fume-choked avenues of the official city, the *sois* establish a quiet locus for urban activity. Different structures of passage and place, distinct worlds of invisible occupation.

While the Bangkok of the avenues feels larger than its twelve million, the *sois* generally maintain a village-like texture. Their basic structure is inherently feudal, with large plots subdivided for domestic inhabitation. The major roads take care of vehicular life and urban transit in general, while the cross-alleys protect smaller-scale pedestrian realms. These *sois* support Bangkok's local markets, traditional houses and indigenous commerce – the avenues, banks, office buildings and shopping centres. There is little in between.

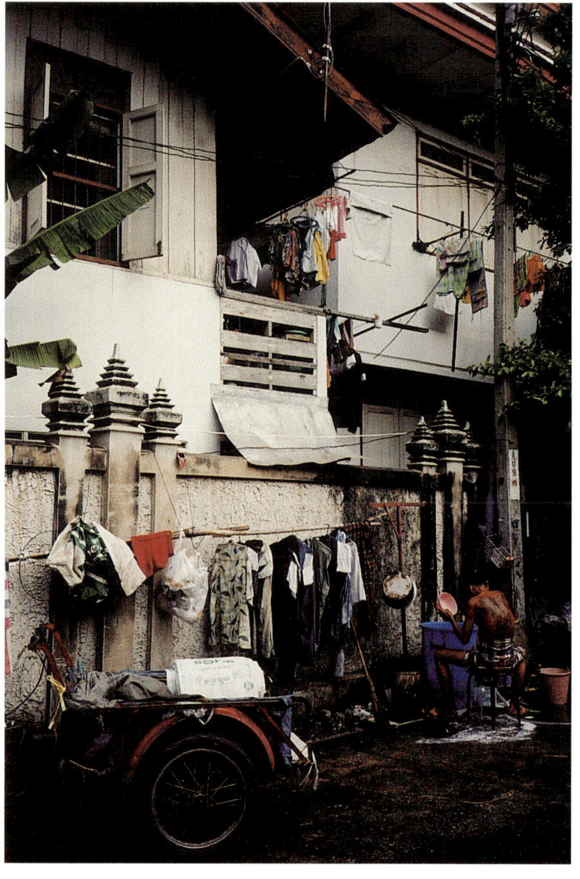

In the juxtaposition of the massive avenues and the profusion of alleys, the life of the city is found. It presents relationships of spatial contrast and contrasting vitalities, a pairing of extremes. This curious dialectic is arguably the root cause of Bangkok's infrastructural challenges. The city's legendary traffic chaos develops where each dead-ended *soi* connects to a single supporting avenue alone. As the *sois* slowly feed into the main streets, traffic flow is seized with arterial failure. The *sois*, designed for residential-scale habitation, are increasingly asked to support larger buildings, overburdening both their physical context and circulatory capacity. Yet the

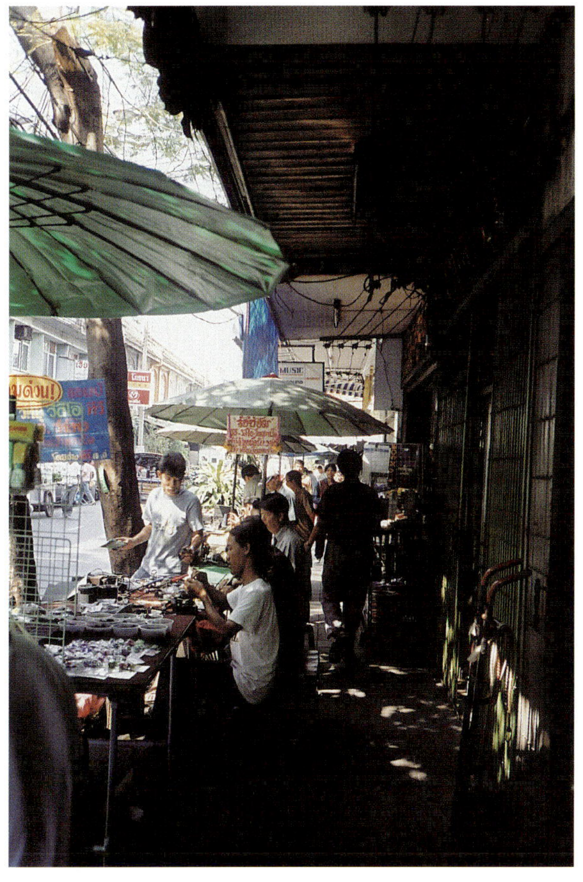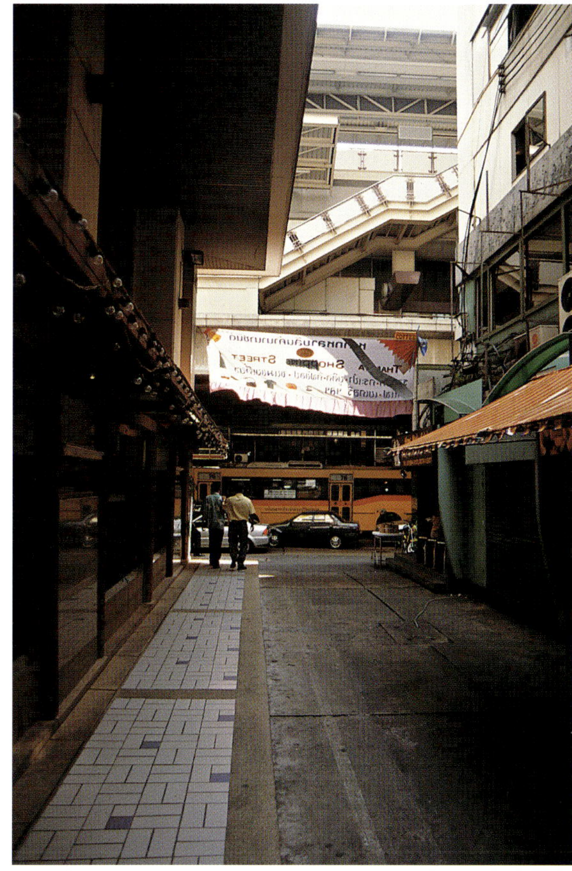

same difficulties provide urban benefit, in the *sois'* ability to protect indigenous life in the face of generic development.

The clear orthogonal *soi*-avenue structure of the contemporary city appears to be fairly recent: a reaction to the modern taste for roads over canals. In Bangkok Noi, the remnants of the proto-Bangkok on the west side of the Chao Phraya river, urban interaction remains more canal-based. *Wats* and houses face on to differently scaled waterways, often with no land connection between them at all. The *sois* that do exist are labyrinthine in quality, creating a dense experience of crooked, dead-end paths.

Fragmented passage links private occupation; the place of public meeting are the canals themselves. Although more evenly planned, the later *soi* structures re-create the introspective atmosphere of this earlier city. Small pockets of local concern are outlined within the greater whole, hidden away and protected. It is a structure of exclusion, of separation. Proximity to the larger public city is maintained, yet an independence of experience is created.

The pairing of avenue and *soi* is indeed an interesting structural model. While a recipe for disaster from a traffic perspective, it is also a guarantee of urban specificity. Individual neighbourhoods are sheltered, their idiosyncrasies enshrined. Within these hidden alleys, new worlds await discovery. Ultimately, the singular challenge of traffic in Bangkok, the city of traffic, is surmounted by the very scale of its problems. The *sois*, unamenable to urban circulation, transcend traffic. Their pedestrian realms, fixed in scale, remain independent of the outer city and its concerns. Bangkok is a city eager to accept the modern world, but whose very structure is predestined to defeat it.

Soi as Character

Bangkok is clearly a street city, one whose street patterns are constructed to be as inefficient as possible. They are as strangely made as can be. Movement is accentuated on the avenues, resisted within the *sois*. While no squares exist as urban alternatives to the roads, the *sois* take over this social role. They are pedestrian plazas first, and barely places of passage second. Spatial hybrids, inhabited in strange ways. Places of distinction in the urban field.

The contrasts of avenue and *soi* are present throughout the city, in varying degrees of rigour and clarity. The *sois* of Silom Road are more corporate, supporting the smaller-scale restaurants and shops that serve the avenue and its offices. Sukhumvit Road's collection offer more striking contrasts of scale and character. The perpendicular passages establish a rhythm along the main avenue, measuring out its linear extension in regular intervals of diverse events. Each alley is known officially by its number, more socially by its associated inhabitants. Perceptually, the avenue bisects a strange and dense net, exposing brief flashes of otherness along its directed travels.

Places of relative tranquillity, the *sois* construct Bangkok's social interior. Cut off from the major streets, this city is experienced in its fine grain of domestic life. The small alleys lead to residential neighbourhoods. Houses rest as freestanding pavilions within their walled yards, the *sois* defined by their modestly articulated perimeters. Often a collection of buildings within family precincts, the houses protect a sheltered, inward focus. Domestic life is defined in close proximity to the large-scale commercial city thriving just a few steps away.

One of the by-products of this unique street pattern is an increase in social density. From within the *sois* there is a limited sense of opening, or potential escape, towards the larger city. The world is viewed through long narrow passages. This local specificity constructs a special kind of focus, increasingly identified with particular activities. Interconnected or adjacent alleys form precincts, filtering out the general city to create distinct programmatic zones. These small alleys create urban-scale figures through their gradual accumulation of similarly intended functions and events. Bangkok's markets develop in this way, from a collection of *sois* adhering to a shared purpose. Variety is encouraged between the *sois*. Within, a form of seemingly unconscious specialization takes place. Their internal focus allows a clarity of concern and intent.

Soi as Escape

Worlds hidden from the world; separate precincts of activity. Whether as market or more distinct programme, the *sois* create a focused attention, and develop their own distinct personalities. An acceptance or even celebration of diversity is structured within the defined frames. A clarity of purpose, if modest urban expression. The *soi* structure supports the creation of mini cities interspersed within Bangkok's general fabric. These dedicated zones assume an internalized quality, one reinforced by the extension of private roof canopies over the public passages. The new ceilings further obscure the *sois*' public nature, as their infrastructure becomes commercially or socially possessed. Increasingly dark and private, the *sois* support increasingly private activities.

Bangkok's notorious side, its precincts devoted to commercial sex, are direct descendants of the *soi* structure. While programmatically extreme, they follow the *sois*' predilection for the definition of internal and exponentially vivid worlds. Patpong, the most famous version of this urban phenomenon, is an offshoot of Silom Road. The precinct was created as a real estate venture, where the large block spanning between two major avenues was cut with minor cross-streets (*sois*) to create a series of smaller building plots. A pedestrian market constructed within the official city. By day it is a sleepy refuge for lunching office workers, patronizing a few local shops. By night, a transformed nether world. Home to go-go clubs, massage parlours, music pubs and the ubiquitous beer-bars (small outdoor bars open to the *soi*), the area celebrates an exaggerated separation from the official city and its practical concerns. This distinction is reinforced by its metamorphosis each evening into a thriving night market. Densely packed stalls selling fake Rolexes, Ralph Lauren knock-offs and imported hill tribe crafts partly screen the sex bars behind. Bright neon, dense crowds of shopping tourists, and private activities made public. The market, like the clubs, disappears in the early hours of the morning to be reborn the following evening.

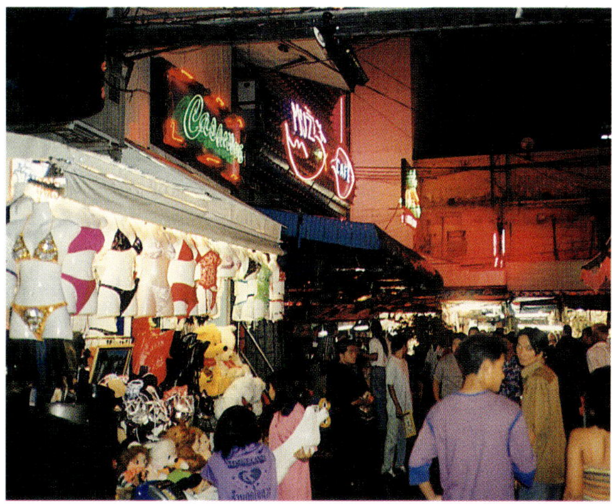

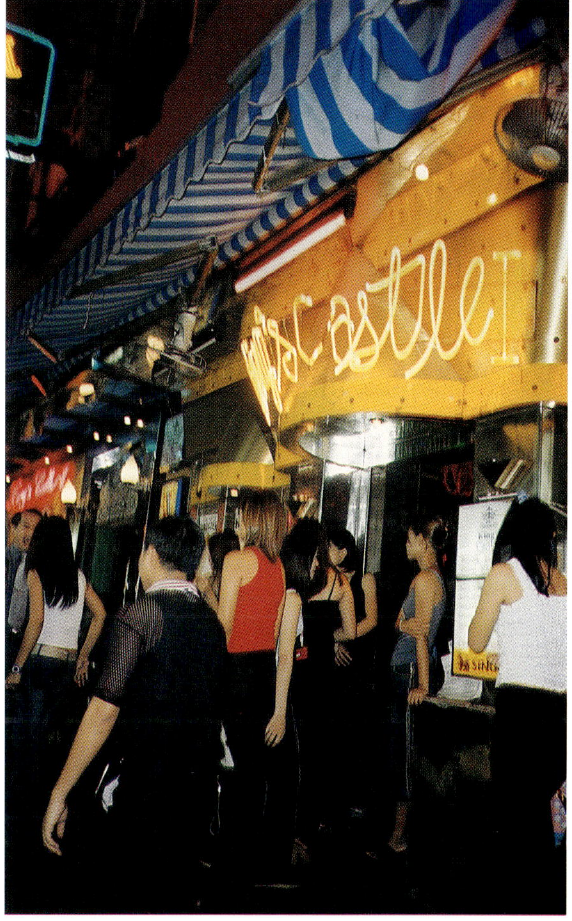

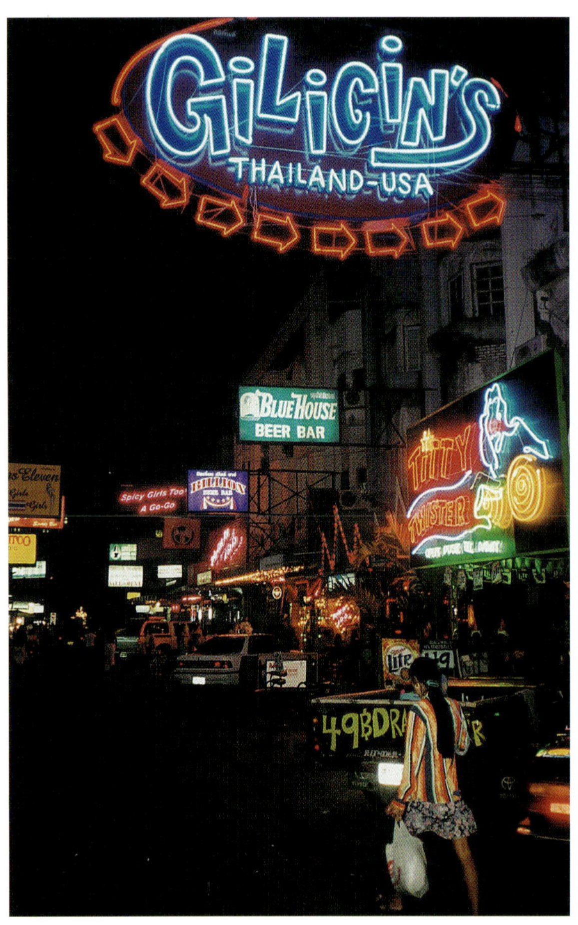

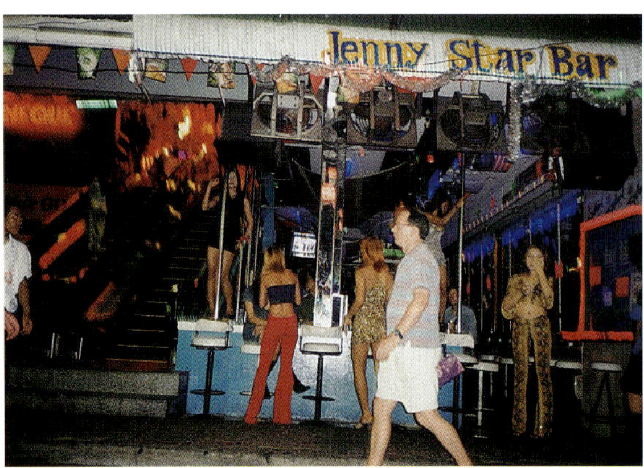

This collection of alleys presents an introspective world of entertainment like few others. Shut off from the city, dark and dense, Patpong identifies a strange and artificial floating world.

Other versions of nightly intensity appear through Bangkok, all enclosed within focused precincts, all populating the dark. The *sois* of Sukhumvit provide many examples, immediately adjacent yet distinct from the official avenue of grand hotels and offices. Smaller and more focused than the broader tourist appeal of Patpong, they heighten the contrast between the interior and the public, the dark versus the lit. Places where the public city truly ceases to exist, though it remains in close proximity. Programmatically extreme, these entertainment areas exaggerate Bangkok's general structural principles. All the *sois* thrive on their introspective nature, and differ in degree rather than sensibility.

An escape into private darkness, an inverse city to the Bangkok of the temple roofs. Life in the *sois* eliminates the power of the visual city altogether by replacing it with an environment of immediate experience. Yet similarities between these extremes exist as well. Both cities present intangible realms. Both are distinct from the concerns of the official metropolis. Both thrive on their heightened contrast with the responsibilities of the practical.

Disconnected elevated roads; overlapping rail systems. Strange ribbons of concrete. Constructions of modern motion raised above the city; salvation through imported technology. Place replaced by mechanisms of efficient movement; the suppression of reality achieved. Streets below in shadow; an underworld of urban life. Above, mythical views created, contrasts heightened.

Dystopic City

The effort to solve Bangkok's traffic problems is heroic. Massive raised highways cross the city. A new Sky Train careers along its major commercial avenues. A subway is due for completion in 2004. The scale of the recent constructions is remarkable. And the scale of its difficulties. Over-budget, rife with corruption, the infrastructural projects encapsulate the modern political city. Process aside, there are also challenges in the form of these infrastructural insertions. Messy, disconnected and expensive, the new transportation networks do not create any unified or idealized order. They remain, instead, dependent on the confusing and circumstantial patterns of the city itself.

Challenged by the complexity of the small-scale *sois*, and with limited control over private land,

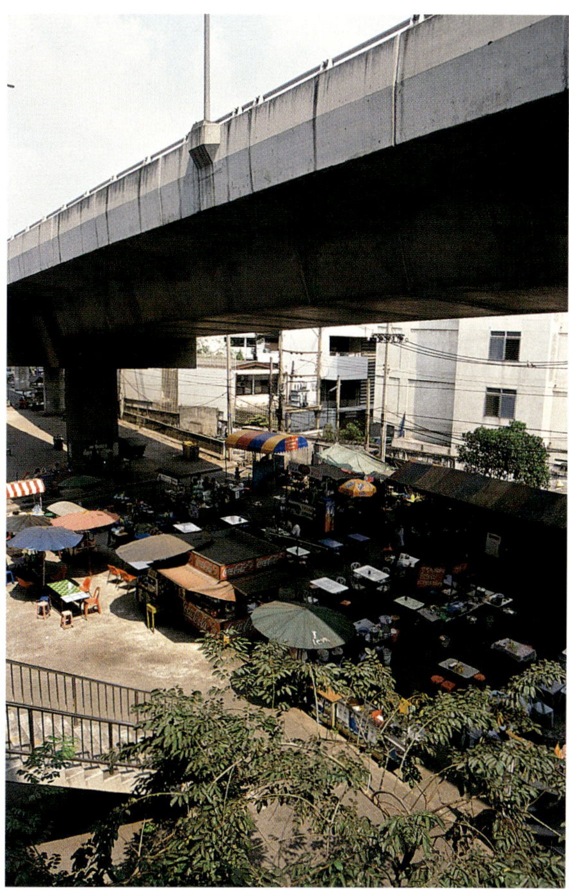

Bangkok has elected to conquer the sky. A series of multi-level circulation systems has been super-imposed over existing roads. Pedestrian overpasses create a rhythm of bridges crossing major avenues – the texture of the *sois* confronting the linear street. At major intersections, more exotically, they create diaphanous networks of elevated links. The junction of Rama i and Thanon Phaya Thai, adjacent to Siam Square, is celebrated with a remarkable composition, a veritable spider's web of passages. This creation reinforces the significance of the intersection while simultaneously floating above it. The overpasses create breaks in the flat terrain, providing temporary respite from the mechanistic flow beneath, and the dubious pleasure of viewing it all the more clearly. While designed for pedestrian convenience, the walkways foreshadow new spatial possibilities, later to be realized at a grander scale.

Two major raised highways have been built. The Phayathai-Bangkhlo Expressway, also known as Thanon Rama VI, runs north–south, bisecting the city before extending to the suburbs and countryside beyond. A massive construction, it defines the perceptual break between the new city and the old. Further east, the Chalern Mahanakhon Expressway creates an additional north–south line, and articulates the edges of Bangkok's contemporary transformation. In terms of urban impact, however, the new Sky Train is the most dramatic and intriguing. Two lines meander in different directions from their intersection at Siam Square. Both skirt the historic core to focus on the commercial city. More significantly, the Sky Train system follows Bangkok's major commercial avenues, reinforcing the city of contemporary life and affecting its experience. Centred above the roadways, the tracks bring a curious addition to the already manic avenues.

The streets below are shaded and transformed, an underworld obscured by the alien structures above. Travel has been elevated to a new status, with earthbound life degraded in the process. Movement is deemed more valuable than place. Yet the value of this movement is illusory. With little original city remaining in the light, where is there left to go? Indeed, these interventions create a dystopic image of the futurist city. The elevated expressways carve through neighbourhoods, virtually colliding with long-existing buildings and covering formerly grand streets. Trains shoot off at speed in new directions, though not extending far enough to reduce significantly the city's reliance on cars.

Is the city legible in these massive insertions? Do its newest forms reveal Bangkok's underlying order? These constructions create the impression of grand repairs. Large urban bandages struggle to heal a damaged condition rather than propose new forms of order. A fatalistic reaction to a challenged infrastructural state? A reaction plagued by local politics, with its accompanying corruption and political infighting? There is a circumstantial quality to the interventions. They follow the seemingly accidental layout of avenues rather than re-create the city anew. Even the map of the Sky Train system avoids any temptation towards ideal order. Unlike, for example, the official map of London's Underground, Bangkok's Sky Train doesn't reveal any coherent intent in its graphic representation. Not ideal even in image, the Sky Train is equally unable to achieve order in its reality. Bangkok has, perhaps, sacrificed its last great chance to reorder itself: an opportunity lost.

Yet it is also possible that there is a subconscious intent to these strange conditions, manifesting a taste for direct experience rather than the easy abstractions of plan. While the circumstantial route reveals little, the actual experience of riding the Sky Train is far more significant in revealing this urban intent. Through its infrastructure Bangkok is becoming more true to itself, rendering its contrasts more extreme. Bemoan the unexpected or revel in its odd specificity.

Underworld

The city of infrastructure: a dystopic ruin or the exaggeration of existing tendencies? Entering a

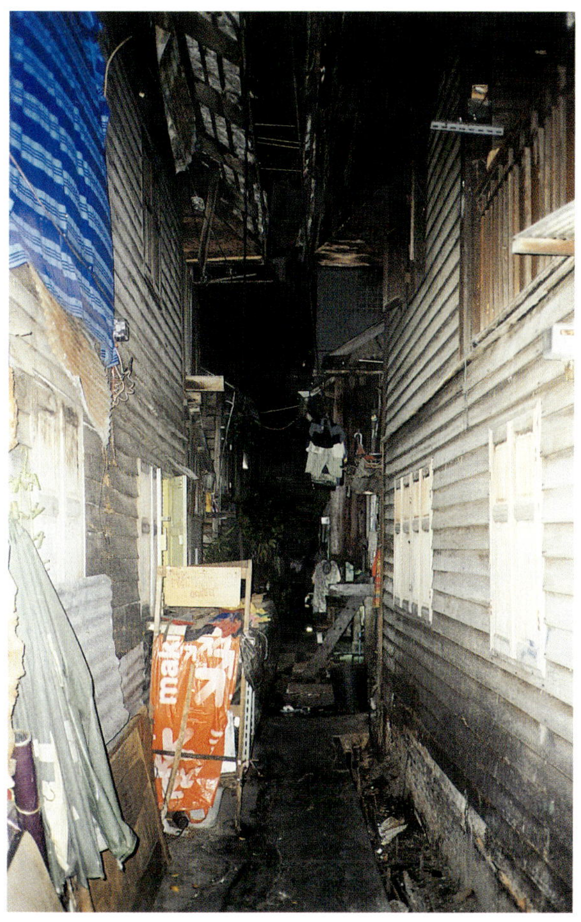

The new underworld created by the highways, and more specifically the Sky Train, mirrors this experience within the city at a larger scale. The slender Sky Trains transform the previously frantic, though relatively normal, avenues into linear caverns. Streets become urban remainders, the ground abandoned in the search for faster travel above. Historically significant avenues now become underworlds of darkness and mystery rather than the face of the official city. The Sky Train, designed to remove traffic from the avenues, may have cured the disease but killed the patient.

Yet, perhaps counter-intuitively, the actual experience of these spaces is not unpleasant. The streets are shaded and cool. While the ground may not have been of paramount importance to the infrastructural design, the consequences are interesting. Small niches provide shelters for commerce, the underside of stairs and escalators ideal for protected activity. Though seemingly degraded, the ground is not uninhabited. In some areas it is increasingly active, with commercial stalls crowding what little sidewalk is left. The air is a little grim, since the ground traffic within the cavernous volumes is usually stalled, and the exhaust has little venue for escape. But it is not insufferably so. The partial glimpses of sky open strange fragmented vistas: a spatial mystery reinforced. The structure and staircases of the floating rail system intersect with the street in idiosyncratic ways, creating a novel visual field. The place beneath, Bangkok's new urban underworld, is a curious civic promenade.

A further manifestation of a shared cultural taste for density? A subconscious will to compress shapeless experience into tightly contained packages, with clearly defined edges? Or perhaps it expresses a

Bangkok market, the outside world has been edited. Tarpaulins cover the small passages, the sun blocked except for the occasional flicker entering through the fabric's cracks. Dark and intense, focus is internalized towards the products of the market. Crates of dried fish, Buddha statues, clothes. The small-scale shops extend their canopies over the *sois* to further exaggerate this sense of enclosure. Only partial light and view are allowed: fragmented glimpses of a distant city. A desire for interiority is manifest in these temporary constructions, with a limited sense that any greater clarity would be a preferable state.

desire for fragmentary experience, avoiding any sense of an illusory whole? The density of this underworld prevents any simple comprehension of the orders of the street, reinforcing its partial appreciation and its experiential intensity.

The modern Bangkok of the grand avenues is imitating the small-scale markets of the traditional city. Attention is focused; external distractions are eliminated. While similar in kind, this development is remarkable in its scale. Entire avenues become dark and introspective. Their earthly quality is accentuated, their lack of connection to the city's spectacular roofs made explicit. The daily life of the street is divorced from the idealized city of aerial figures, and in its place a focus on the tangible, the shaded, the immediate. A taste for enclosure, a taste for darkness. The underworld becomes urbanistically visible. An intense realm is created through manipulating the infrastructure of travel.

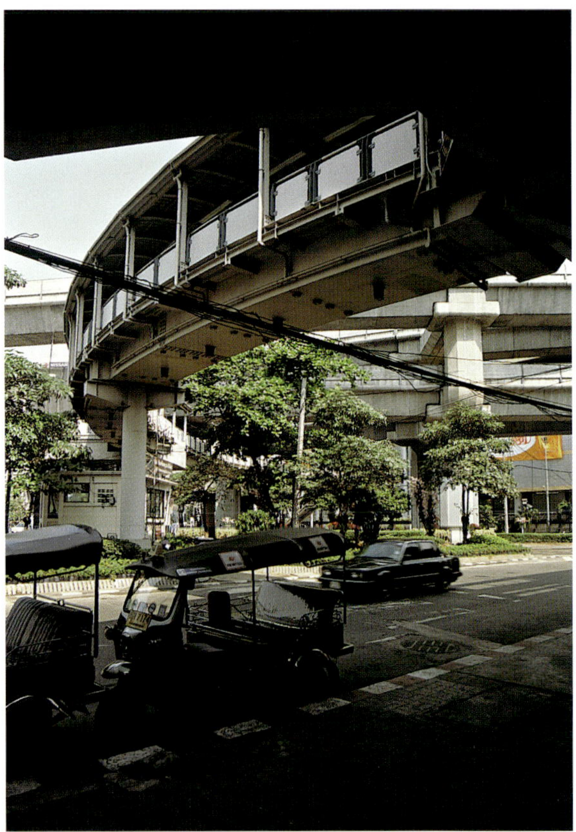

Overworld

The undersides of the walkways, roads and Sky Trains are arguably accidental, the unavoidable consequences of an infrastructure elevated above the street. More curious perhaps is the experience of the raised passages themselves. For if their underworld reinforces a condition commonly perceived in the smaller-scale markets and *sois*, the overworld experience is physically new, previously only artistically imagined.

Through the elevation of travel Bangkok becomes a sectional city, in a topography that has no natural experiential section. These strange figures of travel present, as a result, a form of urban fulfilment. For the first time one can publicly view the city's sheltered precincts, peering from above into their private domains. This creates in life what was previously foreshadowed only in the city's landscape paintings. Side effect or intent? No longer is it necessary to construct imaginary axonometric projections. The city's interiors, its courts, wats and gardens expose themselves to view, fulfilling the promise of the temple's frescoes. Private sanctuaries reveal their structure, but they pass by at speed. Visible but fleeting, always seen in motion. No longer only imaginary, interior urban life becomes real but transitory, their brief appreciation a different form of intangibility.

The infrastructure of travel creates new experiences in the city of heightened contrasts. A darker

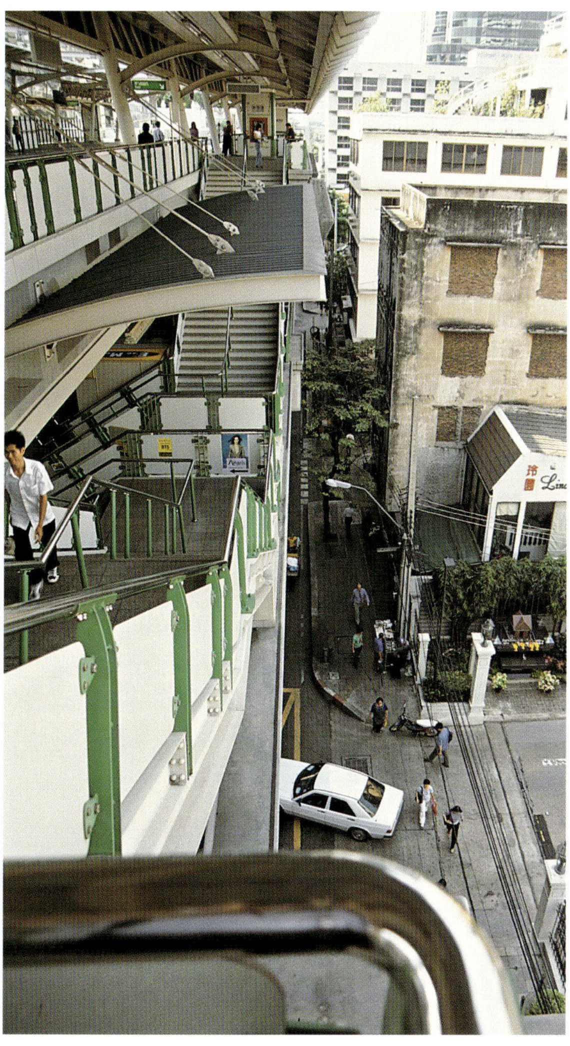

darkness and a new floating panorama of aerial appreciation. Modern construction accentuates the historic city and exaggerates its narrative qualities, but at a distance. Bangkok is a city whose spatial ideals are paradoxically accentuated by travelling over and away from their direct experience. This new section has transformed Bangkok's roads into essential spatial narratives. From darkness to the novel view, the value of vertical passage has been heightened, its contrasts rendered extreme.

A sensory richness is created through this focus on practical realities. Neighbourhoods become more intense, *sois* more enclosed. The fragmentation and localization of parts is fulfilled through the insertion of large-scale infrastructures dealing with linkages and passage. The unintended consequence is that Bangkok becomes more true to itself.

FOUR

City of Characters

PART ONE

Domestic activity at an urban scale.

Precincts of calm amid manic urban life.

Roads deform around oases of singular activity:

shopping, reflection and prayer. Adaptation

and transformation; particular events

rendered urbanistically significant.

Precinct as Character

Bangkok's small *sois* create an urban lattice of internally focused spaces. Yet throughout the city these contained strands gradually cohere into larger wholes, creating recognizable neighbourhoods identified with specific activities. While Patpong and its Sukhumvit brethren are the city's most extreme, Bangkok has a predilition for the creation of functionally discrete precincts. Sheltered from the public avenues of manic travel, the precincts of grouped *sois* internalize urban experience within intense introspective worlds. The city becomes legible as a patchwork of characters, each precinct a form of domestic experience expressed at a civic scale.

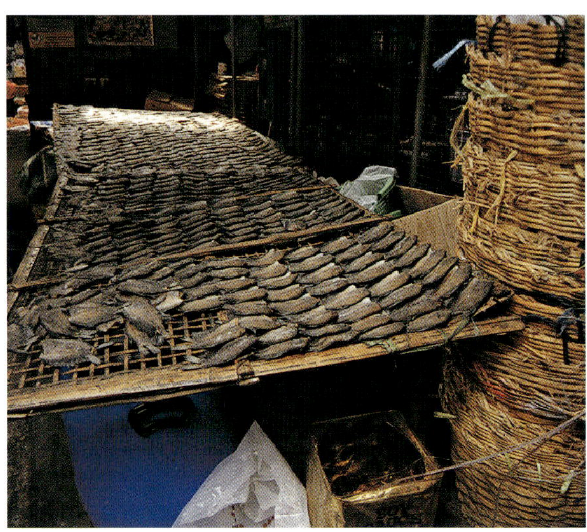

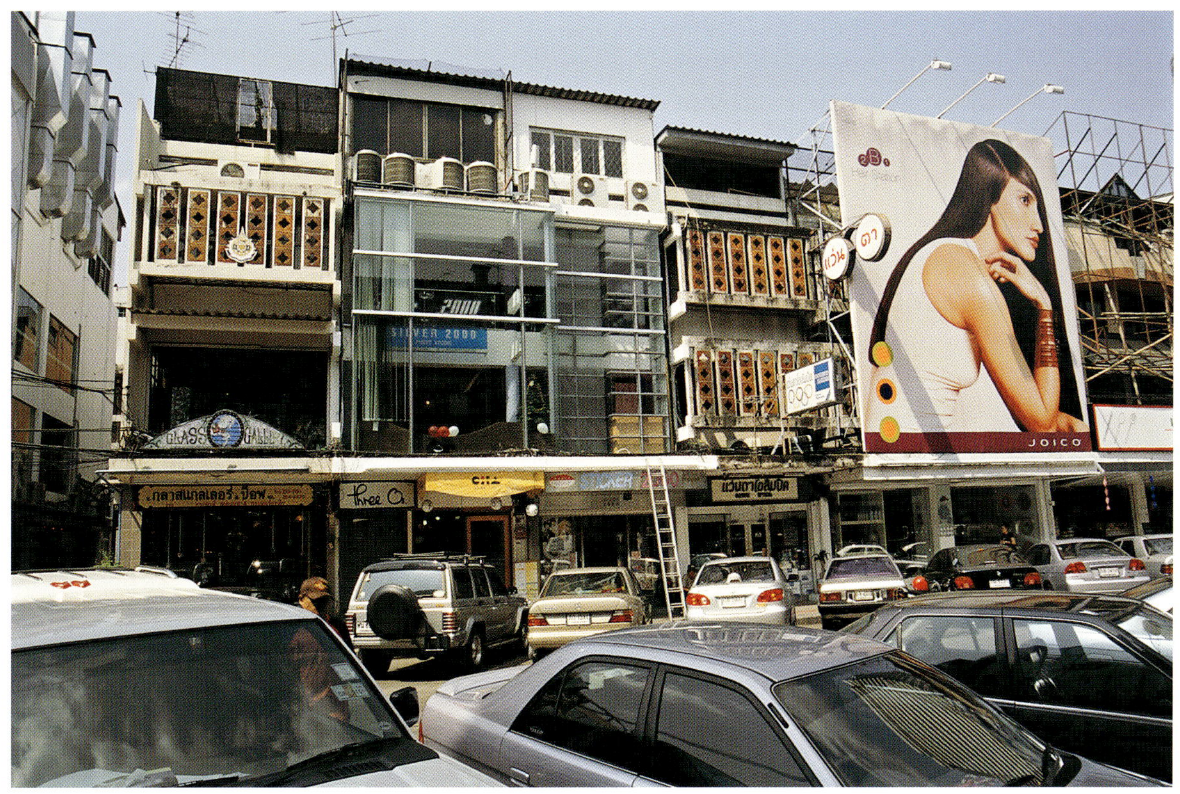

The fish market adjacent to the Grand Palace:
a dense warren of dried squid. Beside a river port,
occupying an early commercial block, the market is
a key functional event in the traditional city. A public
facade, a mysterious interior. Narrow rows of crated
fish. The *soi* structure is compressed, the sun filtered,
the exterior world more severely edited. Within its
boundaries, all is fish. Their scales flicker in the
shadows, lit by the few shafts of fragmented light
allowed to penetrate and enliven the heavy darkness.

The tin-recycling quarter, adjacent to Wat Arun,
manifests similar spatial preoccupations. Within
the dense structure of Bangkok Noi an entire
neighbourhood, with its *sois* and buildings, is
set aside for collecting and flattening large cans.

The delivery mechanisms of choice for processed
foods and oils find their way here, to be redirected
to new lives. Metal reconstructed in the darkness,
a focused task. A historic guild of workers, located
over time? A hereditary family possession?
The congruence of a specific activity and a particular
urban fragment is remarkable. An impromptu
electrical market takes over the streets centred on
Thanon Tanao, a few blocks east of the Grand Palace.
The sidewalks are lined with portable tables, covered
in dishevelled electronics in varying states of creative
repair. Within the buildings the small shops sell
televisions and stereos, their content paralleling
the activities on the street. Siam Square, far more
officially, demonstrates similar principles of urban

definition. A collection of international fixtures (7–11, the Hard Rock Café . . .) and various local outlets are packed into tight alleys, combining to construct a considerable urban figure. Its immediate neighbours are even stranger. Large buildings house multi-level air-conditioned markets. Part shopping centre, part three-dimensional *souk*, these urban precincts masquerade as individual constructions. Icons of shared preoccupations, manifest in varying states of formal clarity and scale, collectively define Bangkok's social geography.

Historical and anthropological analyses argue that Thai society is fundamentally grounded on flexible relations of shared dependencies. Compared to the more arbitrary notions of legal codes or consti- tutions, these bonds are personal, adaptable and enduring. Historic village structures provide the model for social, commercial and even legal practices. At each scale traditional allegiances progressively establish the links between individuals, their social context and the more abstract (and fairly recent) notion of state. The structures of family, village, confederation, government department, country; all present different variations on this essential social order, a condition that underlies the fluid nature of Bangkok's legal, commercial and political structures.[1]

Arguably these models of personal and social cohesion are expressed analogously by the prevalence of Bangkok's urban precincts. A hierarchic and compartmentalized society is constructed within each diverse urban figure, with the city as the composite result. Each precinct a society, each a constituent member of the larger whole.

Business Bangkok, royal Bangkok, sex-precinct Bangkok. The city is composed of its multiple centres, all dedicated to specific activities and their adherents. Each finds what he or she needs, acting within a fairly defined set of choices, all active within the tapestry of the greater city. Even in situations where the outside world most intrudes, Bangkok's precinct sensibility manifests the artistry of its daily life. One of the most oddly distinctive of these fringe areas is the 'traveller' precinct, the site of backpacker culture in the City of Angels.

Banglamphu's Khaosan Road, resting just north of the royal quarter, just west of the river, presents a striking example of the street as urban character. Home to guest-house culture and its inexpensive lodgings, it is, unlike the grander hotel areas, also uniquely close to Bangkok's historic centre. It is a dedicated personification of flexible urbanity: alien yet central, international but historic. Khaosan Road manifests Bangkok's intriguing contradictions in its own strange and compelling way.

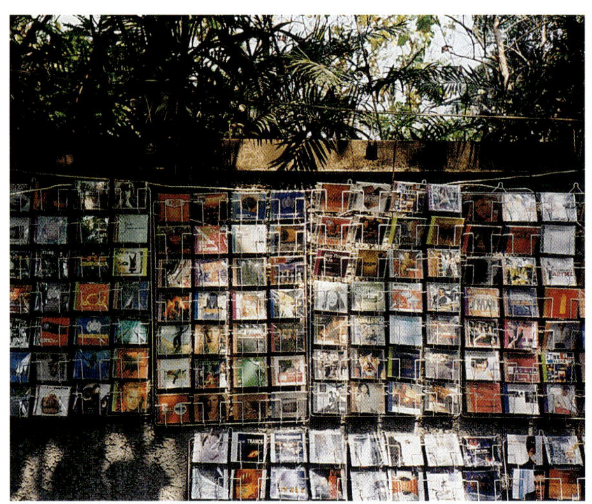

Khaosan Road is a conscious and adapting creation, a place of conflicting images and contrasting demands. Possibly nowhere, or anywhere, it describes an international ghetto (utopia?) of preconceptions and expectations. A crossroads of peoples, a place of generic international otherness. Aboriginal wind-catchers for sale alongside Nepalese jewelry and Burmese teak chopsticks, all pored over by a cross-section of the world's travelling youth. Tanned Scandinavians, under-dressed Israelis, freshly tattooed Californians. A place of sanitized restaurants and transient travel agencies, Khaosan Road is not of Bangkok directly, but rather serves to repackage it for the convenience of budget travellers. The ones glued to their email screens at the countless internet shops, or watching the ever-playing American movies or First Division soccer matches alongside. The street provides the agents who organize the minibuses (and air-conditioned executive coaches) to the islands and hills, guest-houses across a spectrum of prices and propriety, souvenir shops, international CDs on order, and every snack under the sun – some of them even Thai. 'Travellers', a group at least as universalizing as the more corporate tourists of Silom and Sukhumvit. Khaosan Road is truly a place to challenge urban specificity. A microcosm of international convention battles with the very culture it is there to visit.

It is easy to dismiss the area as an overly crowded playground dedicated to the unconscious hypocrisies of Western rich kids (of all ages). Yet, at the same time, Khaosan Road reveals qualities essential to Bangkok. A street specific in its own functional clarity, centring a larger zone. Part of an urban fabric of distinct parts, it is a place of tolerance

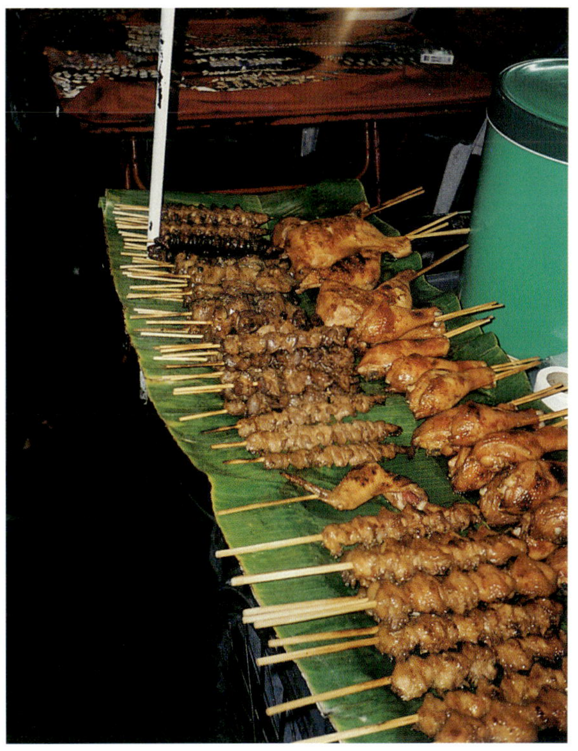

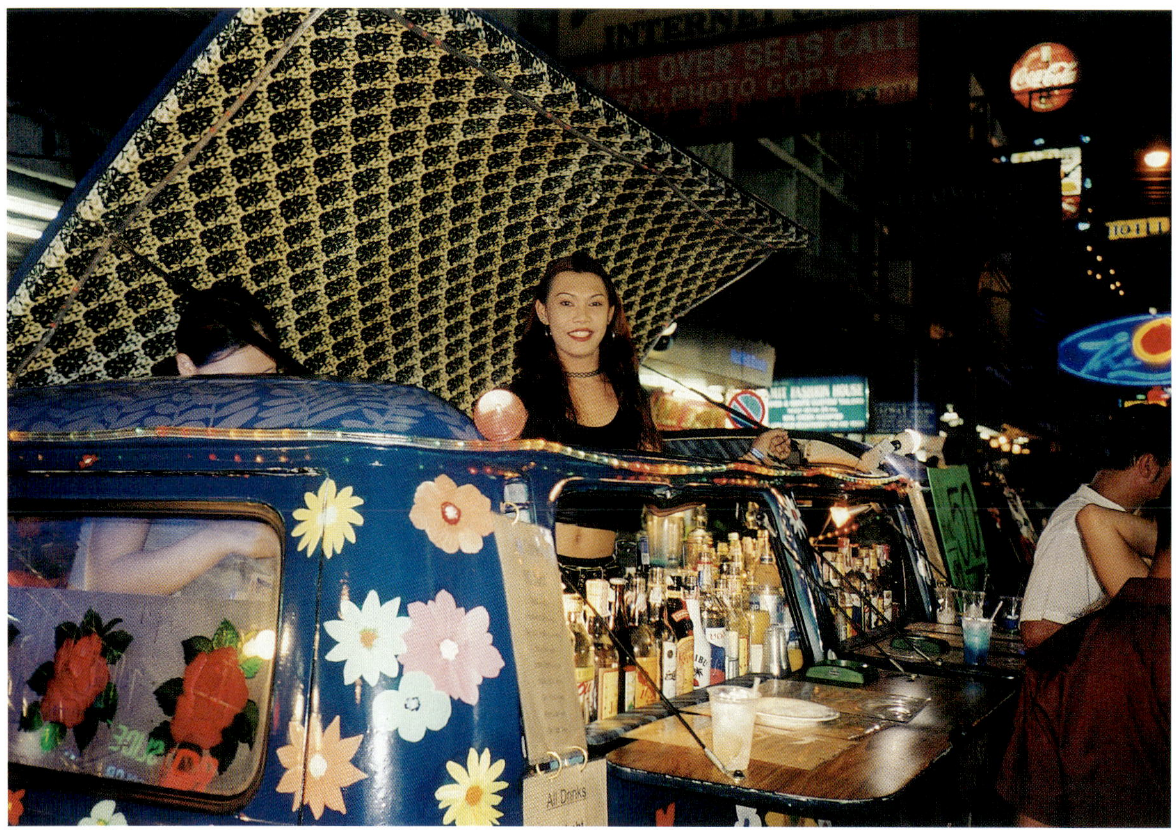

and amusement, dedicated to convenience.
A social centre with a thriving entertainment
culture. A precinct increasingly shared by Thais
and foreigners alike.

Indeed, Khaosan Road is becoming increasingly
Thai. No longer solely for backpackers, it has been
assumed into the larger city, most specifically by its
youth. This reverse takeover of Khaosan Road is
intriguing. While still commercially oriented to
foreigners, the street is increasingly a shared event.
Thai kids patronize local clubs. The trendy and
expensive ones are almost exclusively Thai; others are
more mixed. The cheapest, for visitors only. There is
an easy sense of acceptance and shared inhabitation.

The two solitudes have come together, with intense
results. Just as foreign travellers search out their own
mythical Asia, young Thais are curious about, and
becoming converted to, a fictional internationalism.
Tapping into social visions first perceived via the
strange visitors and their movies, they flock to the
visible manifestations of the novel culture. February
2002, St Valentine's Day. It was a significant event in
Bangkok, remarked on in the Press, but only for the
locals. Schoolteachers and the police were on special
lookout for any overly amorous youths inspired to
misbehave in public due to the day's imported romantic ideals. Popular clubs undertook a careful watch
for underage visitors. Khaosan Road, the street that

articulates this cultural intermingling, is indeed a strange urban and social hybrid.

Khaosan's economy has changed along with this social transformation. The tailors' shops, travel agents and guest-houses are still there. But there are also more Western blouses and T-shirts for sale to the locals; more Michael Jordan than the fake batik favoured by the travellers. This local youth establishes a new layer to the street: crowded, festive, socially interesting. A commercial creativity flourishes. An old minibus rests quietly parked during the day, to be converted into a cocktail bar each evening.

It is an intriguing economy. Small transactions, catering to modest needs, quickly adhere to become significant. Guest-houses earn extra commissions from laundry, selling stamps and the internet, all inexpensive conveniences for their patrons. The small profits pay for new buildings, and a Mercedes for their owners. While Banglamphu's image may be generic backpacker, its workings are much more indigenous, more idiosyncratic: more like Bangkok. Money recycles quickly, among many hands. It travels in a fluid and almost festive way. Even in commerce a sense of fun exists, a recognition that life is a kind of game. Here it is a contest played largely with foreign kids, but also with the authorities of the city itself.

A wave of energy washes down the street. The small outdoor kitchens disappear, partly grilled shrimps are hastily covered. Plastic chairs are whisked away. Seconds later a truck carrying impounded furniture drives slowly by, the police confiscating the materials of illegal sidewalk occupation. Incorrect licences, insufficient bribes? Both stories circulate. A cryptic early warning system operates, though it is difficult to perceive. A bicycle bell, a special car horn honking? If the vendors react in time, their furniture is saved. If not, it is piled on to the back of the truck, taken down to the pound, to be later ransomed. It is a nightly ritual for those of the precinct. They follow its special code; each knows his role, and the area maintains its idiosyncratic energy.

The older, quieter Khaosan sensibility is now positioned further out, filling in the streets around Wat Chanasongkhram. New guest-houses are being built, slightly up-market. The street spreads. Small-scale commerce thrives as it extends and transforms. Along Phra Athit Road, at the western edge of the area, new restaurants redefine this spirit of cultural integration. Benefiting from the nearby universities, Thai art students and the more culinary travellers, a kind of art gallery cum café culture has been created. A cultivated internationalism of quirky restaurants provides the respectable face to the hybrid creations of the Banglamphu precinct.

Tradition and transformation. Vitality and flexibility. Bangkok's urban characters develop to become increasingly specific through their processes of adaptation. The city of mirrors is identified by the many varied reflections of its urban figures. Visitors and inhabitants are equally represented via the precincts they inhabit, the city an accommodating receptacle of desired appearances. Too recessive? An ambition too restrained for a respectable city? Bangkok does not impose its ideas of order or proper behaviour brusquely. Yet, however reticent, some of these appearances are more challenging than others. Like all mirrors, Bangkok's demand self-reflection as well.

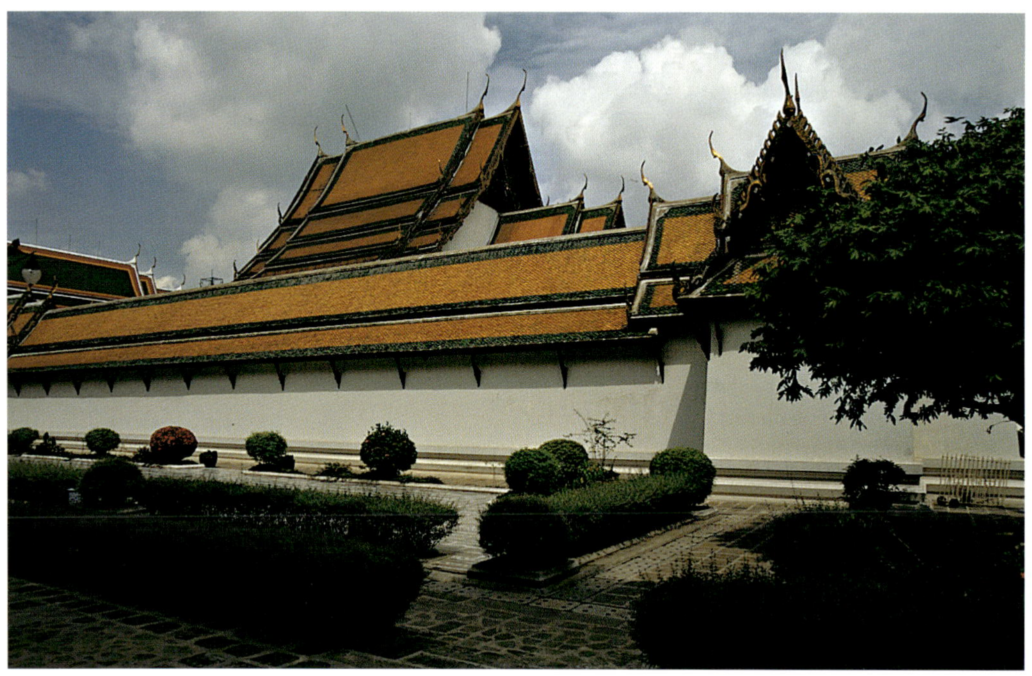

Icon in the City

Both destination and obstacle, Bangkok's temple precincts are part of its living religious culture. Known as *wats*, their urban influence extends far beyond their physical boundaries. The multi-coloured roofs float over monochromatic houses, just as their monks colourfully enliven the surrounding streets. Temple roofs act as markers within the city, reminding the practical world of these special places of value. They establish beacons of difference, through form and material distinction. Glazed ceramic tiles, guaranteed to shine in sun and rain. Orange, blue and green, their colours establish an intentional contrast to the mute city of wood and concrete. Yet in themselves the *wats* are carefully delineated, focused precincts. Urban characters within the whole; oases of an intense architectural calm.

Bangkok's *wats* bear a seemingly tangential relationship to the physical city. Their grounds are protected by walls, their gates articulated. No internal axialities follow the city's roads, no explicit links have been created between the precincts and the city at large. The *wats* present large obstacles to the orderly flow of traffic. With the exception of some general principles of orientation, they manifest little in the way of physical connection to the outside world. But they never disappear. Their roofs are but figures, ever visible above the noise of urban life. *Wats*: sheltered fragments of the utopic city or foils to read the city by? These roofs are in contact perhaps with the city's fundamental desires rather than with its daily realities. Intentional difference, or manifestations of the city's ambitions, expressed in more subtle and refined ways?

PART TWO

Sacred precincts; active architecture.
Clear boundaries and enigmatic
interiors. Lively social worlds. Ideal cities
or special events? Walls protect the
monastic city from the commercial, just
as images of Rama, the Indu / Thai
god–hero defend temple interiors from the
forces of evil. The city's heart is both
microcosm and foil.

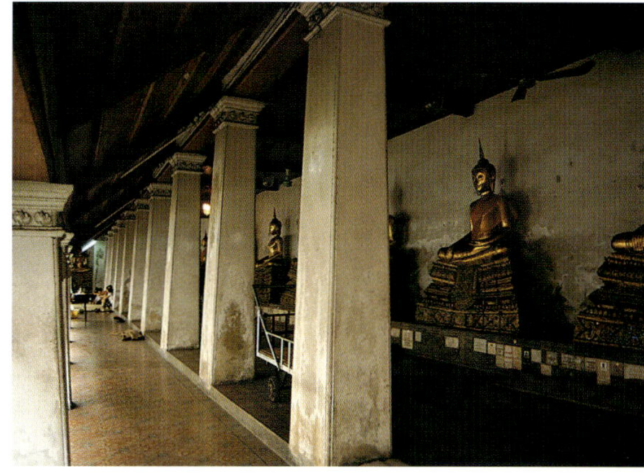

Form and Experience

Wat roofs are generally seen from a distance,
floating over the city to locate their special interiors.
In closer proximity their precinct boundaries join
the composition. Blank walls are conjoined with
the perfect but physically inaccessible roofs: a
strange combination. Neither easily give away
their secrets.

As urban edges, the precinct walls carry out
multiple functions. Visually they support the roofs,
separating these distinct figures and their protected
realms from the inhabited realm of the ground.
More simply, the walls define the symbolic precinct,
creating a clear delineation between monastery and
city. The *wat* is protected, an interior enshrined.
Openings in the wall, the thresholds to the inner
world, are articulated. Gates are made special to
mark moments of significant passage.

Myriad figures populate the interiors, viewed in a
gradual sequence of revelation. Dense and complex,
the *wats* are composite worlds, composed of diverse
arrangements of objects and spaces. In most cases,
additional sets of inner walls establish further boundaries. Protecting the centre, these internal layers also
frame linear arcades. Long sheltered passages; spaces
of gathering and reflection. The arcades provide a
buffer, a moment of tranquil repose in the transformative journey from city to temple. But they also
create spaces of narrative. Paintings, sculptures,
stories, teaching: all occupy the linear galleries. With
their roofs controlling a visual horizon, these active
boundaries are further articulated by subtle level
changes in the ground plane. The sequential layers of
entry are reinforced. Cool and often low, the arcades
prepare the visitor for arrival into the sacred

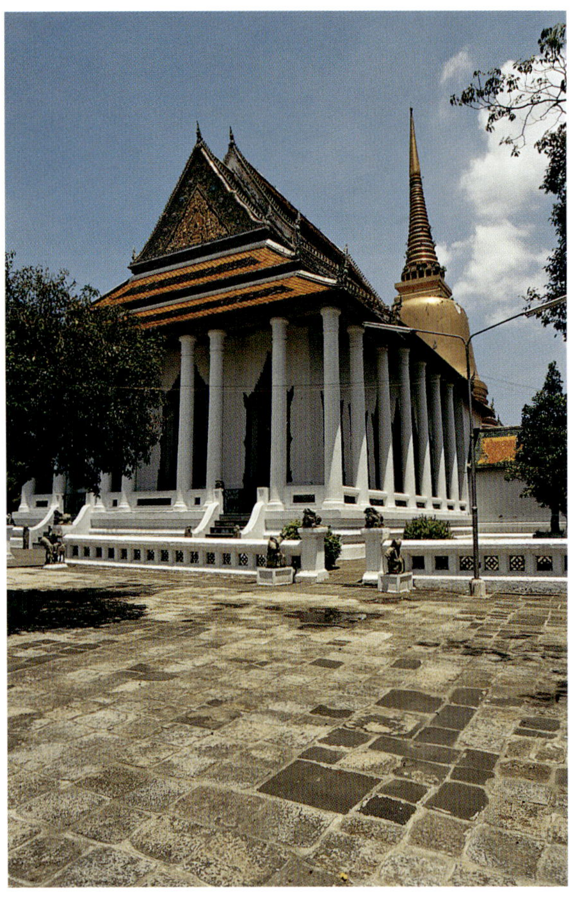 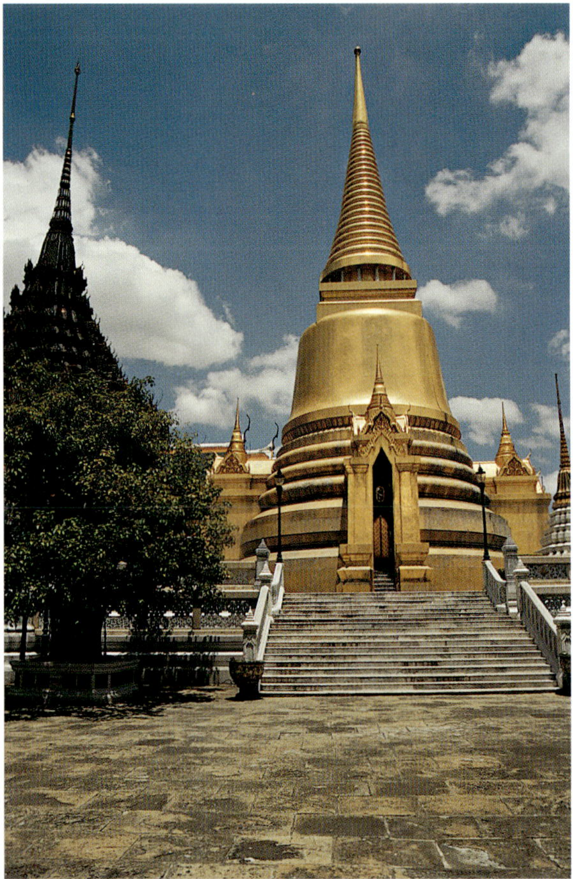

precinct, both physically and symbolically.

The principal temple figure encountered there is the *bot*. Home of ritual, the house of prayer and residence of the principal Buddha image, the *bot* centres the Bangkok monastery type. They are the bodies residing beneath the great roofs that loom over the city. The *bot* exteriors are often fairly mute, though not always unadorned. Large rectangular halls, they are usually oriented east–west, with an uneven number of small windows piercing each side. One enters from the city, moving towards the Buddha, who faces back towards the rising sun. Spatially simple, the columnar halls are richly adorned. Often painted with Buddhist iconography, the bot interiors are composed of dense reds, blues and black. Their ceilings are dark. Attention is internally focused; shoes are left outside.

The *chedis* are complimentary figures, placed as sculptural objects in fluid conversation with the great halls. Housing relics of the Buddha, or ashes of the devout, the principal *chedis* and their many subordinates create mountainous landscapes in architecture. Bangkok's *chedis* are usually deferential to its *bots*, the older *wats* of northern Thailand usually the reverse. In either case, an architectural conversation of object and interior is created. *Viharns* (temple-like figures), teaching pavilions, dining-halls, scripture libraries and classrooms; a series of additional figures populate the sheltered zones. Monastic housing, usually situated to the south, completes the composition.[2]

The Wat Mahathat is a highly internalized example of the type. Set between Thammasat and Silpakorn universities and facing Sanam Luang, the royal parade-ground, this *wat* is central to the official city. Inside, a working monastery. The long roofs of its interior arcades present its most striking aspect. Their low horizon visually controls the sacred world within. The arcades themselves are tight galleries lined with over 200 Buddha statues presiding over thousands of small receptacles housing the ashes of the dead. The *wat* is a living entity, in a continual state of redecoration and refurbishment. New burial spots are created, Buddha images draped in saffron sashes to celebrate the event. An active school occupies the north side, dense residential quarters to the south. Long coherent streets order the housing, a literal urban quality well defined. A large *bot* and modest *chedi* centre the composition. Unlike most *wats*, however, the land between the principal figures is treated as a garden. Planted with decorated trees, the interior precinct of the Wat Mahathat is an Edenic oasis within the heart, and heat, of the city. One special tree becomes a shrine, adorned with coloured fabrics and offerings to represent the site of the Buddha's enlightenment. Form, history and event.

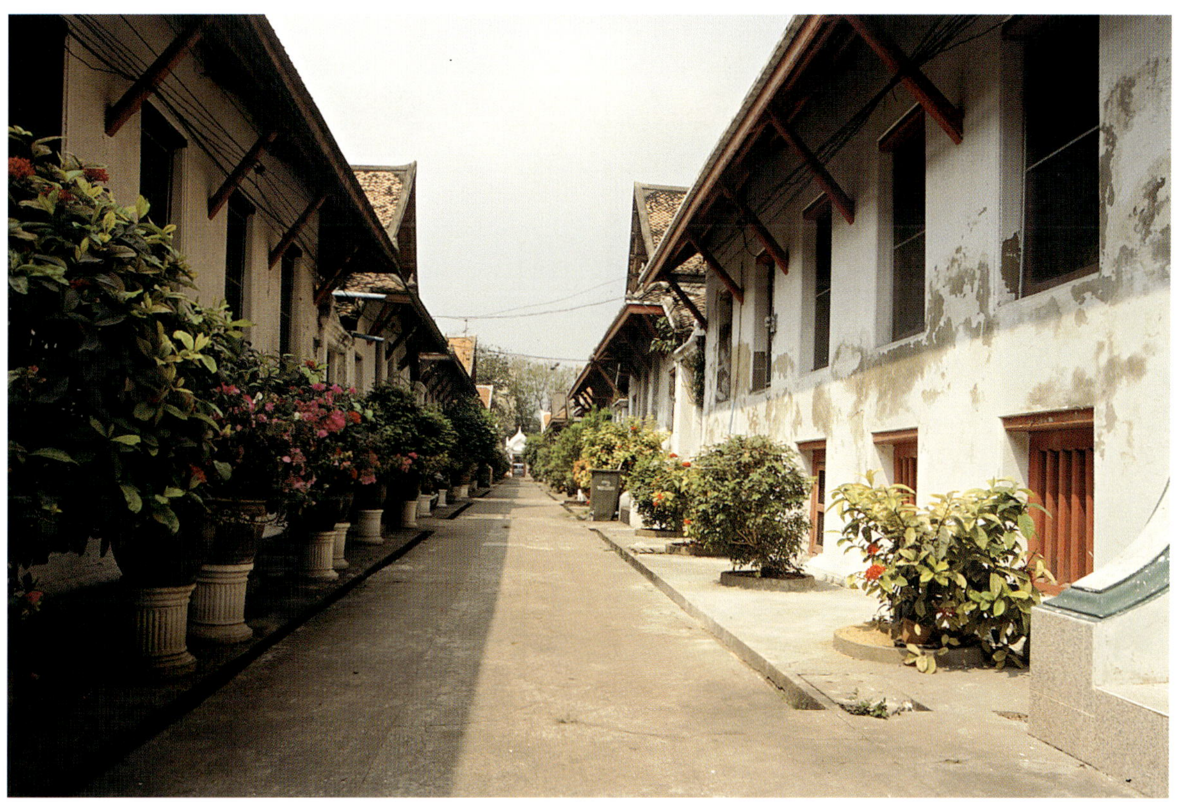

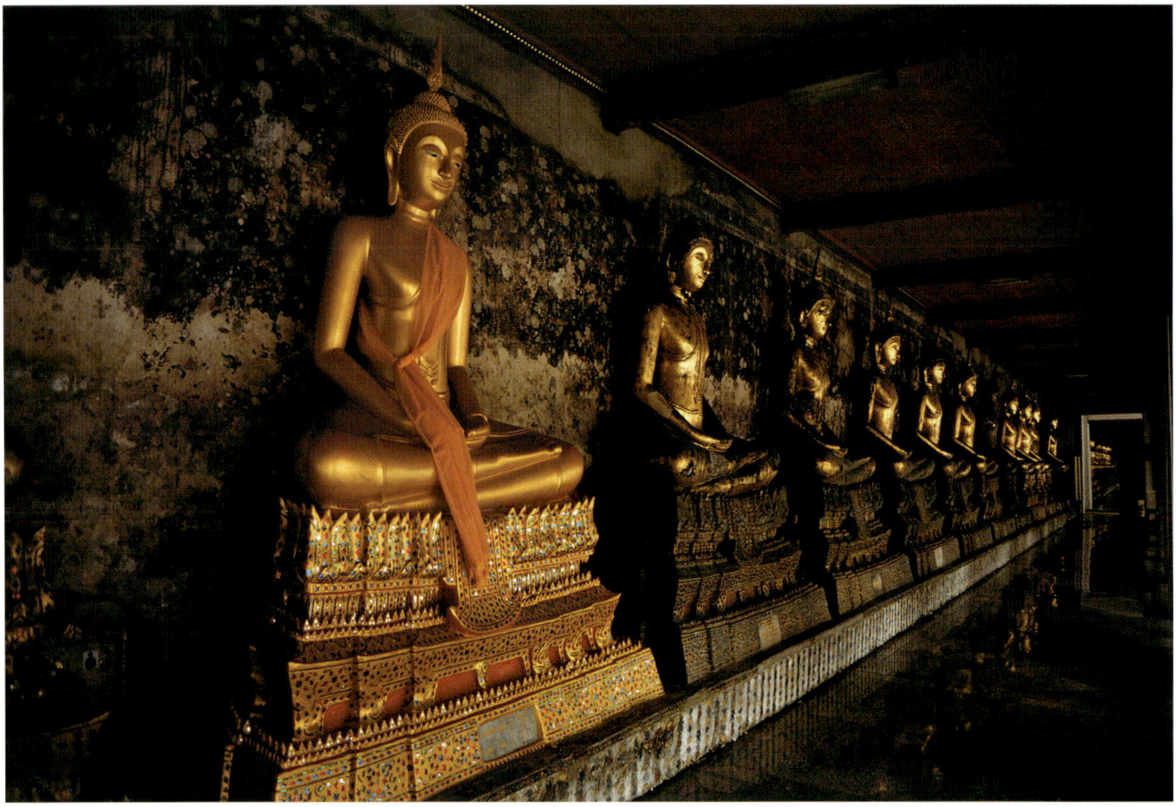

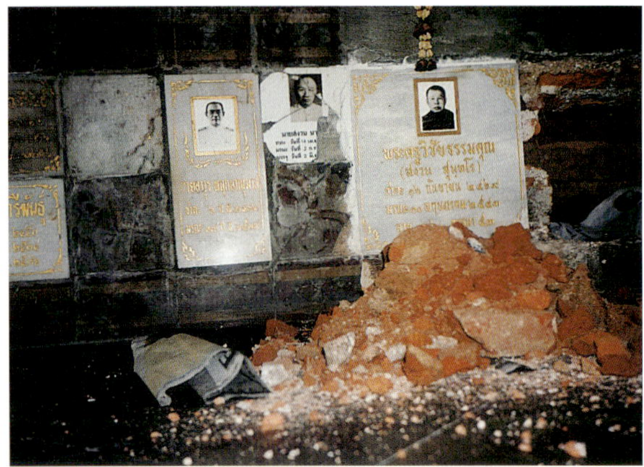

Wat Mahathat, a microcosmic city with a defined social and cultural focus, a symbolic character. In structure, a precinct of diverse parts and activities outlined within the larger whole. Different elements, different functions; Bangkok's *wats* present provocative fields for urban interpretation.

Sacred Foundation, Sacred Boundaries

Traditional Thai rituals governing the construction of houses pay special attention to the relationship between centre and periphery. After the astrologers have determined the propitious moment for commencing construction, a divination rite establishes the exact layout. Columns and their

location are identified according to their
personalities (victory, love, wealth . . .) and gender,
and given a ranked hierarchy. The village mystic
stakes out the plan of the house, and digs a hole in
the precisely determined centre. The excavation is
filled with food offerings, and celebrated by prayer.
Special rituals then accompany the erection of the
perimeter columns, governing both their sequence
and orientation. Although highly charged, this
ceremonial boundary is experientially notional in the
final building, constructed as an invisible line linking
a series of points in the ground. Idealized perimeters,
connected moments, the piers that tether the house
to the ground also define its value.[3]

Similar orders are established within the
seemingly fluid structure of the *wats*. The inner
realms, defined architecturally by the *bots*, are first
identified by eight small stone markers named Bai
Sema. Placed on the corners and the cardinal points,
the Bai Sema, resting over ritually placed stone
foundation blocks named Luk Nimit, outline the
sacred precinct. A ninth Luk Nimit is located at the
spot where the principal Buddha will be situated.
The Bai Sema are often adorned with divine (Hindu)
personages, to keep away evil spirits and establish
the sacred territory. Within the boundary of the Bai
Sema, worldly judicial power ceases; the *bot* is a place
of asylum and priestly authority.[4]

The rituals of *wat* construction, like those of the
house, establish complex diagrams of symbolic
points and lines. Invisible orders, sacred boundaries.
In both cases the founding rituals stress the
significance of the perimeter, even if its physical
definition may be subtle. At a skeletal level, the *wats*
can be best understood as sets of overlapping
concentric rings, expressing varying degrees of

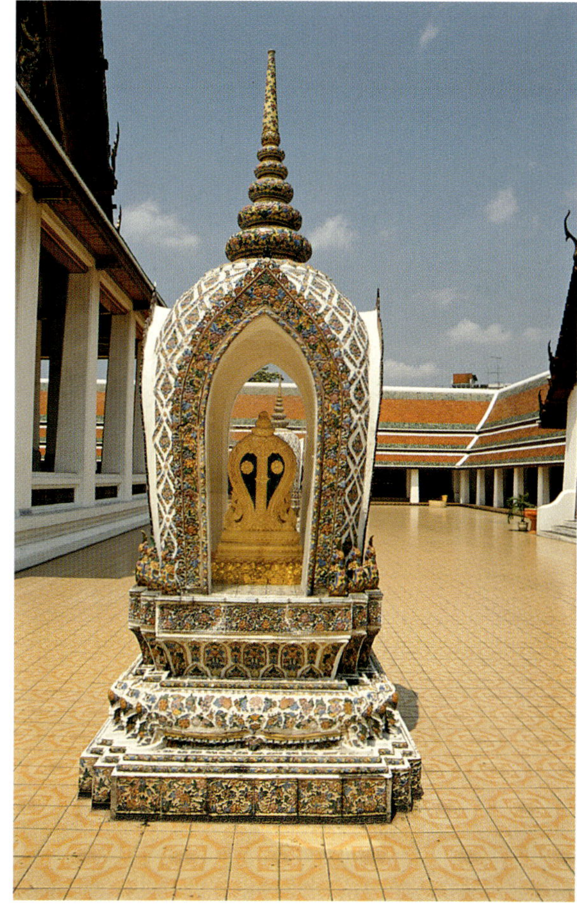

exclusivity. The line of the Bai Sema is the most
sacred. The *chedis*, the internal arcade, the perimeter
walls; each establish expanding layers for observation
and experience. Yet no single centre grounds the
composition: a concentric sensibility with no
overarching focus.

These significant delineations do, however,
articulate independent hierarchic moments in the
plan. Similar strategies are equally applied to the
wats' volumes and surfaces. Planes are subdivided,
thresholds thickened. The dissolution of form
stresses the coexistence of different internal

moments, but also signifies the value of passage between and among them. Individual objects manifest a myriad of internal journeys and lengthened passages.

These sequences of layers separate the *wats* from the city, establishing places of otherness within the urban realm. Yet their inhabitation is surprisingly public, even casual. Subtle and distinct forms, centres of active social use.

Social World

Urban conscience? Social beacons, identifying the continued presence of the monastic community? The *wats* not only identify an idealized urban landscape, they also signify the presence of idealized lives. They are dedicated to Buddhist practices, and to those who serve them. The spiritual lives of these inhabitants articulate more perfect expressions of Bangkok's general religious sensibilities.

Monasteries and monasticism play a central, if paradoxical, role in the city. The *wats* and their monks are ever-present visually and socially accessible. Yet they are also sacred. Monks are deserving of charity, cannot be touched by a woman, and have a special status in law. Their urban presence, like that of the *wats*, reminds one of a higher purpose. Part of the city, but not really; always present, but never fully integrated. Thai monks are also familiar in other ways. While representative of Buddhist principles, they may also be a friend, uncle or brother, or even a briefly inaccessible boyfriend or husband. In addition to the permanent orders, there is a tradition of Thai males joining the monastery for temporary periods. Part of a coming of age or a reflective sabbatical,

the sojourn may be a gesture of gratitude to one's parents, a way of regaining one's soul, or of giving thanks. The strict life of the monastery may also provide, perhaps, a necessary if temporary vision of idealized order before the return to the world of the practical city.

Also potentially paradoxical, the *wats*, normally quiet retreats, are places of festivity. They may be separated physically from the city, but they remain integrated socially. The rituals of Buddhist prayer, celebrated in the *bot*, bring periodic celebration to their usually tranquil interiors. On more special occasions the *wats* fundamentally transform. Urban-scale social events animate the microcosmic cities.

Wat Bowonniwet, a thriving shrine. It was King Mongkut's residence prior to his accession to the throne, and is the current seat of Thailand's supreme patriarch. Its ritual precinct of *bots* and *chedis* is fairly small, the residential and administrative component more extensive. Criss-crossed by canals and alleys, the *wat* constructs a convincing labyrinthine city. Strange dead-end passages, small courtyards and urban squares, ponds with the fattest, ugliest carp imaginable within. And on Sunday 3 March 2002, home to a collective feast.

The ceremonies were dedicated to monastic initiations. Young men entering the priesthood were being blessed by their friends and families, photographers in hand. In one popular ritual the wellwishers lined up to cut small locks of hair from the new disciple. Once the memorial fragments were removed and carefully collected, a monk, razor in hand, carried out a more thorough symbolic shaving. Hair, eyebrows; all shaved down to the skin. The novitiates were then dressed in white robes, ready for their new life. The extended family celebrates the

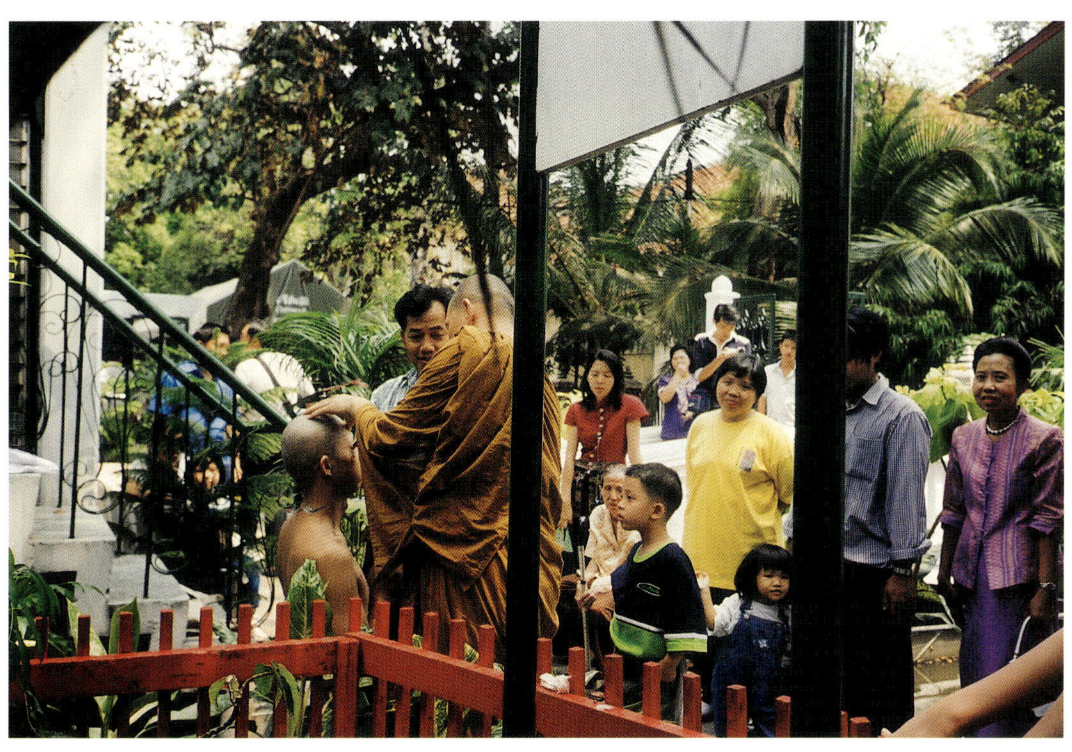

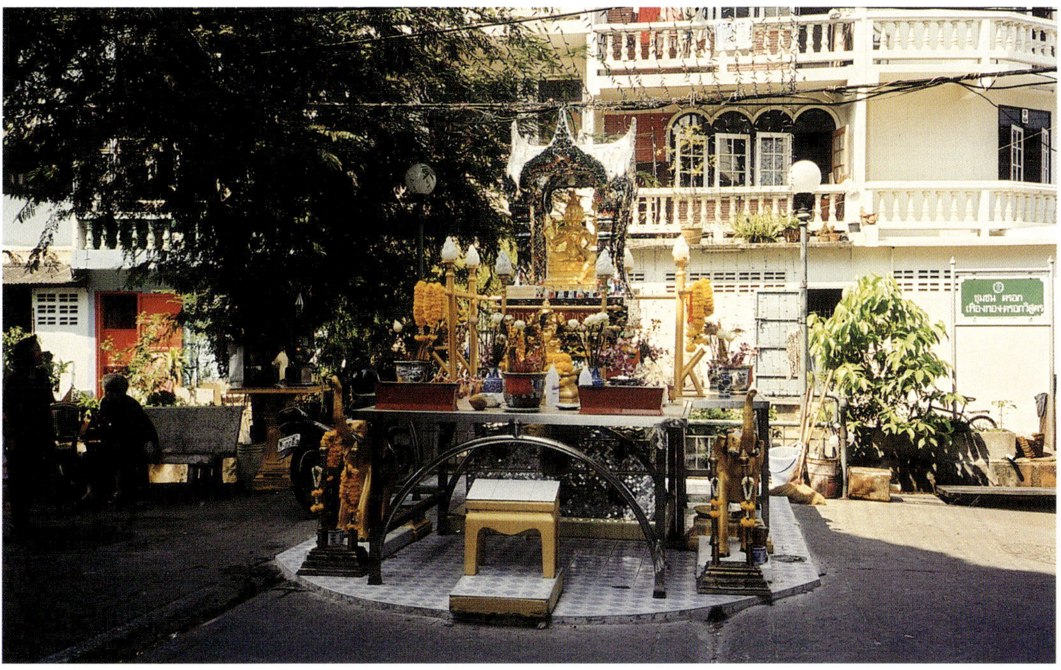

event with food. Food cementing social and symbolic events within the ritual micro-city. Extra or idealized urban states, animated by feasting, the *wats* are experienced through their special social moments.

The rituals of Bangkok's monasteries celebrate the life and teachings of the Buddha. But they also articulate the structure of the monastic order itself. They celebrate the community as a model, through its relation to the annual cycles of nature and its position in Thai society. Its values stand as exemplars for the larger city. A social construct, the analogous orders of monks are always available for appreciation. The *wats* demonstrate this contrasting spirit, but with no direct engagement with urban form. They identify a presence whose message remains ambiguous, yet whose qualities are unmistakable. Neither city nor *wat* subsumes the other. Rather, they take turns, each a binary and symbiotic counter-influence. Structures whose social and physical attributes create friction with their settings.

The institution is a part of the city as well as being its idealized model. Simultaneously excluded and central, home to a reclusive society and a vehicle of public religious education. The *wats*' architecture enshrines this social order, and brings form to its fundamental practices. But as manifestation of its message? Architecture can house religious activities, without necessarily assisting in their articulation. Do the *wats* physically demonstrate Buddhist teachings through their own form as well? Striking architecture, social focus, certainly. An explicit symbolic message? – much less clear.

PART THREE

Social focus: ambiguous architecture.
Conflicting signs of architectural value
and intent. Missing or multiple centres.
Perplexing sources and references.

Experiential Oddities

Places of social ritual and religious festivity, Bangkok's *wats* focus the city's attentions. Ideal cities, presenting a heightened spiritual order within a world of aimless activity. But are the *wats* physically exemplary as well? Do they manifest an angelic architecture, whose message awaits decipherment? The principles of orientation, structure and spatial experience found in the *wats* may present cryptic fragments of analogous urban revelation. Clues, perhaps, to Bangkok's formal mysteries.

Bangkok's *wats* constitute dense worlds of overlapping figures and events. Places of negotiation, arenas of multiple arrangements, they reveal significant form and behaviour. Yet at the same time these dynamic realms present seeming redundancies of formal significance. Duplications of focus, contradictions of intent. In the oscillation of their elements a myriad of interpretive possibilities are presented. Yet the clues conflict, with few easy interpretations apparent. In this respect, Bangkok's *wats* are appropriately related to their urban home. A profusion of partial meanings and contradictory messages characterizes their experience. Obvious architectural concern; perplexing symbolic purposes.

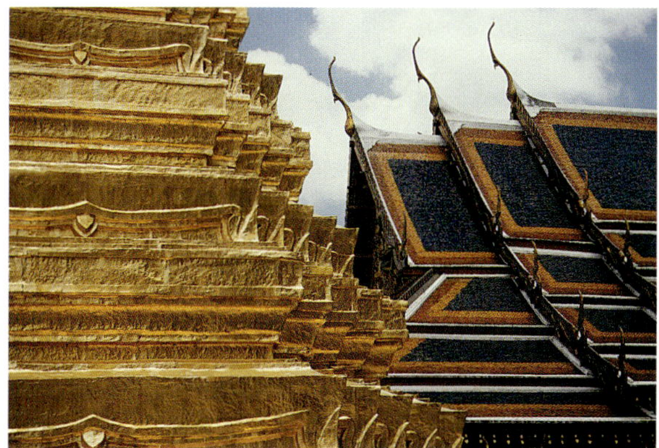

Buddhism rejects the pleasures of the world as meaningless distractions. Yet Bangkok's *wats* manifest a striking taste for material exuberance. Glistening ceramic tiles, profusion of gold and enamels, their physical realities are opulent, even ostentatious. Roofs, columns, *chedis*; all flicker in the sun. *Bot* interiors are lit by their shining Buddhas, golden figures casting an ethereal glow in the relative darkness. Wat Phra Kaeo in its entirety is like a jewel, sculpted from precious stones and polished to perfection. A conspicuous luxuriousness is maintained, especially in comparison to the modest life of the monk and the dishevelled nature of the surrounding streets. A hierarchy of worldly delight, rather than any rejection of its pleasures.

Architectural quality as temptation? Physical and artistic pleasure articulating the challenging task of spiritual transcendence? The celebration of ephemera as foil, contrasting a proper destination? The *wats'* material splendour sends perplexing messages of architectural and social intent. Potent sensory worlds, they exist to celebrate their own replacement.

The role of form is equally ambiguous. The exterior spaces of the *wats* are dramatic. Roofs, so striking in the landscape, dynamic *chedis*, the collage

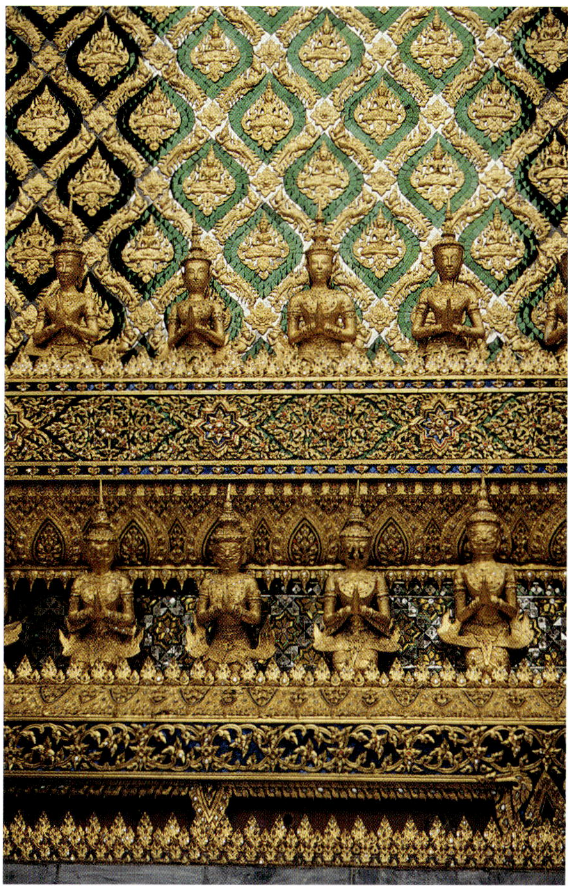

of objects. Yet the architectural manipulation of form, so clearly significant in the roofs and *chedis*, disappears within the more muted interiors of the *bots*. An axis runs through the centre, defining an easterly focus for the simple volumes. Yet this practice is rarely legible, since interior experience is divorced from the orienting conditions of sunlight and view. Attention is internalized, directed towards the Buddha at the end of the perspectival hall. Microcosmic completeness is established, not through architectural manipulation, but rather by narrative and image. The painted lives of the Buddha define the scope of an ideal life, the sculpted images

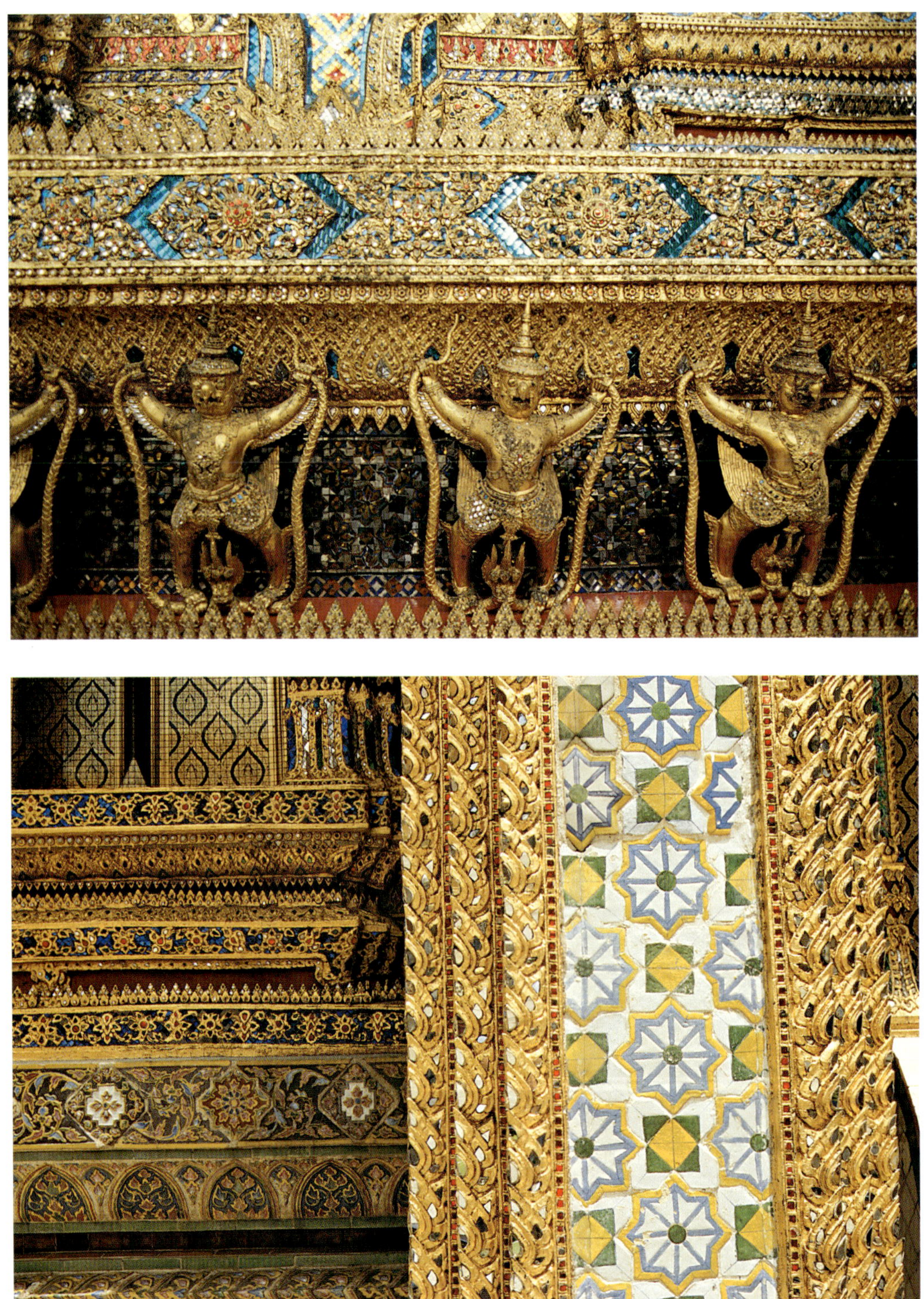

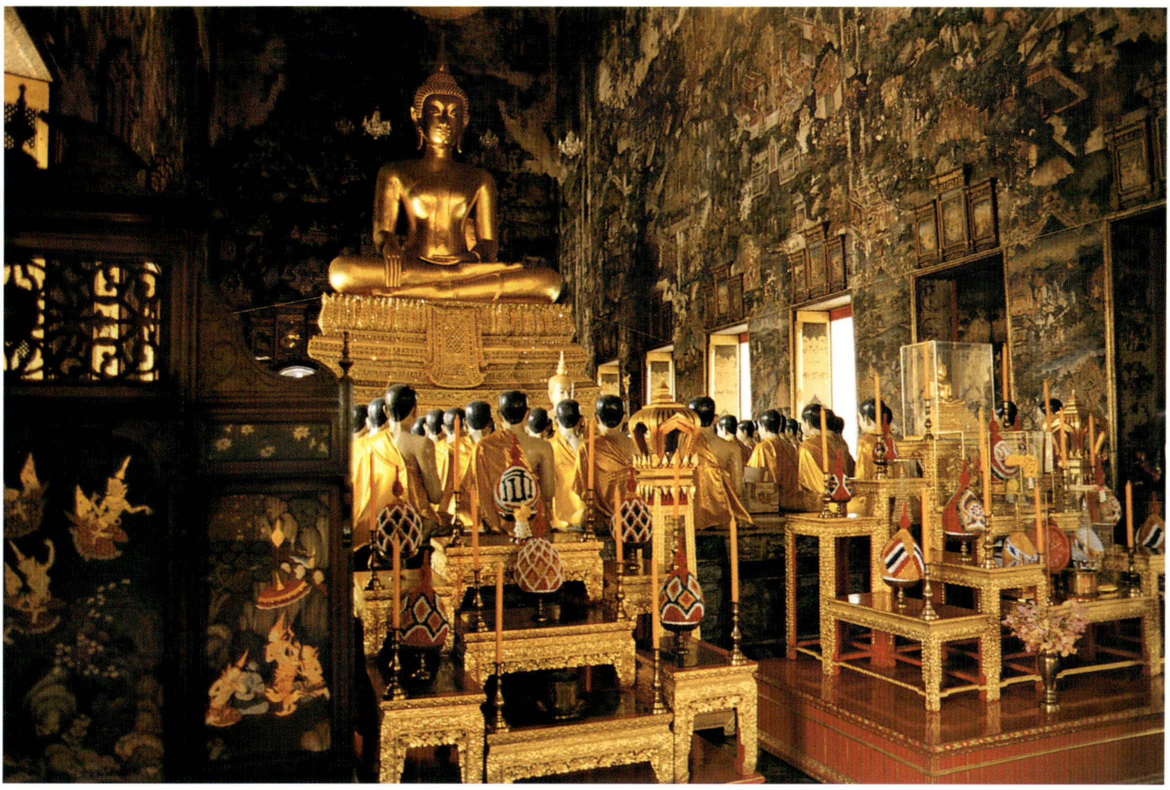

encompassing the necessary totality of wisdom. The rituals of prayer outline one's proper path. Active figures telling stories, creating events. But these figures and practices do not engage with the architecture directly. Building as shelter rather than spatial articulation, a shell rather than a sculpted experience. With the exception of a modest interior landscape of raised platforms, providing dedicated seating for the monks, the *bot* interiors reject the narrative potential of architectural form.

Arguably, the interior spaces support different activities, and perform to different audiences from their exteriors. Yet even in the larger precinct, the role of form is perplexing. Each courtyard presents an architectural landscape, a special kind of city that controls passage through distinct spaces and objects. Yet the *wats* manifest no single route, or demonstrate any obvious controlling order. No longer striking urban beacons alone, they construct ambiguous spatial messages of greater subtlety and complexity. Differently dramatic, their arrangements of parts pose new questions of directed experience and meaning. The perceptual absence of clear formal intent creates its own special kind of mental dislocation. Indeed, Bangkok's *wats* manifest very odd utopias. Amid the architectural field, no figure or spatial ideal clearly presents itself for appreciation and emulation.

The most noticeable formal curiousity is the absence of a figural centre. With a few extraordinary exceptions Bangkok's *wats* do not culminate in a controlling summit, or create any singular focus of attention. They are composed of distinct figures, evenly displaced. Idiosyncratic formal and material expression highlight their apparent independence. Unlike the unified architectural mountains of Angkor or the great *wats* of Ayutthaya and Sukhothai, Bangkok's temples are conversations of independent parts. Nor do the elements cohere around a centralized space. The notion of centre is diffused and attentions distracted. Bangkok's *wats* are less a focused hierarchy and more a complex dance.

This general sense of displacement is made explicit in the *bot–chedi* pairing and occasionally further complicated by the pressure of *viharns*. Two radically different buildings, their qualities present distinct essays on diverse approaches to sacred architectural experience. An oscillation of attentions, a competition of orders. The *bot–chedi* relationship is central to the image of the city's *wats*. A recurring conversation of necessary difference; a tensile balance of characters.

Bots and *chedis* manifest complementary variations on the themes of physical passage, form and space. Aside from the urban function of their roofs, the *bots* are primarily self-enclosed rooms. Large spaces directed towards the principal Buddha, their focus is spatially clear and architecturally simple. *Chedis*, however, demand a clockwise circum-ambulation around their physical forms. They are highly centralized, articulated figures. Faceted, sub-divided into layers; geometrically rich. Their precise shapes attract speculation on their objective intent. Physical passage is defined as circular and terrestrial, referencing perhaps the cyclical motions of nature – the seasons, the sun's passage, time in general or the endless frustrations of earthly existence. But the *chedis* also centre a vertical axis, which is further stressed by their stepped profiles. Episodes are marked as stages on a journey to gradual invisibility, as the earthly and stable give way to the barely tangible summit. This more imaginary journey is first a visual one, directed by the *chedis'* formal transformation: broad, complex base to pure point.

The *bots*, though they contain vertically ordered shrines, remain relentlessly horizontal. Their programme fulfils the demands of entry and travel towards the Buddha image, and provides places for prayer, which are also directed so. Yet neither ceiling nor roof recognizes this sculptural focus. The halls maintain undifferentiated horizontal ceilings. The value of verticality, so comprehensive in the urban presence of the roofs and the forms of the *chedis*, is ignored in the *bots'* interior development. The *bots* and *chedis* establish different forms of directed passage, different foci. Different fields of symbolic expression.

Both figures present different forms of sacred mountains. In the *bot*, the Buddha figures are usually composed into large pyramidal constructions. Set on terraces, often flanked by subordinate figures at the corners and populated by vases of flowers and incense, a compressed landscape supports the principal Buddha image at its summit. The *bot* is spatially defined by the view towards this symbolic mountain: a landscape contained. The *chedi*, conversely, is a landscape figure in its own right, resting independently on the ground. Perhaps a simpler and more self-contained architectural version of the *bot*'s interior landscape, *chedis* are viewed in the world, juxtaposed with the sky and earth. They maintain visible profiles in nature.

The distinction between iconic and interior worlds is further explored in the differing presentations of object and relic. Both *bot* and *chedi*, at least symbolically, contain sacred artefacts. Fragments of the Buddha, or mementos of his life, are buried, literally or notionally within the great *chedis*. Conversely, the *bots* display their honorific figures clearly, the Buddha statues visible in multiple variations. The *chedis* hide their relics, their value presented by analogous architectural form. An abstract architecture housing actual sacred fragments. In the *bots*, the sculptural reinterpretations create the primary spatial focus. Differing artefacts and their appreciation, both types manifest ambiguous physical centres. The *bots* define a linear passage towards the Buddha: centre as travel or destination. *Chedis* obscure their interiors, their solid volumes cloaking geometric centres as imaginary locations. Hidden from view and protected from harm, the centre remains largely imaginary.

These shifting approaches to abstraction and tangibility are also materially present: otherness established in distinctly physical ways. Chedis have precisely articulated forms. Their presence is established through mass, geometry and surface. Yet their construction is indeterminate. Earth, brick, air: great volumes, invisible structure. The *bots*, though spatially simple, are intensely crafted. Refined carpentry, intricate inlays, carefully articulated parts – they demonstrate the refined processes of their own making. Carved wood versus brick and stucco; constructed assembly versus monolithic surface.

The figures are differently specific in their materials, and their expression of artistic history and intent.

Bots and *chedis* make strange pairings, their combination a curious model. Their symbiotic balance – a subtle clue to Bangkok's spirit?

Floating Model

The figures of *bot* and *chedi* reference different families of architectural experience and symbolic order. Conjoined within the microcosmic cities of the *wats*, these overlapping metaphoric structures join others to create complex systems of meaning and potential. Rama and the Buddha, object and passage, sacred shrine and festive destination, the *wats* present provocative challenges. At the simplest level they establish spaces of sacred difference. Clearly symbolic, the question of more precise meanings, however, remains open. Bangkok is populated with countless utopias that defy comprehension: celebrated puzzles to be deciphered.

The Wat Mahathat is in a constant process of renovation. A sacred duty shared among its devotees maintains the shrine. Wat Phra Kaeo, home to the royal chapel, records its history through significant moments of rebuilding. Remade at a scale requiring rededication, the *wat* has frequently been reborn. These momentous occasions, usually involving a member of the royal family as custodian *of* the process, renew the city's spiritual centre.

Other *wats* throughout the city fade into disrepair. Constructed of lacquered wood and inlaid mosaics, the *bots* are especially fragile, easily succumbing to the ravages of humidity and torrential rain. Yet this is not due to any dissipating religious concern. While significant *wats* are left to ruin, new constructions

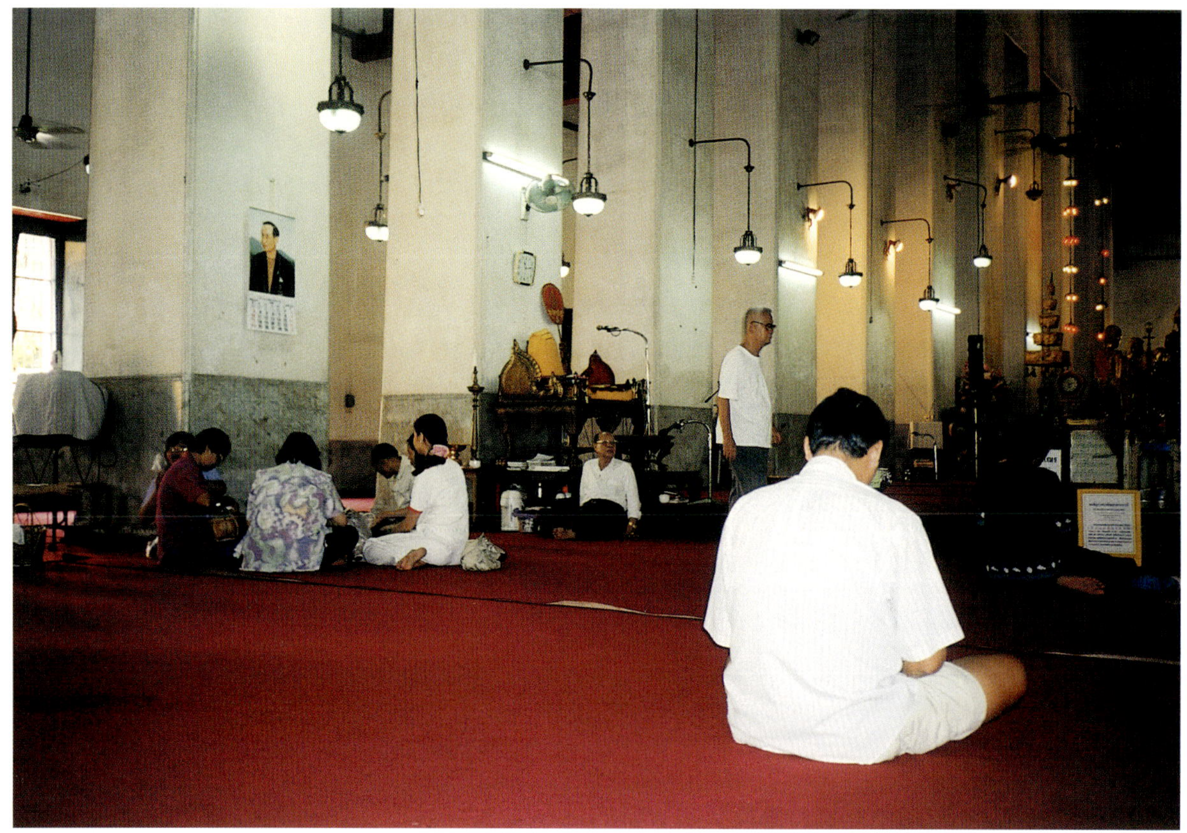

appear alongside. Parallel creations existing in varying stages of completion and collapse. Indeed, *wats* are generally replaced rather than repaired. Founding a new institution is perhaps more valuable to a patron's spiritual future than maintenance or preservation. Or perhaps the process of building itself is the key: dedicated action more valuable than any resulting object.

Bangkok's *wats* continually manifest these parallel processes of rebuilding and replacement. Yet they rarely reaffirm a fixed form. Form is special though fleeting; vibrant but temporary. Construction is more significant than spatial or historical experience alone. Floating worlds in constant change; artistic metaphors for the larger city.

Canals

PART ONE

City as refuge, water as escape. Canals cut

within the marshy terrain, a prime urban act.

An aqueous state, a return to essence.

Venice of the East, in distant memory.

Corrupted structure; enduring spirit.

City as Refuge, Water as Escape

Bangkok, a self-conscious construction springing from an inauspicious beginning. The city was founded in reaction to the Burmese sack of Ayutthaya, the preceding capital to the north. Ayutthaya, a thriving metropolis and major regional power, a city rivalling any in South-East Asia and perhaps the world. On 7 April 1767 Ayutthaya was laid to waste, burnt and abandoned, its population murdered, raped and starved. Prior sacks had presented reconstruction opportunities, fresh chances to remake the ever-transforming capital. This version, however, proved more drastic. The city demanded a total rebuilding, and its location was sacrificed along with its shattered monuments. Urban capitulation in service of transient civic re-creation.

The sack of Ayutthaya also destroyed much of the kingdom's documentary history. With the written records and physical legacy of its fractious past gone, a fresh beginning was both physically and symbolically possible. A city poised for a rebirth, to face an open future unburdened by historic baggage. Bangkok, succeeding Ayutthaya, may be the last (or latest) in a long line of capitals, historically linked to Thailand's foundations. But it is also a new city, a child born of accident. Contemporary with the modern world and its

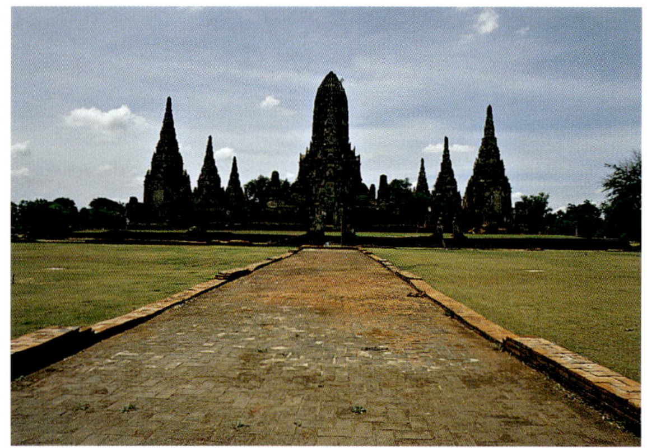 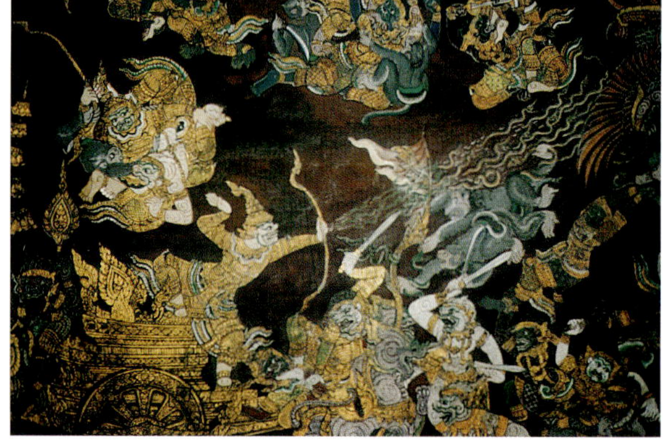

forces, Bangkok is an open creation on a largely
blank slate.

This cathartic potential was not, however, wholly
embraced. Neither the acceptance of a uniquely
modern outlook nor the adoption of available
Western technological sensibilities took precedence
in the new creation. After a period of military
retrenchment and stabilization, Bangkok was indeed
refounded. Yet the new city was structured on an
ideal past rather than on any imported vision of the
future. More provocatively, the creation of Bangkok,
highly coloured by the forms of Ayutthaya, was based
on a text. The city as a dream. The city of Rama,
rendered sacred by its relics and renewed Buddhist
principles, was reborn in its new and idiosyncratic
landscape as an improved version of its mythical self.[1]

Bangkok, under the leadership of Rama I,
undertook a renaissance of Buddhist practices,
legal structures and royal rituals. Monastic
conventions were held to re-establish the canonic
Pali-language *Tripitaka* (sacred text) that had fallen
into disrepute. In parallel, earlier Brahmanic rituals
were redesigned and reinstated. The traditions of
monarchic representation, and their symbolic
relation to the landscape, find revised urban

expression. Rama I and his court were further
responsible for the renaissance of Thai literature,
most notably by transforming the *Ramayana* into
its extensive Thai version, the *Ramakien*. The
memory of Rama's struggles, like the shadows of
Ayutthaya, became embedded into the cultural
fabric of the new city.[2] Yet the personalities and
actions of its characters are inflected, indicative of
the social and cultural sensibilities of their new
home. Simultaneously, the rigid, even ossified, forms
of Ayutthaya's political culture were relaxed. Rama I
was considered more a 'first among equals' than the
distant and sacred monarchs of Ayutthaya. Bangkok
was created as a royal city of purified historic myth,
law and religion, all juxtaposed with the forces of the
modern world.

Physically, Bangkok's reconstruction directly
referenced Ayutthaya as its ideal model. Significant
temples were remade, their names maintained.
Even historic landscape features were reconstructed,
geographically articulating the links between the
two cities, or, more accurately, the rebirth of the
same city in its new location. This transposition
was, however, more than only symbolic. 'Thousands
of boatloads of bricks were taken from the ruins

of Ayutthaya and used in constructing the city's walls and public buildings.'[3]

Bangkok and Ayutthaya have fundamentally geographies. Bangkok is further south, further from Burma. It is closer to the sea, a fact significant to the international trade increasingly essential to Thailand's economy. Yet the congruence of its landscape with Ayutthaya's is more striking. The Chao Phraya River waters both cities, each located on its great central plain. Flat (Bangkok perhaps more so), prone to regular flooding and fertile. An ambiguous terrain of water and land. This landscape is defined by the symbiotic relations of rice fields and modest villages, flooding and harvest. A landscape of subtle sensibilities and regular rhythms.

Canals present the most significant human intervention within this fluid terrain. Patterning the land, they identify collective inhabitation, supporting both agriculture and community. Significant to the cultivated fields, the canals are equally central to the city. Ayutthaya was a city of canals. They defined its form and grounded its sensibilities. Bangkok borrowed these canals as its strategic means, used to outline the principal structures of civic design.

Urban boundary and its image are typically defined by a city's walls, and both Ayutthaya and Bangkok partly follow this convention. Perimeters of brick outline their central precincts. Yet their real boundaries were the fluid ones, combining river and canal into defined aqueous edges. Canals as walls, whose civic role is arguably first one of defence. The fall of Ayutthaya was due to internal political turmoil and moral lassitude as much as to the superior military skills of the attackers.[4] And indeed, while the actual site of Ayutthaya was abandoned and its society reformed, the practice of water as defensive edge was not. Bangkok's infrastructural principles followed Ayutthaya's model. Both cities were based on the extended relations between canal and river, constructed into careful compositions of aquatic order. Defence demanding infrastructure; city wall as symbolic form. Yet in this case, a barrier of water.

A type of virtual edge protects the city from terrestrial attack, whose layers of concentric protection are extracted from the context itself. There is indeed an aspect of expedient defence latent within a flat and marshy land. Unlike the strong and heavy mountains of Burma, implying a defence of solidity and weight, Bangkok's approach relies on the multi-faceted qualities of water. Water, with its unique ability to challenge weight, allows brute force to defeat itself. Light and flexible; a celebration of intangible strength. The canals – formed water – provide the effective barriers and means of urban definition.

Bangkok was a new city, consciously carved from the amorphous terrain. This is, perhaps, the most accurate analogy embedded in its historic title as the 'Venice of the East'. Both cities were founded as refuge in times of trouble, both adapting to flat and marshy conditions. A fairly inhospitable aquatic landscape provided a defence from terrestrial predators; survival a quasi-naval, amphibious operation. Venice and Bangkok, cities whose sensibility developed through the extrapolation of their sites, and the creative celebration of their qualities. The city as retreat leading to the rediscovery of a forgotten essence.

Escape to Essence: Water as Culture

The first official settlement in the new location took place at Thonburi, the proto-Bangkok situated

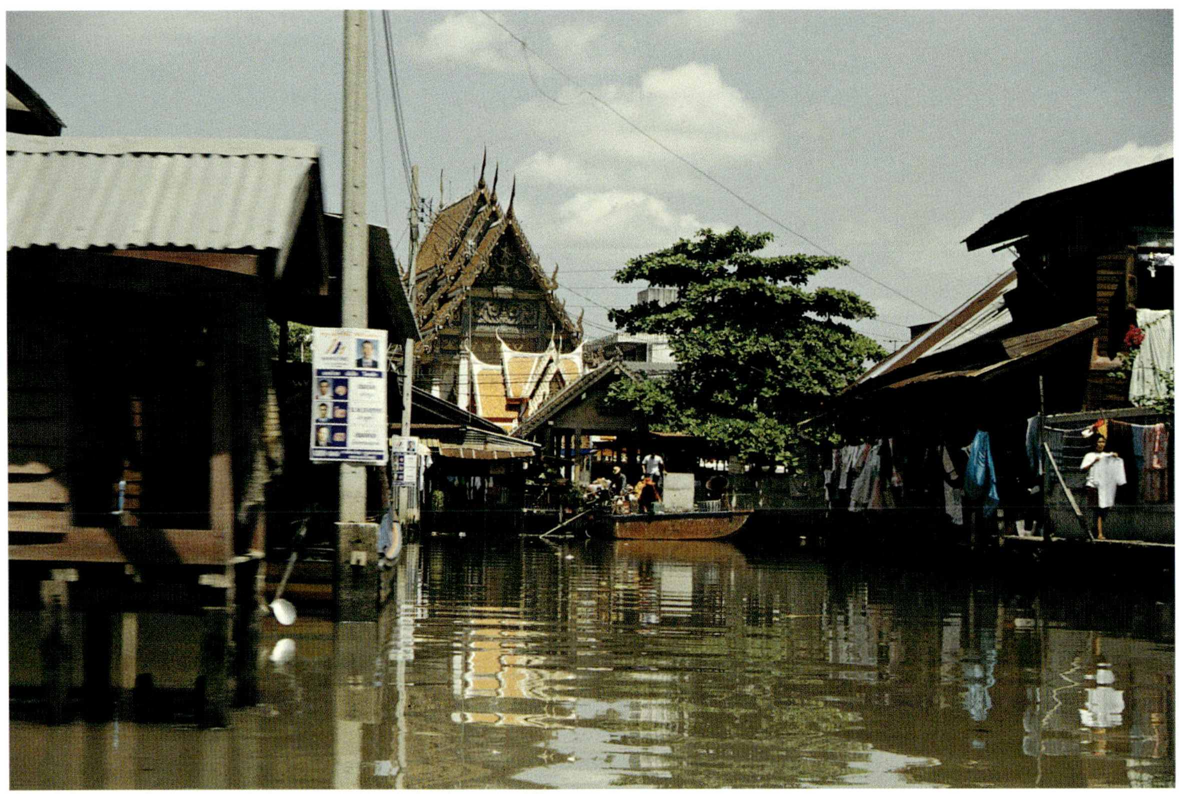

on the west side of the Chao Phraya river. More an
emergency military encampment than a new city, its
form was likely indicative of accepted practice rather
than creative design. Its replacement by Bangkok five
years later, a proper royal city founded on the east
river-bank, has allowed Thonburi, to retain these
indigenous qualities. The necessary pressures of
urban development having occurred elsewhere, the
earlier site is the most historically representative:
the traditional city made experientially accessible.

Thonburi's canals carve urban order from the
suspect materials of mud and water, a tenuous and
seemingly fragile grounding for urban construction.
Yet the resulting forms are still perceptible, just as
the area's labyrinthine qualities vividly express the

spirit differently present in the new capital. Dense
and introspective, local and secluded, Thonburi's
spatial experience is guided by the particular and
personal rather than any larger-scale urban image.
Low houses and tall temples constitute the historic
fabric, with few modern buildings obstructing their
traditional relationship. The temples occupy slightly
higher ground, the houses blurring the boundaries
of land and water. Flexible thresholds; thickened
edges of amphibious inhabitation. Temples, houses
and shops, the fundamental building blocks of the
traditional city. Water, roofs and strange precincts,
interacting in intriguing ways.

Boats are the primary means of negotiating this
aquatic world. Boats – ranging through a spectrum

of official and casual, fast and public, slow and local. Boats, whose seeming fragilities reflect their contexts, unstable yet durable over time. Floating houses render these qualities large. The canal houses are barely more grounded. Neighbourhoods remain in flux, always ready to relocate with the transforming water. Floating markets establish mobile commercial centres. Individual vendors crisscross their aquatic field in small boats, their collective groupings forming dense carpets of bobbing produce. Water-buses ferry children to the schools of the official city; domestic boats perform more local tasks. Boats: each is assigned according to need, supporting fluid activity within the linear canals.

Intersecting canals create urban squares. These aquatic forecourts accentuate view, presenting figures and their mirrored images in conversation. Canals: linear forms with perplexing, non-linear passage. Canal travel is indeed disorienting. With no apparent allegiance to directional coherence, space becomes pure quality. This experiential instability defines Thonburi's civic foundations. Casual form is conjoined with a density of overlapping experience; social orders are commingled together. Later Bangkok is foreshadowed in its essential foundations.

Thonburi's canals once provided its sole means of transportation. Now, though still functionally active, they are less central to contemporary life, forming just one part of a composite transport system. Roads and interconnected alleys have been superimposed over the original waterways. This multiplicity of choices exacerbates curious local sensibilities. No single movement system exists, though there is little to connect the different modes. Like Bangkok's contemporary Sky Train, floating above the traffic beneath, these independent systems create dense layers rather than any single coherent order.

Thonburi / Bangkok: temporal contrasts in urban ideals and their appreciation. While eventually surpassed by its successor, Thonburi remains the best physical reminder of an original Bangkok. Its structural legacy remains present, but obscured. Its experiential qualities are still legible, if unconsciously registered beneath the capital's grudging acceptance of terrestrial modernity. The city's canals have been gradually sacrificed to the supremacy of the roads. Yet analogous traces of this essential aquatic Bangkok still percolate within civic sensibilities and their revelatory moments.

Life in Motion

Order as experience, medium as message. The distinct modes of canal living create idiosyncratic urban realities. Boat as defining culture, reflecting an amphibious state and its fluid sensibilities. The ebb and flow of the waters, the temporal cycles of the seasons; each contributes to a sense of transient ground. One negotiates with the water and learns its lessons. Accommodating practices. Houses on stilts allow water to flow unhindered beneath. Domestic platforms float in front, their docks adjusting to varied levels without stress. Flooding, an annual reality rather than a calamity. Water: a defining context, always in immediate proximity.

Canals establish a different experiential ground for the terrestrial city. Life on the water demands distinct skills, and rewards different imaginations. Rapidity and agility versus stability; quickness over security. Few things are fixed, as the mobile forces are always more powerful. Go with the flow. Bangkok

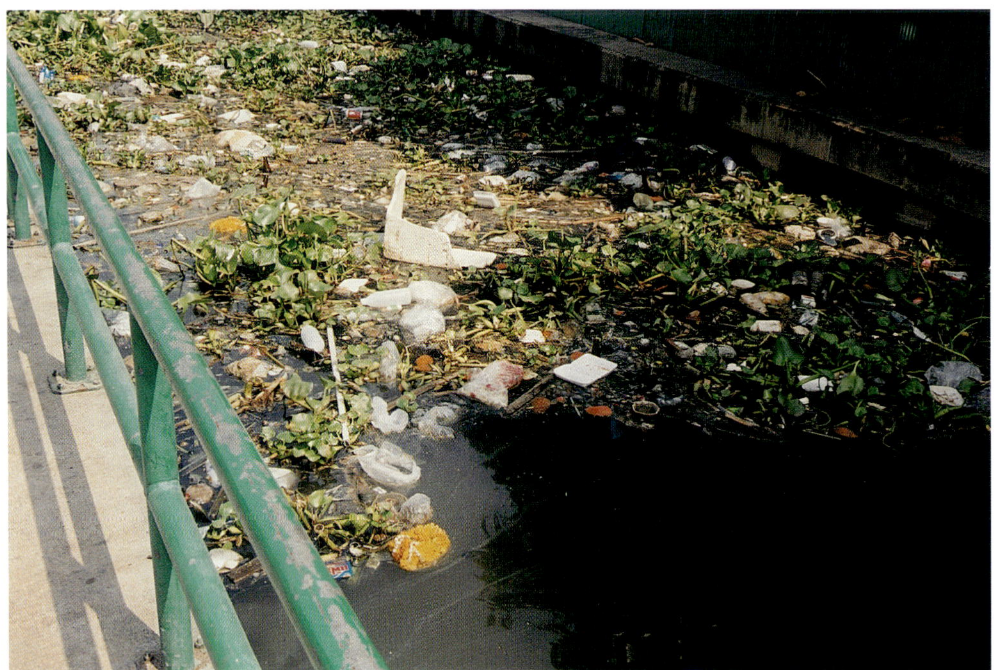

and its occupants respond to these lessons in ways that become essential mental pre-dispositions. A famous Thai folk tale, the spirit of quickness and flexibility materially manifest: Sithanonchai, a legendary hero, convinced the sovereign of Ayutthaya to challenge the Burmese to a pagoda-building contest, the first to finish becoming the victor. Having agreed to the contest,

> The Burmese immediately set about mobilizing a large labour force and brought in large quantities of brick and stone. On the Thai side, aided by only a few people, Sithanonchai, an architect par excellence, very quickly erected a wooden structure, wrapped it in cloth in the agreed shape and size of the pagoda, and duly won the day.[5]

An architecture of sticks and fabric, an architecture of boats, successfully challenges the heavy constructions of the earth.

This water culture is central to Bangkok's sensibility. Old habits die hard. A Thai acquaintance explained (but not justified) Bangkok's accumulation of litter based on these aquatic foundations. Vegetal refuse was traditionally jettisoned into the canals, to be carried away by the ceaseless current to the river, and ultimately out to sea. Casual but efficient garbage removal, the aquatic decomposition also served to fertilize the flood plains each year: the earth fed by the nutrient-laden water. A symbiotic relationship between city and land. These practices are less effective when the canals become roads, and the refuse is plastic, but they linger. The idea of living on a moving, transient and self-cleansing foundation is an essential constituent of the city's psychological life.

PART TWO

Tenuous boundaries, largely obscured.

Aqueous form; ambiguous grounding.

Order remade in spirit, superstition as

structure. Sacred corners: fragments of

imagined stability.

Existential Instability

Life in fluid motion. While most explicit in Thonburi and the many aquatic villages of southern Thailand, this amphibious state is equally fundamental to Bangkok. The city enshrines an intangible essence, and renders it through ambiguous experience. Flexible form, shape in motion; Bangkok's relation to terrestrial stability is indeed distinct.

Canal as boundary, a fluid defence. A city is protected by water, an island constructed as refuge. A city that requires agility to circumnavigate its forms and seasons. Celebrating lightness over weight; water as urban sensibility. This exchange of stability and instability, inverting expectation, is central to Bangkok's identity. Floating or grounded, Bangkok manifests the paradoxes of the amphibious city, a paradox that finds its way into the country's iconography. A royalty that claims authority from the grounded Khmer traditions of Angkor, but is also ritually bound to the river and the flooded fields. The sacred figures of royal tradition, elephants. Active in farming, logging and warfare, as well as royal ceremonies, elephants are integral to Thailand's culture and central to its representation.

Elephants, rather heavy, set adjacent to the slender boats of aquatic ritual. A continual balancing of forces, a quality of existence. Lightness and weight in symbiotic tension.

Most of Bangkok's canals are now impassable, registered as distant memories of their former selves. Yet the remaining few expose a different world. A working canal. Beginning at the Golden Mount, immediately adjacent to a historic city gate and fragment of its wall, the Khlong Mahanak transforms into the Khlong San Sap to lead past the commercial mountains of Siam Square and the new city beyond. Along the way it cuts a section through the city's living fabric, revealing a more personal realm than the Bangkok of the avenues. Different lives. Houses face the canal, their terraces and balconies exposing introspective worlds: social microcosms and dense gardens. Formal aquatic gates lead to grander estates. A historic moment: the Jim Thompson House. A residential complex, an idyllic retreat, constructed from a series of teak pavilions imported from Ayutthaya. Built by an American architect turned Thai silk trader, it embodies a domestic ideal clarified by an outsider's eyes. The historical, perhaps romanticized (and highly popular) vision is juxtaposed with the realities of the transforming city. Face to the canal, its pavilions floating in luxury above the densely planted sculpture gardens beneath. Celebrated architecture as benevolent observer, its flexible artefacts as guide.

Canal life is a curious urban foundation that changes with the seasons, rains and drought. Water as ground; ground as time. The city reacts to these transforming natural forces in cyclical ways. This aqueous foundation also reinforces Bangkok's inherent instability: a psychological condition

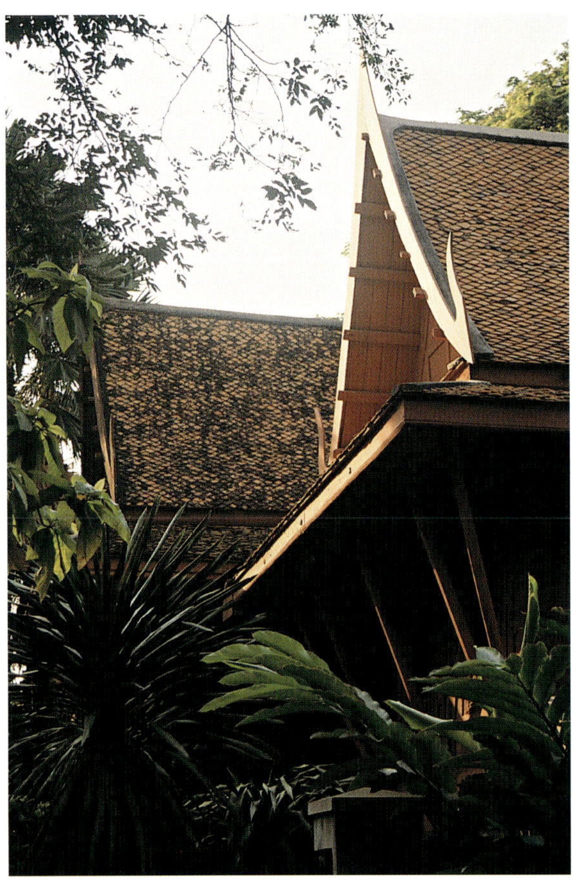

essential to its personality. The city and its artefacts glorify the qualities of surface, while fully cognizant of the more enigmatic realms remaining hidden beneath. Perplexing images; possibly coherent depths obscured. This existential instability is created by a city of striking appearance, the city as a mirror whose flickering surfaces reveal partial, if enticing, clues to its submerged realities.

A clearly intentional state. Yet life within the disorienting fluidity of Bangkok's competing orders has the potential to challenge sanity. Existential angst occasionally surfaces within the city, its seemingly placid society erupting into bursts of unexpected violence. How does one deal with a relentlessly floating world? For youth, a well-publicized amphetamine problem. For adults, a highly developed taste for luxury and power. Traditionally, different foils. The creation of points of symbolic stasis.

Imaginary Precincts: Sacred Tethers

A transient life, in ceaseless motion. Yet even Bangkok accepts the necessity for moments of urban order. Socially, the family and village clan, the historic precinct. Architecturally, similar desires are met through symbolic orders, formal ideals expressed via miniature models. More clear than Bangkok's inhabitable forms, these representational architectures articulate the city's hidden life, coexisting within the real.

Most famously, Angkor Wat is reconstructed within Wat Phra Kaeo as a stone model. Brahmanic and Buddhist authority is joined in a single reference – symbolic for the royal chapel and its city. A reminder of the historic values arguably still implicit within Bangkok's buildings and its religious practices. Yet the representational confection serves to clarify the city's architectural ideals primarily by contrast.

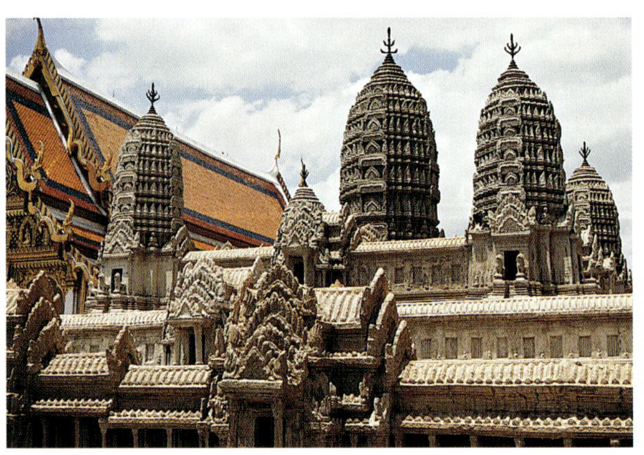

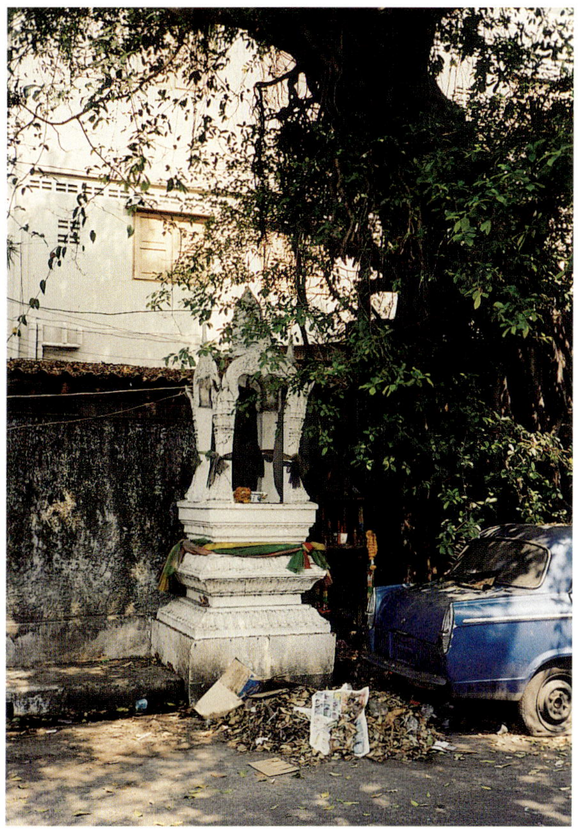

Angkor manifests a symbolic and material clarity largely avoided in Bangkok's indigenous constructions. Its explicitly ordered sensibility is rejected in the city's architectural trajectory. The city's manifestations of essential order follow other models.

Countless smaller architectural mascots appear throughout the city. Known as spirit houses, they identify sacred moments at a domestic scale. Constructed as cities, temples or stylized domestic scenes, the miniature buildings provide homes for local guardian spirits. The spirit houses are generally not geographically referential, as in the case of the model of Angkor, but rather point to imaginary worlds of idealized order. An architecture of local responsibility. Attached to temples, office buildings and houses, personal territories are celebrated through their private architectural totems. And the spirits who live in the little mansions? Beneficent souls, or more representative of the divine pantheon, some more ambivalent than others? The spirits are generally seen as protective, the special shrines standing in for the well being of the whole.

The spirit houses circumscribe a virtual precinct. Conventionally they are set on freestanding pillars, close to a significant entry. Fragments of boundary, usually positioned at a corner, a line of significant, if subtle, order is superimposed over the fluid ground, defining a precinct and rendering it safe for habitation. Defended by the good spirits, protected from the bad. Bangkok's dense alleys necessitate a different response. Houses crowd together, seemingly lacking architectural concern. Their interiors appear jumbled, families and possessions packed in without order. Yet above the densely inhabited spaces spirit houses float as symbolic talismans. Miniature but architecturally complete, they speak of a different and more comprehensive world than the expedient building below. Aerial mobiles; spirit houses in a different form. The light figures capture the invisible wind, its power changing shape. This material transformation is celebrated through the tinkling chimes. Hanuman, the white monkey hero, and perhaps the most endearing (and Thai) character of the *Ramakien*, was the son of the wind god Pai. Able to transform his appearance, to assume different personalities, he was strong and mischievous simultaneously. A fierce fighter, intensely loyal to Rama and key to his success, Hanuman was always attentive to his own pleasures as well. Hanuman, flexible in form, enduring in sensibility.[6]

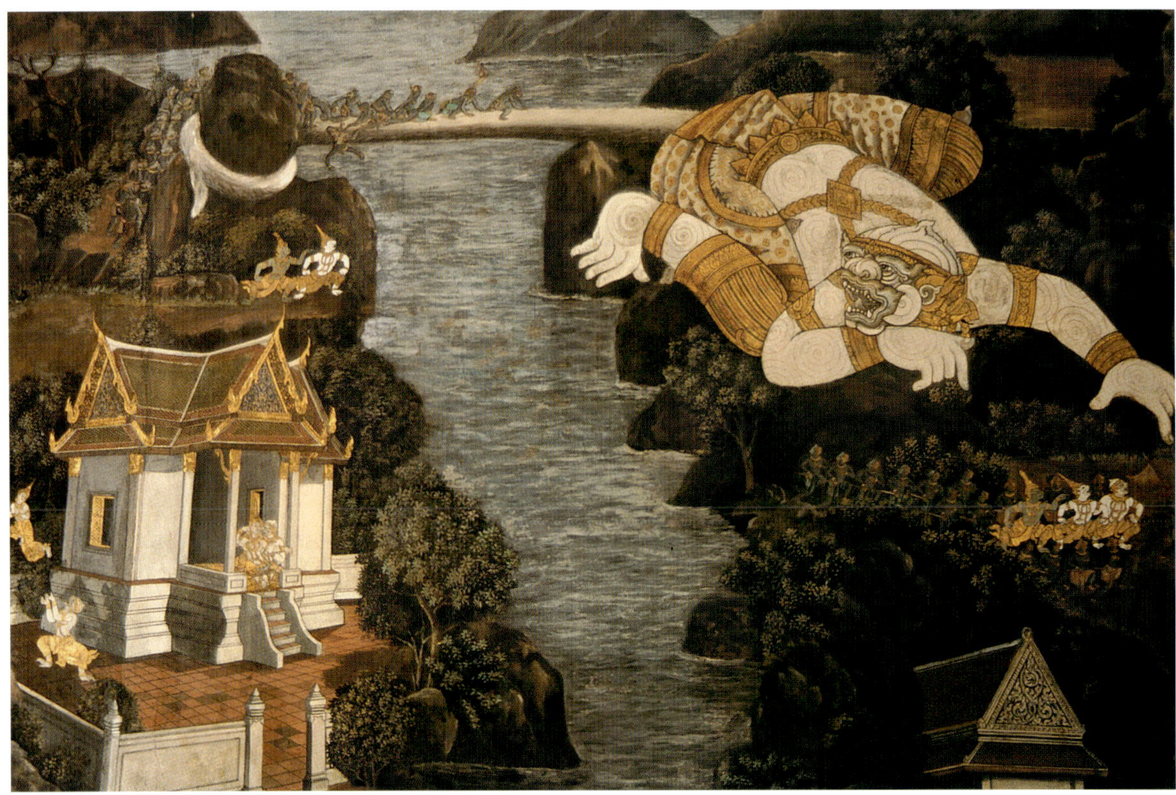

The traces of this latent superstition are pervasive. In the city, coloured shrines punctuate the monochromatic streets. Garlands of flowers and offerings of rice and fruit appear as symbolic moments, celebrating the transient and the decorative, the tangible and personal. Statues are dressed with saffron sashes, the acts of devotion temporarily bringing living colour to the sculpted figures. The Emerald Buddha, the most important statue in Wat Phra Kaeo, and perhaps the country, has three luxurious outfits; each is ritually changed in royal ceremonies to mark the passing seasons. Like the wat roofs at a larger scale, these signs of personal devotion colourfully animate the experiential city.

The city's totemic sensibilities are further manifest in personal devotional figures. Alongside shops dedicated to school uniforms and herbal medicines, Bangkok's principal amulet market occupies an extended space between Wat Mahathat and the river. Each small *soi*, while also residential, is part of a dense warren dedicated to selling religious icons and statues. Thousands of Buddhas, in varying sizes and postures, populate the narrow alleys. Repeated in smaller versions elsewhere in the city, these pockets of sacred commerce stand out as places of protected difference: market life supporting – and supported by – private devotion.

The *Bangkok Post*, 2 February 2002: 'Religious rite to get rid of ghastly ghouls.' An urban exorcism.

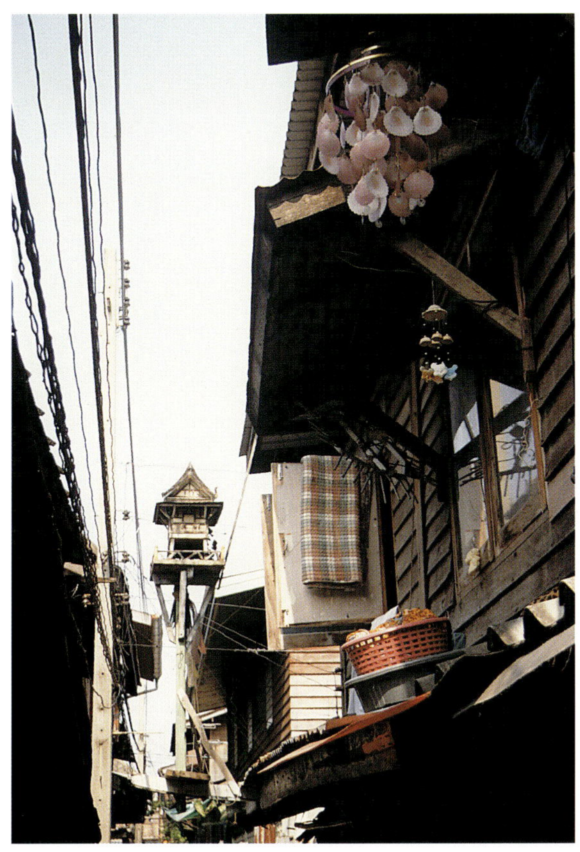

Governor Sanguan Chanaksorn has raised
eyebrows by organizing a religious rite next
Saturday to get rid of ghosts many locals believe
are haunting an accident-plagued intersection
known locally as the Roi Sop (100 corpses
crossroad). Some local people believe the intersection was haunted by ghosts who wanted more
people to die so that the spirits of the dead would
guard the road for them.

A few days later, a more festive occasion.
Bangkok Post, 6 February 2002: 'Jumbo Valentine'.
Pattanapong Hirunard reported on an engagement
party celebrated for Plai Ngathong and his fiancée

(two elephants) at the Ayutthaya elephant shelter.
Visiting children offered their congratulations for
the upcoming wedding, to be celebrated at the zoo
on St Valentine's Day.

In certain *wats*, caged birds are purchased to be
then released; one's financial generosity guarantees
a future of good fortune. Within temples gold leaf
is applied to statues, and coins are offered, as rites
of passage. Incense burns, accompanying prayer.
Physical (and financial) devotion establishes tangible
connections with the Buddha figures. Yet this desire
for earning earthly merit, for good luck, would seem
contradictory to the more official tenets of Buddhist
practice and Buddhism's message of earthly
renunciation. In situations that ideally appeal to
a more abstract sensibility, tangible ritual takes
precedence.

An animistic spirit remains latent to Bangkok,
coexistent with the city's public Buddhist sensibility.
A paganism submerged but not eradicated.
Or perhaps these moments arise within Buddhist
practice as the physical expressions symbolic of
its more mysterious core. Abstract values are
necessarily communicated through perceptible
images. The city, a world in symbiotic balance, held
in place by structures of competing, if barely visible,
symbolic orders. Individual sensibilities, local
values, subordinated to a shared destination.

Points of Stasis

Foreshadowed by the canals and spirit houses,
Bangkok's principles of sacred definition and control-
ling order are equally present at the scale of the city.
The Lak Muang, Bangkok's city pillar, was erected by
Rama I in 1782. Pillar and pavilion, it is a mooring

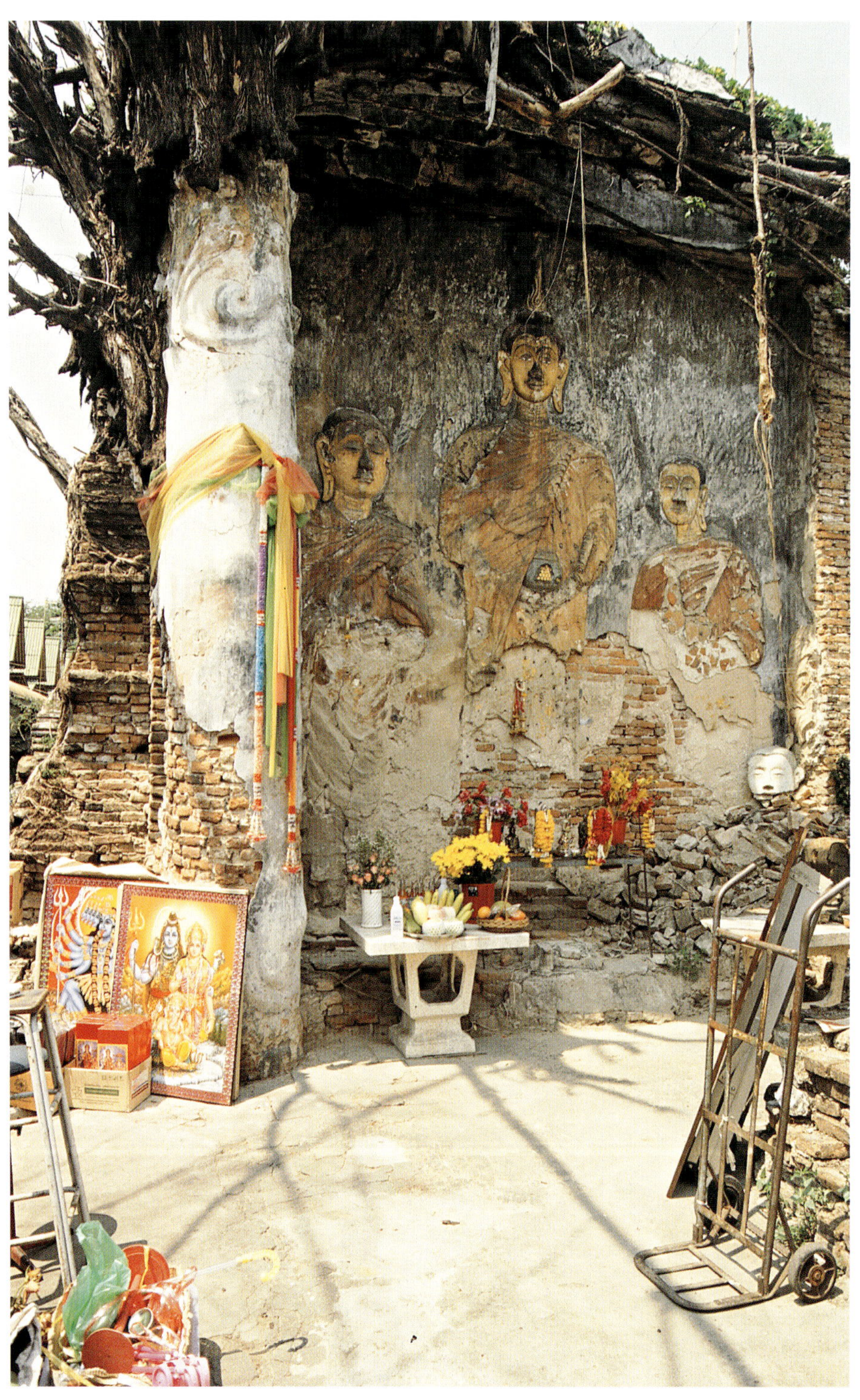

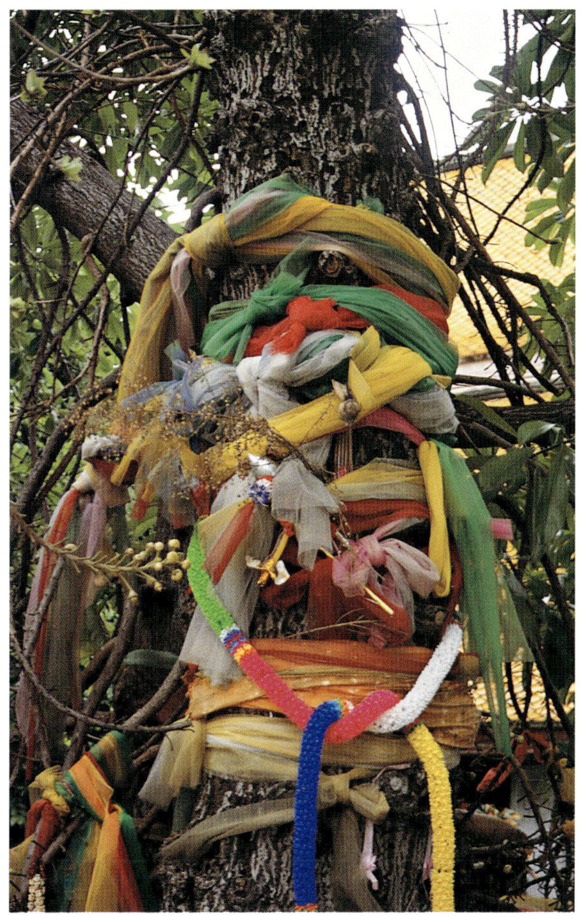

doesn't really look much like anything. A post. Unlike the sacred peaks of Angkor or Borobudur, celebrating sacred centre as architectural mountain, or Delphi's ompholos, articulating a celebrated passage into a mysterious earth, the pillar is a fragment of an edge. Bangkok's symbolic 'centre' is a corner, a piece of a virtual boundary. Its function is supportive, serving to hold the city in place and memorialize its transient stability. A monument that celebrates a practical purpose rather than a venerated form.

Yet the Lak Muang is not urbanistically insignificant. A place of popular ritual and collective event, it celebrates the link between the city and its site. It is the representational founding of the new capital, and the home of its guardian spirits. A temporal and spatial moment commemorated by distinctive sacrifices. A collection of severed pig heads is arranged beside the principal shrine, arrayed to observe the scene. Like the spirit houses, the Lak Muang punctuates a flexible terrain. A figure holding place in a fluid land; a temporary mooring. And the character being tethered? Bangkok is a sculpted object whose original canals delineate its form. Even if now largely implicit, the city's canals reveal its essential order.

device for the city at large. A spirit house for the collective whole.

The Lak Muang is situated opposite the north-east corner of the Grand Palace. It is a curious place. Like the *wats*, it defines a precinct, housing a collection of sacred objects within its walls. Yet the most significant figure is neither *bot* nor *chedi*, but a *linga*, a phallic symbol of Brahmanic origin. Set into a sunken frame, housed in a centralized pavilion, the pillar's physical form is underwhelming, easily overshadowed by the Wat Phra Kaeo nearby. In spite of its ornate surface and gilded home it

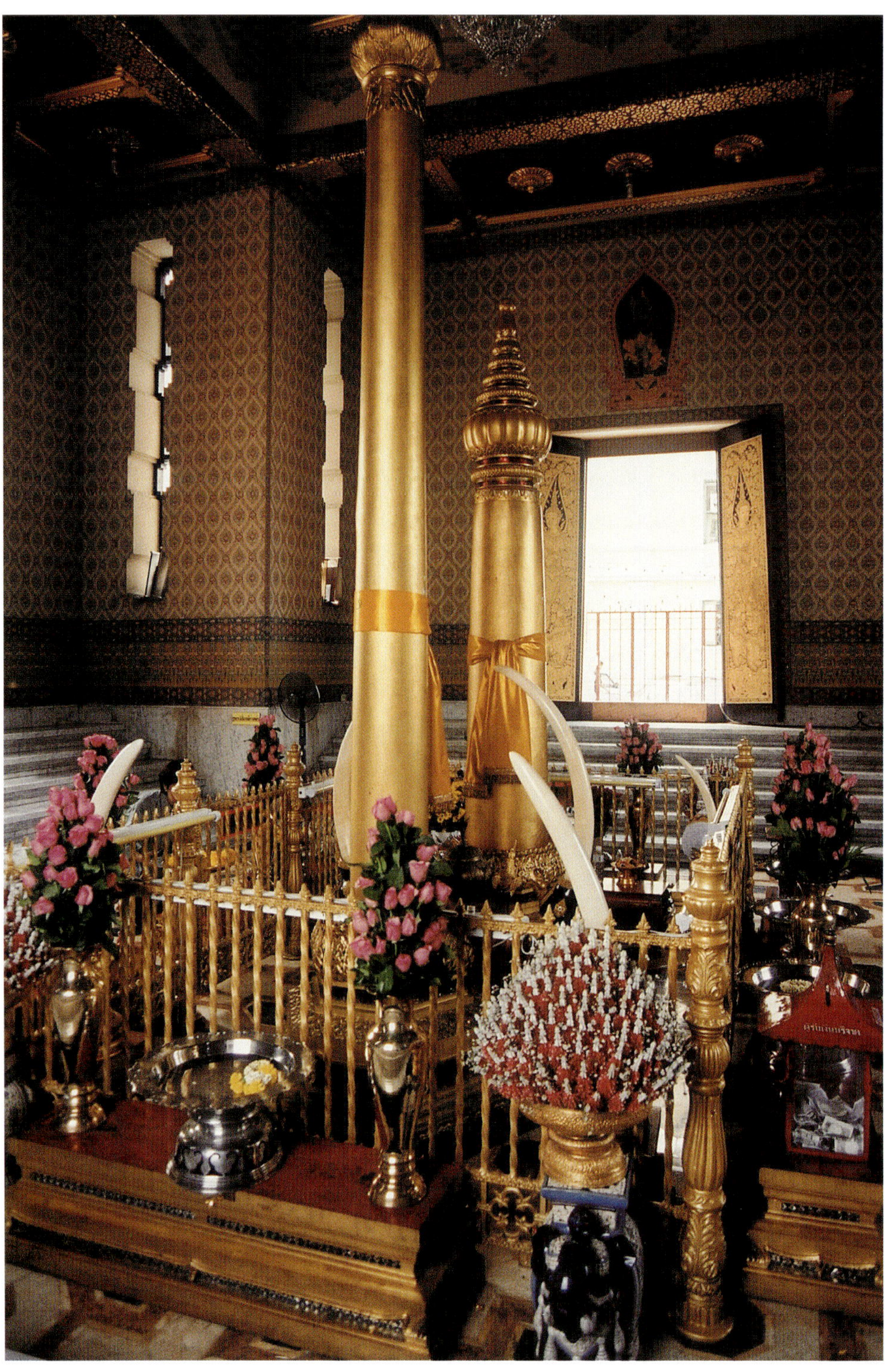

PART THREE

Venice of the East, in distant memory.

An anti-Venice, with a more permeable edge.

Corrupted structure. Tenuous aqueous

boundaries, largely obscured. Historical intent;

missing urban design.

An order rejected, or sublimated to the

greater land.

City as Form: Concentric Order

Bangkok's boundaries are subtle. The flexibility so necessary to its survival finds expression in its multiplicitous orders. Overlapping concentricities and profusions of centre. Every house, temple and precinct identifies an intact and protected whole. Networks of relationships; microcosms of the larger city.

Attentions within these figures are constantly directed to the edge. Spirit houses outline protected precincts. The city pillars identify an imaginary boundary that frames a civic centre by contrast. Similar properties of ambiguous centre and concentric periphery are portrayed by the city's canals. Situated on the site of an earlier fort, Bangkok's terrain was previously populated by modest houses and villages, evenly arrayed along the river. The foundation of the new capital established a centred focus within this field, and articulated its value within layers of aquatic definition.

Civic design; a pattern cut from the amorphous land. More accurately, Bangkok's creation transformed the featureless terrain into an island, or a series of islands viewed in sequential definition. A hierarchy was established, the marsh clarified into a grouping of concentric figures. Rhythms of water and earth. As both the means of travel and urban design, Bangkok's canals articulate a vision of religious and monarchic authority within the structure of the city. Form, use and even ethnicity are arranged by their location within its concentric orders. In the centre, Rattanakosin Island, the royal foundations of palace, ministries, galleries and universities. The next layer, more casual government, urban fabric and the city walls. Outside the walls: markets, industry and the areas inhabited by foreigners.

Commerce. Chinatown, by far the largest precinct, is a vast conglomeration of shops and markets located south of the royal city, just outside the walls. It is the commercial heart of Bangkok, but is not in it exactly. Western commercial influence, more recently significant, takes form equally outside, further south and to the east. The city's historic centre remains protected for more significant concerns.

The order posited by the canals is further supplemented by controlled building heights. There are no tall buildings within the area defined by Bangkok's original walls. Though the Grand Palace is rarely visible in the flat land, no other figure is permitted to take precedence in the skyline. The effective boundaries of this inner city are now marked by two condominium towers, each positioned on the river just outside the historic precinct. Modern secular construction frames the symbolic centre. Reminiscent of the earlier forts and bridges, which equally avoided touching

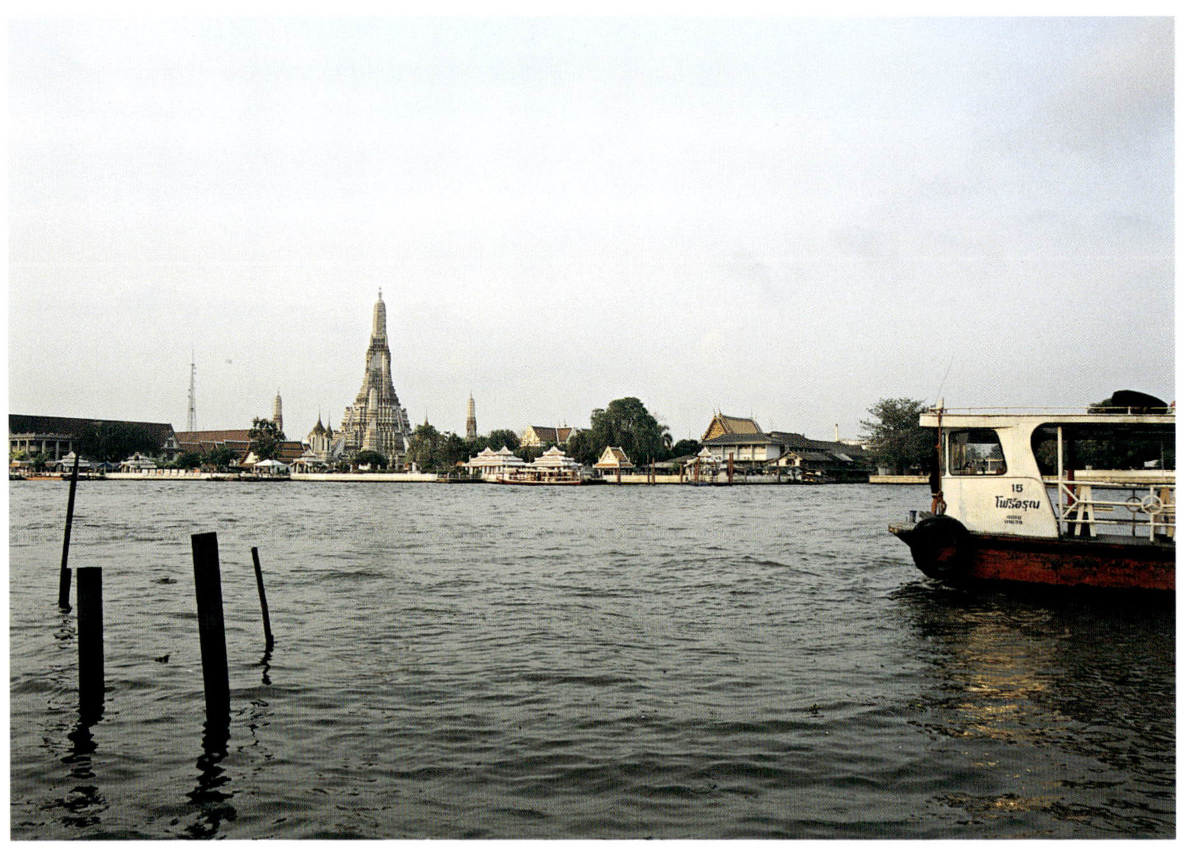

Rattanakosin Island, they identify the sacred precinct by contrast. The city's modern commercial skyline, rising to the south and east, presents an inversion of historic value, a contrasting indicator of social worth.

Gates: symbolic and actual. Bangkok's original walls, still visible in fragment, follow the outer canal and reinforce its shape. Historic forts punctuate the perimeter, acting as hinges between the canal and the river, the city and its hinterland. The recent construction of a public park at Phra Sumeru, a restored fort (one of the original fifteen), marks the northern point of the historic city. At the meeting of canal and river, the antique infrastructure is celebrated as a popular public amenity. Other gates, visible only in traces, establish places for public gathering. Frictions in the concentric order create public moments, the impermeable edge defined by contrast. Outside the walls, the oddly formed wilderness of the modern city: towers, markets, commerce. Contemporary life surrounds the protected antique core of the representational city.

Now largely obscure, this centred form has always been perceptually tenuous. Striking in abstracted plan, the distinction between water and land regularly disappears. At times of annual flooding the entire city becomes aquatic, obscuring the lineaments of designed order. The inhabitation of the canals by houseboats and barely grounded buildings equally blurs their clear figural appreciation. Urban forms are conceptually present yet barely visible, centralized but arrayed on a flat and undifferentiated landscape. Each significant centre is obscured by a precinct wall. Bangkok's order surfaces in brief moments of enticing tangibility, apparently in spite of its best intentions.

Concentric Order: Perfect Centre

The Grand Palace and its chapel, Wat Phra Kaeo, establish a royal focus within this notional island. With the palace at its centre, the canals define an ideal city: an ordered artefact of aquatic definition. Abstract and clear (once distracting experience is edited away), the city springs from the palace, extending out through successive layers of descending value. Sacred and centred object, precinct walls, canals; the concentric edges validate the reticent centre.

And the symbolic significance of the Wat Phra Kaeo itself? Its roofs as referential mountain? In Hindu and Buddhist cosmology, Meru, the centre of the earth and path to heaven, was a Himalayan mountain surrounded by rhythms of subordinate hills and layers of circumscribing water. Canals, like seas, provide both protection and definition for the sacred figure within. Bangkok's canals may articulate a fractional trace of this larger mythical realm. Wat Phra Kaeo, however, is an ambiguous centre in this centred composition. While the forms of the *chedis* and Buddha compositions point upwards towards their celestial destinations, the orientation of Wat Phra Kaeo, its *bot* and the general composition of its many elements, maintains a transverse focus. Vertically inclined

centres are juxtaposed with horizontal inflections. This combination of *wat* and palace manifests a curious centre, one that points up but also leads out, orientated to the west. Most immediately west, the Chao Phraya river. Across the river, Wat Arun, the Temple of the Dawn, a striking spire viewed against the horizontal water. Further out, the setting sun; the real west.

Island as Figure: Form and Motion

Figure as centre, but not a centred figure. The composition of the palace and its chapel inflects horizontally. Equally, Bangkok's canals do not form perfect concentric rings, but rather scallop out from the strong bordering edge of the Chao Phraya river. The palace identifies both a centre and a boundary, the city's focus and its principal facade. Symbolic icon and link to the outside world.

Bangkok is a concentric city with eccentric tendencies. An island cut from the amorphous terrain, but not centred on its land. A sculpted figure carved from a fluid marsh, temporarily moored in the flowing river. A city that oscillates between form and movement, centre and directed attractions.

Bangkok's canals may identify an ideal city, awaiting rescue from the obscurity created by casual modern development. They equally provide a sense of the strong form that the city could have adopted, if it had been so inclined. Indeed Bangkok's canals are trace remnants of a centralized predisposition. Yet this teasing possibility was a route not taken. Bangkok's design is eccentric in its original foundations. Poised against the river, the pleasures of coherent centrality were sacrificed to the more

significant ideals of adjacency and edge. The traces
of a centred geometry remain subordinate to the
river and the concerns of its larger landscape.

The west and a river, an ambiguous focus for a
concentric city. Yet perhaps this condition was key
to Bangkok's very foundation, necessitating the
replacement of Thonburi for a proper royal setting.
The river, an improved aquatic boundary for defence;
certainly. More fundamentally, the creation of a
crucial view. The river, the setting sun and a distant
architectural mountain. The aqueous landscape
presents both boundary and visual preparation
to ideal destinations, necessarily seen to the west.

SIX

River

PART ONE

Civic spine and edge; spirit and boundary. Source to the canals and viewing platform to ritual. Stable ground for the dream world of the sacred. Linear form, natural boundary. Civic facade; city as body?

Centre: River as Form

Orientation is created within a featureless land, an amorphous context rendered significant. Pinned to the moving river, Bangkok's architectural centre is juxtaposed with a natural edge. The city: a concentric island bisected by a linear vector. Fixed to the land by the Lak Muang, a symbolic pillar. To the west, the slow but relentless water. Centre and incised boundary; curious adjacencies and provocative conflicts.

The Chao Phraya river flows from the north, bypassing Bangkok as part of its unhurried descent from the mountains to the sea. Bending to avoid any disturbance, the soft river meanders over the flat plain. The result is a sculpted landscape, at least in plan. Specific moments are created by the river's sensuous, if arbitrary, curves. New sites of habitation are validated, transverse points defined. Each bend in the river's path creates a centralized form. Bangkok itself? A sheltered promontory, not unlike the sideways oblong shape of Ayutthaya. A proto-city whose latent focus awaits figural completion through the excavation of its supporting canals. Bangkok relies on a circumstantial design, and takes advantage of a found geometry.

Bangkok's canals complement the river's curvilinear flow and follow its inspiration. The result is a striking composition of major and minor forms.

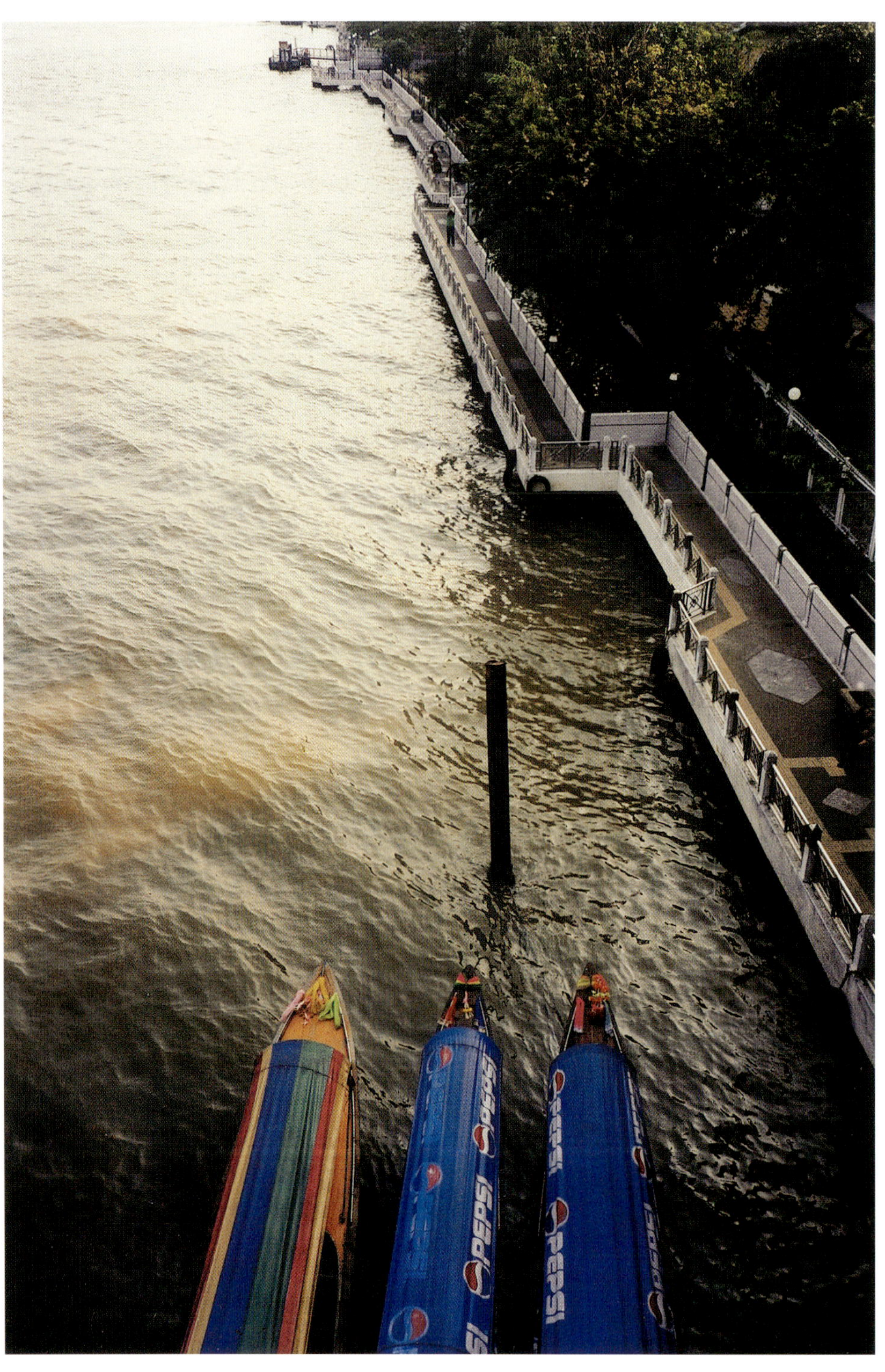

The river, a natural inspiration and urban foundation; the canals, its artistic completion. The city is based on a combination of river and canal, an infrastructure of nature and design. A perfect location and its artificial inflection.

In plan the pairing of river and canal constructs an intriguing figure, oriented through a sequence of hierarchic layers. Located within the river's bend, Bangkok is roughly symmetrical about its east–west axis. The westerly focus is the palace and its chapel, a sacred destination juxtaposed against a natural backdrop. Symbolic journeys find partial completion. One travels from the outer city and its wilderness, from the east, towards the honorific centre. Clarifying a series of aquatic thresholds, Bangkok's figures become more precise, more significant. Culminating at the Wat Phra Kaeo: *bot* and *chedi*. The river to the west. A natural boundary limiting the horizontal journey; a change in state, achieved at the end of lengthy terrestrial travels.

In plan, Bangkok's form follows the example of a generalized temple, a curvilinear macrocosm of the *wat*. An oriented journey through a sequence of layers culminates with a symbolic figure (Wat Phra Kaeo), each perceived through an intensely introspective passage. Just as the *bot*, considered temporally, constructs a route to the Buddha achieved over time, the city frames its focus at the end of an idealized voyage. Gate to palace: Wat Phra Kaeo, as destination and summary.

The same plan, however, can be inverted. Viewed with the west to the top it presents a different image. The abstracted form of the inflected concentric city becomes a more particular, and even personified construction. In 'elevation' the east–west axis identifies a vertical spine, framed by the river's

curvilinear form. A broad base ascends to a figural summit, the sculpted landscape more a body than a mute setting centred by a path. In the conventional plan view, the centralized city is juxtaposed against a linear edge, demonstrating a horizontal inflection. In the imaginary section, the river presents a form of analogous sky, the city a solid body beneath. If the experience of the *bot* is most analogous to the city in its conventional plan orientation, the shift to viewing Bangkok from the land renders it more like a *chedi*. A *chedi* in section or elevation, identifying a series of layered figures leading to a point. The Grand Palace forms the summit: temple as head. The river, a boundary of water and air. Bangkok, a city constructed in the form of a sleeping *chedi*; and a vertical path rendered specific within the horizontal landscape? Different versions of inflected passage are presented for reflection and comparison.

This is perhaps an interpretative stretch, based on coincidences of formal similarity. Yet the transformation from building to nature through a shift in symbolic reference is present in both cases. The official city inflects to the river. And after? Nature as boundary, or a shift in mode? A threshold to a place of different travel? Bangkok's shape orients towards this powerful natural phenomenon, and subsequently transforms at their collision. A civic taste for transmutation finds infrastructural expression in the meeting of city and river. Completion and destination.

Either analogous reading posits a reconsideration of the city's concentric order. Yet these directed concentricities are integral to Bangkok's physical reality. A curvaceous river fixes a significant moment along its southerly journey, preparing the ground for the city's construction.

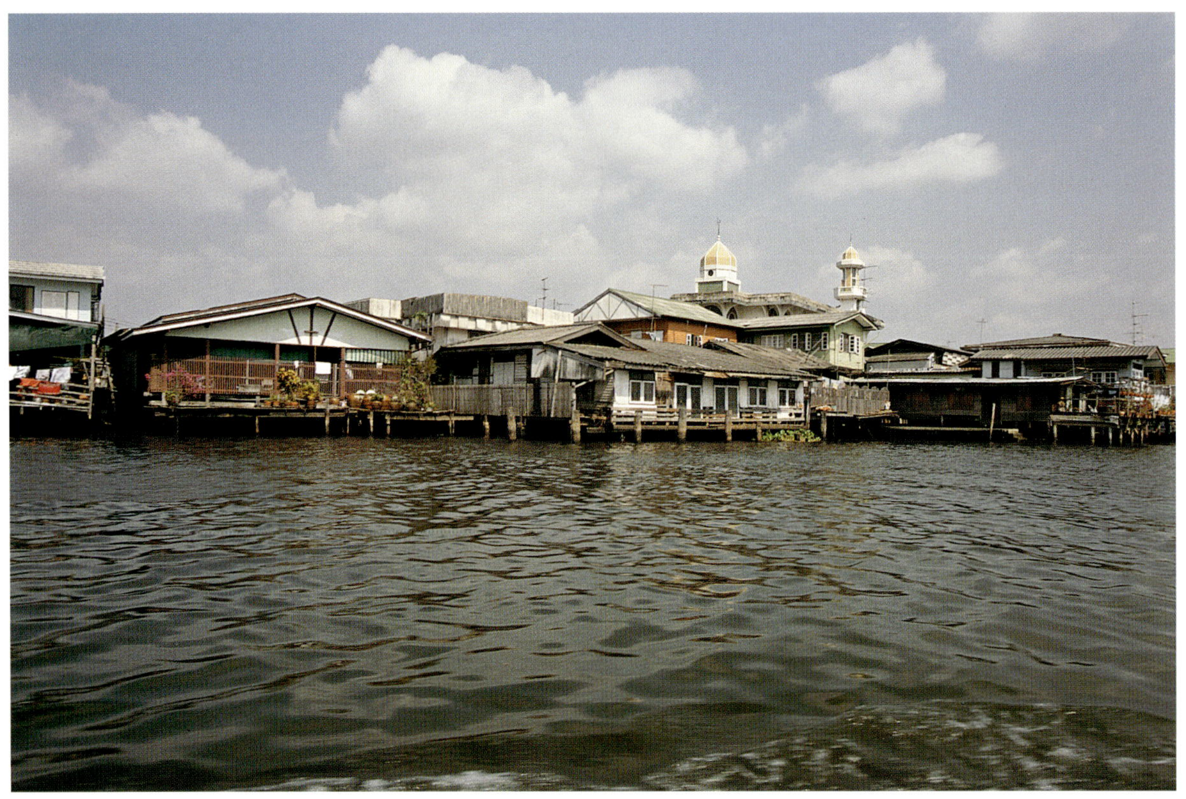

The junction of canal and river defines its form, a generic landscape rendered specific. Subtly defined through the artifice of the aquatic city, the combination of imaginary centre and implied passage is given a geographical definition. If the canals embody Bangkok's domestic life, the Chao Phraya river provides its natural foundations and essential preoccupations.

River as Facade

An eccentric creation, Bangkok juxtaposes its centre and edge in close proximity. A heart exposed; its mysteries unveiled. Perhaps the city is conceived as a gallery to the river, viewing out to the intruding landscape. In the absence of any more evident topography, the Chao Phraya river is Bangkok's actual nature, a landscape legible at an urban scale. This river provides a form of natural theatre, where Thailand's traits are rendered vividly present. View as urban spectacle. It is equally plausible, however, that the river provides the premier location for appreciating Bangkok. On the water one has a privileged position from which to observe the interacting forms of the city. Like its roofs, Bangkok's architectural intentions are more comprehensible when viewed from afar, their appreciation clarified by a perceptual buffer. From the river the city's forms become more legible, their intended significance more easily discerned.

Bangkok presents a wall of densely packed buildings to the water. Yet this compilation does not appear to be defensive. Rather, each building faces the river, with an open, if perhaps cryptic, expression. Observers to the river's flow, these characters form a collective urban facade. Ambiguous barrier and idiosyncratic character simultaneously, Bangkok's river front provides its strongest vernacular image.

This facade is highly animated. Boats crowd the docks, fighting for access to the land. Each building inversely strives for aquatic attention. Yet the surface remains porous, both skin and inhabited boundary. The river may be Bangkok's edge, but it also provides partial openings to the lives of its inhabitants. The definition of the water's limits is equally ambiguous. The buildings form part of a defensive boundary, but they rest on wooden piles. Water extends unhindered into the substructure of the protected city. An oddly permeable boundary. If there is any land to halt the aqueous flow, it remains well hidden. In elevation the individual constructions, collectively arranged, are disconnected from the terrain, poised above the water on forests of wooden sticks. Their stable grounding remains underwater, in shadow. An architecture built on darkened foundations, its support nebulous. Building as urban section? Bangkok appears to float above the water. The image of the city? A large boat or an unstable island, awaiting a fresh current or the next strong wind to direct it to a new home.

The river's edge, Bangkok's principal facade, is indeed a strange kind of urban boundary. Though visually porous, the facade is a barrier to public passage. Collective human entry into the city is largely blocked. Presenting a finer-grained filter,

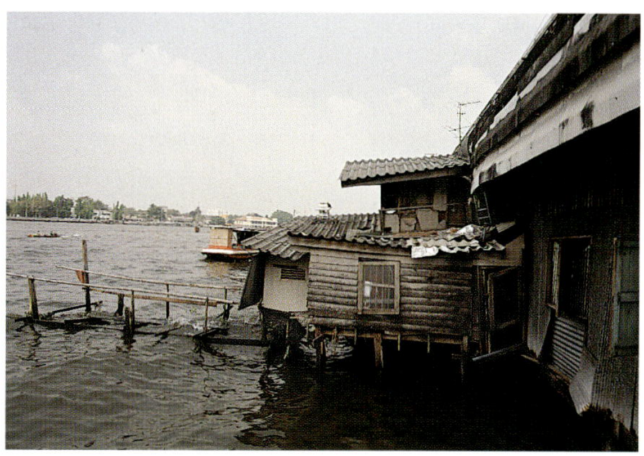

private occupation takes over from shared accessibility. The river, however, flows unhindered, seeping beneath the illusory solidity of the city's forms. Bangkok is poised as a thin line of inhabitation, negotiating between the abstract realms of water and sky while fully integrated with neither. Facade as image, image as reality: Bangkok, floating city. Its ground is fluid, its supports tenuous. The very foundations are fragile, the city ready to slip off its moorings and flow downstream with the monsoon rains. Out to sea. The river buildings foreshadow this implicit destiny, as both witness and progenitors of a future state.

Breaks in the Wall

Breaks in this spongy facade create significant urban moments. Public events; places of commerce and gathering. The ferry landings are the most social. As aquatic gates they provide the proper entries to the historic city. More tangible than the remnants of terrestrial entry, the experience of passing through the visibly amorphous civic facade is experientially rich. Frantic life on the river is replaced by a dense and introspective occupation. Urban infrastructure;

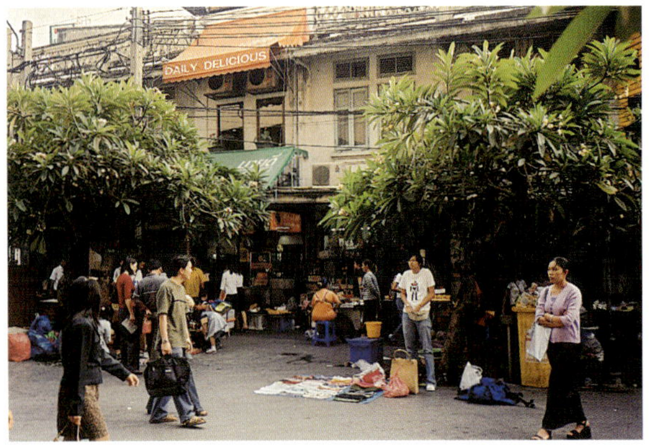 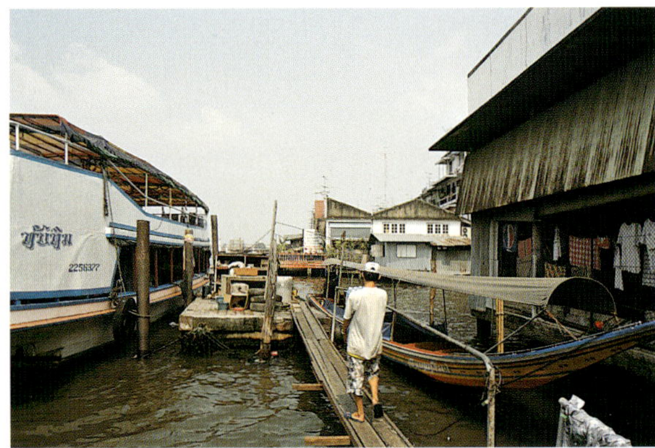

public place as event. Markets and shops occupy the openings in the thickened thresholds. Small restaurants benefit from each landing's dual focus: the junction of city and river celebrated by dining. Activity and view.

The Chang Ferry Pier, just north-west of the palace, is paired with a recently reconfigured pedestrian square. Both market and passage, the combination reinforces urban entry as a place of public gathering. The design is modest but effective. The formal clarity of the historic shop buildings is supplemented by simple planting and paving. Shade is provided by low trees, music by the market's loud-speakers. A lively space, where river, market and landing combine to create a social focus. A smaller version is created at the Prachon Pier, adjacent to Thammasat University. Elsewhere, more casual variations. Each break in the aquatic wall, crucial for the operation of river transport, establishes memorable points in the urban terrain. The city's realities are brought into meaningful conversation through practical necessity.

At the Grand Palace, a more formal relationship is established. The palace, set back in its own precinct, is fronted with an open break in the river's occupation. The dense, small-scale building is peeled away to reveal the honoured figure behind. A foreground, now somewhat obscured by encroaching landfill and casual military installations, is established: a place of symbolic presentation meeting the river, the Chao Phraya itself a place of symbolic action.

The royal facade. The palace roofs float above their defining boundaries, presenting a vision of ideal architecture to the river. A perfect image centres the more general city. This perceptual forecourt allows the elevational appreciation of roofs and precinct walls, the collision of forms that disappear on closer view. The relationship is striking. Royalty and water, symbols of city and country, authority and nature. The immediate juxtaposition of centre and boundary. In the breaks in the river's facade the city is unveiled, its values exposed. Centre and edge; figural object juxtaposed with temporal flow.

PART TWO

Edge and centre; facade and spine, of city

and country. Line of history, as capitals

travel seaward to accompany the rain.

Sukhothai, Ayutthaya, Bangkok; a

sequence of cities along the path of time.

Boats as temporary, superior land.

Monarchic ritual; funerary destination.

Edge or Spine: River as Centre

The river: a space of conversation, a space of reflection. The Chao Phraya river may historically define Bangkok's western boundary, and its most coherent facade, but it is also experienced as a principal urban space. Another version of centre. As Thonburi has become subsumed into the metropolis, the experience from the water is increasingly symmetrical. With the exception of the historic *wats* and the Grand Palace, similar constructions line both banks, framing a centred passage and obscuring the fundamental differences active behind.

This condition, first perceived visually, is also functional. Due to the challenges of Bangkok's traffic, the river provides the fastest and most dependable means of urban circulation (though perhaps now partially surpassed by the Sky Train). In the congested city, exterior boundary becomes a functional spine. Public ferries cruise between the banks, just as the more private long-tailed boats race by, their rapid passage marked by the diaphanous spray of their wakes and the high-pitched whine of their engines. The river is a hub of motion, where a myriad of boats, seemingly oblivious to each other, careen about in unexpected safety. A fixture of urban life, supporting Bangkok's most expedient means of travel.

The Chao Phraya river is equally active at the scale of the country, balancing the concerns of centre and edge for the larger landscape. As edge, the river provides a defence from the Burmese to the west. Yet the river is also Thailand's central artery, its geographic and functional backbone. This north–south axis establishes a complementary orientation to the east–west bias of the city and its temples. A line of varied significances and historic responsibilities.

The Chao Phraya river connects the northern hills to the sea. Along the way it bisects the vast agricultural plains central to Thailand's historic wealth. The river is the means for carrying the rich produce of a fertile land to the greater nation and out to the larger world. Yet the river's waters also participate in creating this abundance. Traditional Thai agriculture is highly aquatic, its products, most notably rice, reliant on the river and its seasonal flooding. Rice springs forth from the inundated plains, the fecund earth fed by the brown waters and their wondrous life generating reappearances.

As a form within this larger landscape? The circuitous aspects of the river's travels are striking, especially for a major functional conduit. It meanders across its plain, in no apparent rush. An indirect voyage, attempting to avoid the inevitable, to delay its eventual submersion in the sea? Or does the descent respond to different needs, required to create a rhythm of distracting episodes along its fated journey?

Passage up-river, against the natural flow; the path of visitors. The Chao Phraya river has historically provided an introduction to Bangkok, and indeed to Thailand, for the Western traveller. Travel from the Gulf of Thailand, the voyage from the sea into the unknown land is a recurring literary trope. Water as initial image, an idiosyncratic culture presented to an outsider's eyes. This traditional armature for historic discovery is also the vehicle for some strange observations. Engelbert Kaempfer, a German physician writing *A Description of the Kingdom of Siam* in 1690, speculated on the relations between the Nile and the Chao Phraya river. The agricultural parallels between the two rivers, with their skilful reallocation of natural flooding, led him to assume Egyptian foundations for Thai civilization. Even the Buddha was deemed to be of African heritage. While Kaempfer based the association on 'This Saint being represented with curled Hairs, like a Negro', the more familiar image of the Nile established the conceptual provocation for his constructed relations.[1]

Foreign observers were fascinated by the life they observed on the river, its conditions and their accompanying social implications. The agility of the boatmen avoiding collisions, the popular rituals of bathing, a people perceived to be indolent on land but feverously active on the water. Water and its image, the source of perplexed observations or grudging respect. 'The Siamese', wrote P. A. Thompson in 1910, 'are an amphibious race, and the finest watermen in the world'.[2] He marvelled at the amount of domestic activity taking place in the docks. Eating, washing, scooping drinking water, all occur in immediate proximity to the river. Travelling upriver, an introduction to Bangkok; an inverse route to the city's sensibility.

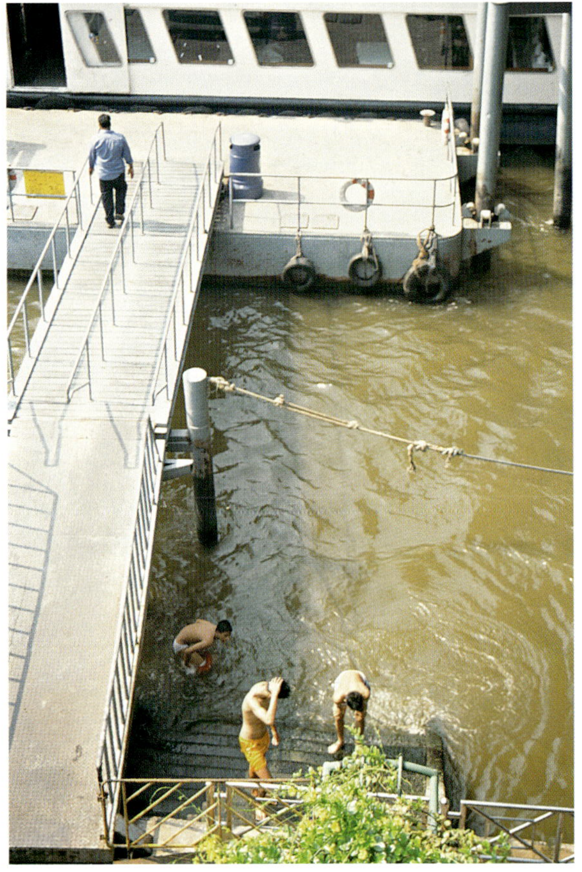

The river, Thailand's essential infrastructure, and the spine of its history. The river's southerly flow encapsulates the history of Thailand's capitals. Gradually descending from the north, fleeing the troublesome Burmese, these cities were sequentially refounded further from their historic source; a journey that parallels the original migration of proto-Thais from China. The passage from Chiang Mai, Sukhothai, Ayutthaya and Thonburi to Bangkok defines a line of successive capitals, or more likely, a single capital in motion. Each city is a momentary flowering of national authority, each eventually surpassed. Directed by the flow of the river, this temporal passage is as tangible as the existence of Bangkok itself. Analysis of the river becomes an investigation into the historic foundations of the monarchic city, and its ultimate, if unconscious, destiny. The national capital survives as an ideal rather than a location. The river constructs the temporal foundations to Bangkok's history, and perhaps its underlying purpose.

Mythically? The Chao Phraya river flows from the north, collecting tributaries from the mountains. The north, equated with Mount Meru both geographically and culturally. The Himalayas are the ultimate source of the sacred waters, the myths articulating their gradual descent from the mountains to the sea. Proper life is poised somewhere in between. The river, viscerally real, is a tangible link to this symbolic landscape. Thailand's inhabited land and its mythic realms are joined, the invisible mythic source rendered aquatically present. Like the water that supports the rice fields, only to be absorbed into the earth, the river flows to the sea, carrying fleeting memories of the distant and generous mountains towards their disappearance.

Royal Time

Flexible but relentless, accommodating, but ever present. A natural figure that orders the passage of time. Its descent to the flat landscape of Bangkok, validates the curious destination. A landscape that requires virtual representation and symbolic reconstructions to gain legibility. River and city; complementary forms, binary visions. Different ideals of spectacle; different modes of action. The most publicly significant events? Bangkok's royal ceremonies.

The Chao Phraya river is a figure of historic and mythical time, a place of destiny. It is also a place of symbolic presentation, key to Bangkok's celebratory life. The primary bond is created at the junction of the palace and the river. Monarchic significance, articulated by the centralized plan of the canals, finds its temporal expression in royal rituals. River and palace; places of royal representation, both central to Bangkok's sensibilities. Early photographs of Bangkok portray the palace as a central figure in the river's image. A small landing separates the palace walls from its docks, their pavilions and the adjoining water. Though now largely (but not irredeemably) obscured by security barriers, tennis courts and a major road, the relation remains. The palace presents a lengthy facade to the river, the intervening space a historic conduit for symbolic meetings.

The royal rituals celebrate historic, sacred and natural time, relying on the river as their seasonal signifier. A symbolic moment, the Royal Bathing Ceremony (Phrarajphithi Longson). Although now largely extinct, the ceremony required the Crown Prince to bathe in the Chao Phraya river. A complex series of temporary constructions bring Mount Meru symbolically to the city, the bathing pavilion conceived as an architectural mountain surrounded by water. The centred architecture supports the ritual coronation.[3]

Each rite articulates a fleeting relation between significant land and water. The Royal Barge processions are celebrated as massive works of architectonic order. Conscious historic constructions, the rituals were reinstated and reconfigured most recently under the reign of the current king, the design undertaken by a princess. Its arrangement, like its predecessors, is based on a cosmological analogy. The boats assume the roles of the sun and moon, the planets and the stars. Their relative locations are structured by a series of parallel rows travelling with the river. These rows are subdivided lengthwise as well, creating a five by five matrix. The arrangement of interdependent, orthogonally disposed figures in motion is not dissimilar to the relationships that order the elements in the larger *wats*. A symbolically rich geometric order is superimposed over a flickering and transient ground. Stability is achieved, an active celestial form set in aquatic motion.

These choreographies are remembered (and were likely created) in striking manuscript images, now on view with the boats at the Royal Barge Museum in Thonburi. Similar to the roofs portrayed in the frescoes, the celestial characters are axonometrically arrayed across their setting. Their appreciation is spatial, planimetric and elevational simultaneously. The flowing order, cosmically arranged, carries out its ritual duties. Each boat's profile is distinct, their locations significant. The cosmological metaphor is most evident in the arrangement, their personalities clearly expressed as elevational image. A celestial royalty, understood through mythic images, meets the river to renew the sacred links between water, mountain and sky. Bangkok's ornate royal barges articulate the legacy of this bond, and provide the most compelling images of temporary order achieved. Boats, choreographed as reminders of the idealized city, manifest on the flowing river.

The Thai Navy was destroyed by the Burmese at the sack of Ayutthaya. In replacement, a fleet of 60 boats was ordered by Rama I, founder of Bangkok and composer of the *Ramakien*. As the text, the new boats were similarly adorned as narrative figures, the mythical characters of the Indic inheritance animating their prows. Hanuman, Vishnu riding Garuda, dragons and monsters: the boats bring the mythology of the epic to visible form. With the heroes of the northern hills recreated in their new aquatic home, royal authority was re-connected with its foundations, mythically intact. The partial destruction of the Thai fleet during the Second World War was more recently traumatic. The boats' subsequent restoration manifested a new commitment to protecting the nation's artistic heritage, one that gradually became extended to the temples and buildings of the city as well. Boats first, buildings later.

The Chao Phraya river itself, blessed by this link with the heavens and the characters of myth, is always in motion. It travels from its mythical foundations towards greater temporal reality, and maintains their connections. Myth, history, life, death and dissolution. Architecture, in the form of the Royal Barges and the symbolic constructions of their rituals, animates this relation, and sharpens their possible conflicts.

The End of Time

Bangkok's royal chariots, now kept at the National Museum, are large constructions used ritually to carry the nobility across the earth. And their image? The chariots are articulated as boats: civic land rendered as virtual water. Indeed, the chariots, primarily used for funerals, so closely resemble the royal barges as to render the distinction between land and water moot. Bangkok: typically overlapping structures of sequence and symbol.

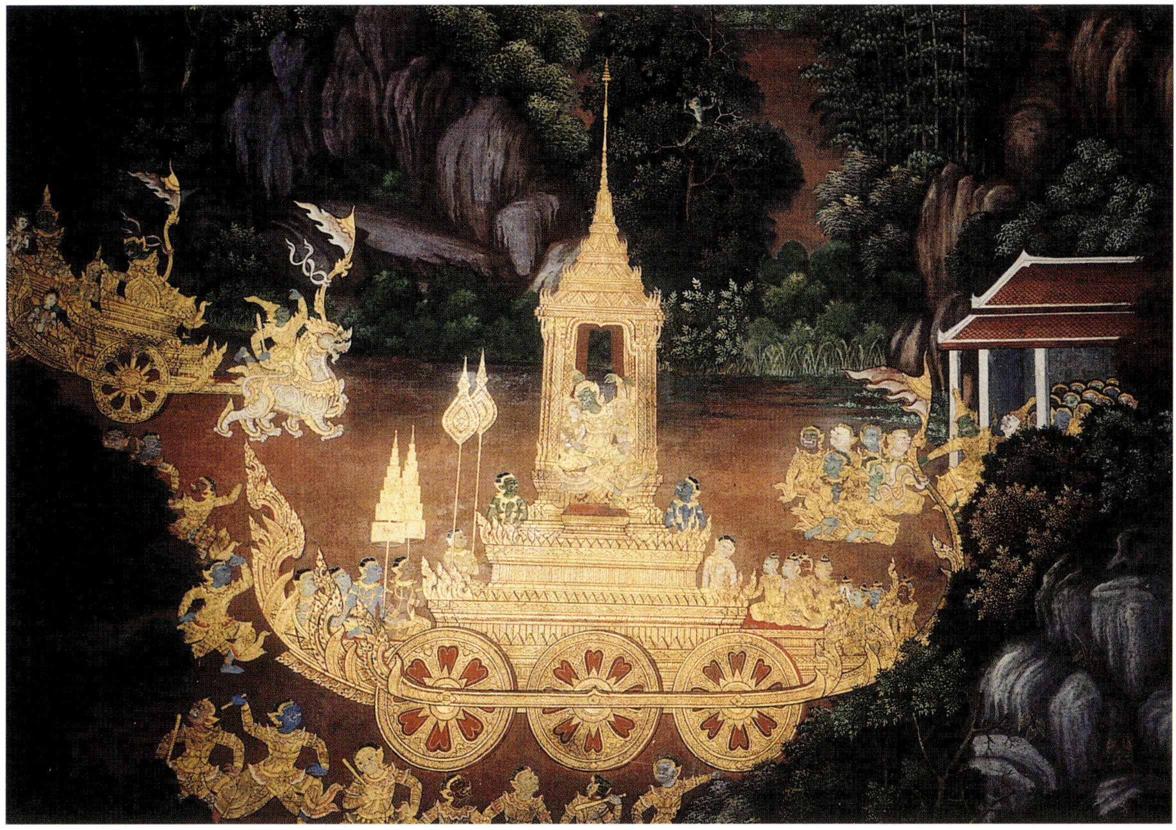

The chariot, as a ship of state passing though life, brings the royal body to its cremation – the gate to a future, and hopefully higher, state. The chariot is drawn towards the specially constructed funerary pyre, the latter's form referencing Mount Meru, or Mount Sumeru (Phra Sumeru in Thai), the centre of the world in Brahmanic and Buddhist cosmology. The ceremony links the deceased, but divine, royal with his celestial home. The boat-chariot carries the body to Meru in a special urn that is then raised up a ramp in the image of Naga the water serpent, to the summit. There the urn is burned, though without destroying the temporary architectural setting. The royal bones are taken away in a new urn to be housed in the royal palace, the remainder of the ashes placed in either the canal or the river, to float away with the transient water.

These Meru-like constructions are traditionally located on the Sanam Luang, adjacent to the Grand Palace. Symbolic mountains, their proximity to the palace creates an association of idealized landscapes, the mythic hills and palace roofs placed in close juxtaposition. Yet the chariots are articulated as boats. By implication the land is water, the city an aqueous terrain punctuated by the symbolic mountains. Overlapping metaphors. But why are these referential Merus not actually located on the river itself, as were the earlier bathing pavilions?

The immense scale of the river processions reported in the historic chronicles makes it clear that it was not due to problems of skill or a lack of commitment to ritual. The reported magnificence of the river processions and royal cremations challenge comprehension. The conscious shift to the land necessarily implies other concerns.

Symbolically, Meru is a land figure, a Himalayan reference. Although it may be accessed by transversing a series of canals, in itself the mountain is the ultimate and grounded source of their waters. It is a figure of fixed concentric stability, its own axis and its funerary significance vertical. The cremated soul enters the heavens at a defined point, the mountain a gate leading to visual and virtual disappearance. Land, point and sky.

The funerary chariots bring the earthly body (and temporal life) to the holy mountain. Through the assistance of the serpent Naga, its horizontal (aquatic) journey is transformed to a vertical one. A change in state; a break in the horizontal plane. This shift requires a concentric land with a vertical focus. The river, trapped in time, remains the locus for transient realities. Physical life and its ashes return to fertilize the flooded fields. Early – preparatory – life, celebrated in the bathing ceremonies, is temporally based, and thus celebrated on the river. Final – essential – life is outside of time and temporal value. The juxtaposition of the boat (chariot) and mountain identify different temporalities, brought into immediate proximity through the ritual of the cremation. The path to a proper future abandons the horizontal river to meet the sky, assisted by the mythical mountain.

The river manifests linear and horizontal passage, articulating earthly, temporal journeys. These may be symbolically potent, but they remain physically tangible. The river describes a relentless descent to the sea, even if delayed by its meandering paths. A place for ashes, not for souls. A path for physical cities, rather than their spirit. Unlike the pyres of Homer's heroes or the Viking longboats carrying a warrior's soul to Valhalla, the aquatic architecture of Bangkok's funeral chariots and barges lives on. It does not disappear in the flames, but rather memorializes the symbolic journeys for future appreciation. The destiny may be a notional one, but the different journeys leading towards it are vividly celebrated. Supporting this passage is an architecture of symbolic mountains reconstructed for the ritual events. The river is memorialized in each symbolic Meru through contrast. Ultimate transformation may take place on imaginary land, but the route towards it is, perhaps paradoxically, more permanent, and more accessible to artistic embellishment.

River, spine of the country. Path of the monsoon rains to the sea. Civic festival, spiritual assistant. The means for washing away sins. A succession of experience that renders the river and its inexorable flow more tangible than the city itself.

River as Spine, River as Spirit

National time, mythic time; all centre on the river. Not surprisingly, the river is the focus for the expression of local and personal time as well. Festivals of movement and balance, constructed in concert with the river. Domestic funerals travel in special boats, personal obligations being ritually blessed by the waters. Physically vivid; spiritually rich. Ebb and flow; water as link.

Outside the gates at Wat Rakhang in Thonburi, a thriving market sells gift baskets for donation to the monastery. Candles, sashes and incense are on offer, ready for submission to the *wat*. Intermingled within, stalls of river life: snails, fish, eels and turtles, sold by the kilo. The slippery creatures are purchased in order to be released into the river. Paralleled with prayer within the temple, the action demonstrates a generosity of spirit and brings merit to the supplicant. Through giving the defenceless captives their freedom, one's soul is purified. The fish do not (seem to) suffer so badly. The plastic

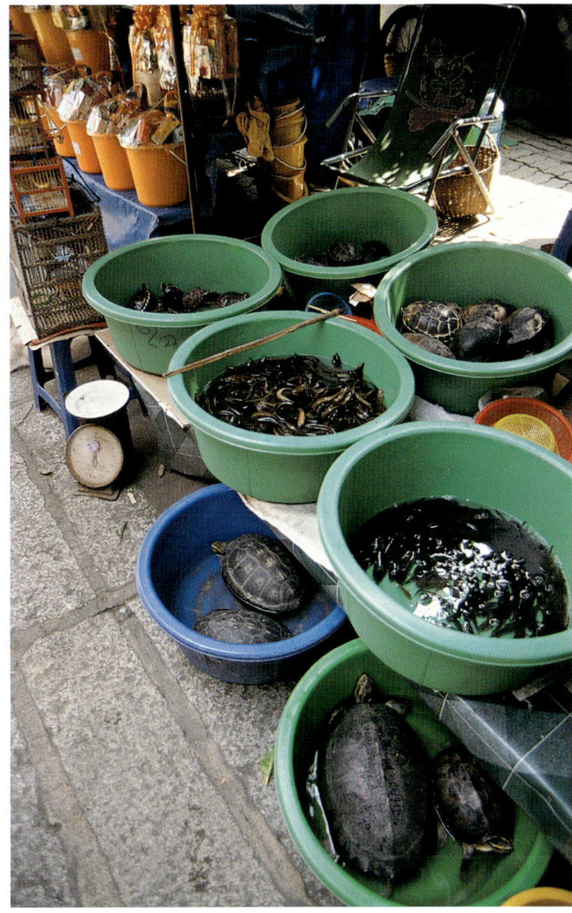

buckets providing their temporary homes may not quite be the river, but they are not deadly. The snails baking in the sun are less lucky. Monastic escargot. Purchasing a few dozen snails not only gives them their liberty, but likely saves their lives as well. While dropping the small shells into the water may not have the visual appeal of watching a fish swimming happily away, it may be the more necessary act. Humility in action. Of course, the riverine hostages were intentionally caught for this purpose, making the circular morality of the process somewhat suspect. Yet in spite of the questionable

logic, the symbolism is clear. The river presents
a path to liberty.

At other *wats* small birds are purchased to be
released from their cages into the sky. Nature as
freedom. Sky and air; river and water. Nature is
a conduit for escape. For the river, its directed
motion is central to this capacity. Travel is explicit
in its ever-present current, a distant destination
implied.

The Songkran festival, commemorating the
New Year, applies the restorative aspects of water to
people more directly. A few drops of sprinkled water,
a traditional form of blessing. The more complete
dousings are now licensed as socially permitted
revelry. Water ritually splashes the occupants
and artefacts of the city, foreshadowing the annual
blessing of the monsoons. The sensual, nourishing
aspects of water find social expression. The rains,
necessary to restore the river to its required
agricultural strength and thereby central to
national survival, are invited back by example.

Through the monsoon, life is brought to the
crops, and by extension to the people. Water,
carried by the intermediary figure of the flooding
river, is a fertilizing, energizing source. Celebrating
this realization, Songkran brings about a certain
giddiness, people washing each other just as the rain
bathes the city and its landscape. Water is recycled,
travelling quickly, just like money in the local
markets. The effect? A bit manic, where the festival's
original modest solemnity has been transformed via
a change in scale. *Sanuk*. A Thai word referring to a
sense of fun, a taste for finding enjoyment or a
capacity for entertainment in all things. In Bangkok
the practicalities of the world may be justifiably
ignored if they are insufficiently *sanuk*. A quality

central to the festival, and perhaps essential to the
universal appreciation of water as well.

Sanuk and the city? Bangkok is built on
celebration. It is physically animated by the
remnants of royal festivals, their buildings, boats
and chariots. Annually, by its rituals. The most
compelling aspects of Bangkok's daily life? Food,
social interaction and fashion, striking and
fleeting simultaneously. Water as provocation
and reminder.

The Loy Krathong festival, held in November,
borrows the river (all rivers) as a powerful force.
At the end of the rainy season and its floods, the
waters depart to leave the terrain dry and the fields
barren. Bidding farewell, the festival blesses their
healthy journey, and guards against the pestilence
that sometimes accompanies their absence. The
descent must be properly celebrated, the waters
ceremonially sent on their way to ensure their
proper return.

The festival borrows the departing waters as the
means to wipe away sin. Past misdeeds, embodied
in the form of small reed-boats bearing candlelit
offerings, are placed in the river to be carried out to
sea and oblivion. With the rafts launched, Thailand's
rivers become constellations of flickering lights,
the dark waters animated by the floating stars.
The celestial metaphors articulated by the
choreographed royal barges are made experientially
explicit in the collective ritual. Large paper lanterns,
fuelled by the heated air of their candles, are sent
into the sky as complementary figures to the floating
rafts. The bright figures, lifting into the night air,
bring this active celestial relationship to heightened
visibility. Darkened sky and water; both are
animated and clarified by the disappearing lights.

And now, like Songkran, the Loy Krathong festival is notable for its excesses. Solemn ideals, frantic reality. Fireworks are casually lit, aggressive explosions tossed about to punctuate the night. Kids populate the river-banks with exuberant parties.

The scene appears more like the up-river encampments portrayed in *Apocalypse Now* than a collective prayer for cleansing souls. Perhaps the racket helps scare the bad spirits on their way. Tranquil beauty and manic intensity are super-imposed, with no sense of contradiction expressed by the participants.

Temporary events as manifest order. With any presumption of permanence avoided, the festivals decorate the city and bring its order to visibility. Food in temples and sashes on statues; the Emerald Buddha ceremonially dressed. Temporary buildings. The sensibility underlying it all; the transience of water as image and quality.

River Life

The river. Form and event; image and experience. While explicit ideals of symbolic passage may underlie Bangkok's river festivals, its daily presence is equally reflective of the city's more essential values. This existential quality is manifest in Bangkok's boats, in both form and action. The celebratory golden barges express official monarchic sensibilities. The virtues of life afloat are celebrated in their idiosyncratic forms and mythical references. Planets and stars flicker on the water, literary creatures and heroes reborn. Yet the sensibility of boat as image and event is apparent at all levels. The brown river, opaque and dense. A dark substructure of fragile piers. In contrast, the boats present bursts of colour,

blurred images of speed and intensity set against the dull backdrop. Boat as image? Boat as splash. The river and its surface are decorated with an intense, if transient, occupation.

Boats in motion, animating the boundary between water and air. In action, Bangkok's boats create a noisy combination of colour and spray. Their frantic activity calls attention to the river's surface, the thin line stretched between water and sky. The boat's hulls are decorated with coloured stripes, accentuating its horizontality. Coloured frames, coloured roofs: a striking contrast to the brown water below. Like the city's low historic skyline they demar-cate a finely defined horizon, a narrow threshold of interaction. A thin seam of contrast, animated, and indeed energized, by the constructions of daily life. Boats and buildings. The river's most prosaic crafts formally accentuate this quality. The long-tailed boats, long and narrow, are powered by large in-board engines, the propeller extended to the water by a long steel shaft. Stretched along its axis, the propeller sits well outside the boat itself, elongating the composition and celebrating the horizontal surface in a noisy spray of colour and water.

Boundary as Event

From the boats, a privileged view; a directed experience. Sheltered passage is focused towards a destination. The ferry's seats are set low, creating an internalized experience. This is accentuated by the densely coloured ceiling and walls, especially when the boat's fabric skin is raised as a defence against the suspect water. A introspective cocoon moving on the water's surface. A circle in cross-section; a tunnel of crimson set against the muddy water. The boats are part of the river but distinct through form and experience. They exemplify the river's qualities by skimming over its surface. Lightness as respect.

This activity articulates the mysterious meeting of water and sky. The lack of any distracting landscape, assisted by the city's relentless horizontality, brings both realms into immediate juxtaposition, and simultaneously heightens their independence. Any moment that articulates this relation becomes special. *Wat* roofs and the ritual funerary constructions create breaks though difference. The royal boats, and river travel in general, animate the point of contact through independent action. Manic motion calls attention to the significant meeting of water and sky, celebrating the horizontal seam.

Descent or Discovery?

The river is a figure of personal and national history passing through the land. National history is animated by life on its surface. A place of commerce, travel and royal representation. A place where the parts of the city become visibly integrated.

The river provides a field of reference for most aspects of Bangkok. Water flows to the sea, cleansing the canals and feeding the fields. Brown and murky, its surface flickers in the sun. It is mysterious and opaque, though populated by flashes of brilliant colour. Like Bangkok, the river is mostly a dull brown, and full of debris. Yet it is also capable of majesty and light. The same dark waters become a fine spray in the wake of a long-tailed boat, the noise signalling the ethereal transformation of the dense water into its opposite. This river is a place of escape. Freedom for one's soul; freedom for the fish, eels, turtles and snails purchased at the *wats*.

Liberation achieved through motion. Restlessness or focused desire?

Ultimately, the river descends to the sea, but in an indirect fashion. Its looping form creates specific moments within the undifferentiated plain. Each twist brings a figural quality to the land, creating temporary centres to contrast the gradual but relentless southerly pull. While the river's final destination is clear, the route is circumstantial, even random. A meandering path to a distant result. It is an ambiguous force whose curvilinear form, while occasionally changing direction, manifests a quiet strength. The Chao Phraya river is a suitable avatar of its country and its restless principal city. The river, as the conduit of primal meetings, brings the real Bangkok to visibility. The city can't resist the power of the river, but must live with it, and learn to temper its idiosyncrasies. A city with an ambiguous relation to its own land, both physical and mythical. The descent to the sea, an ascent to self-knowledge.

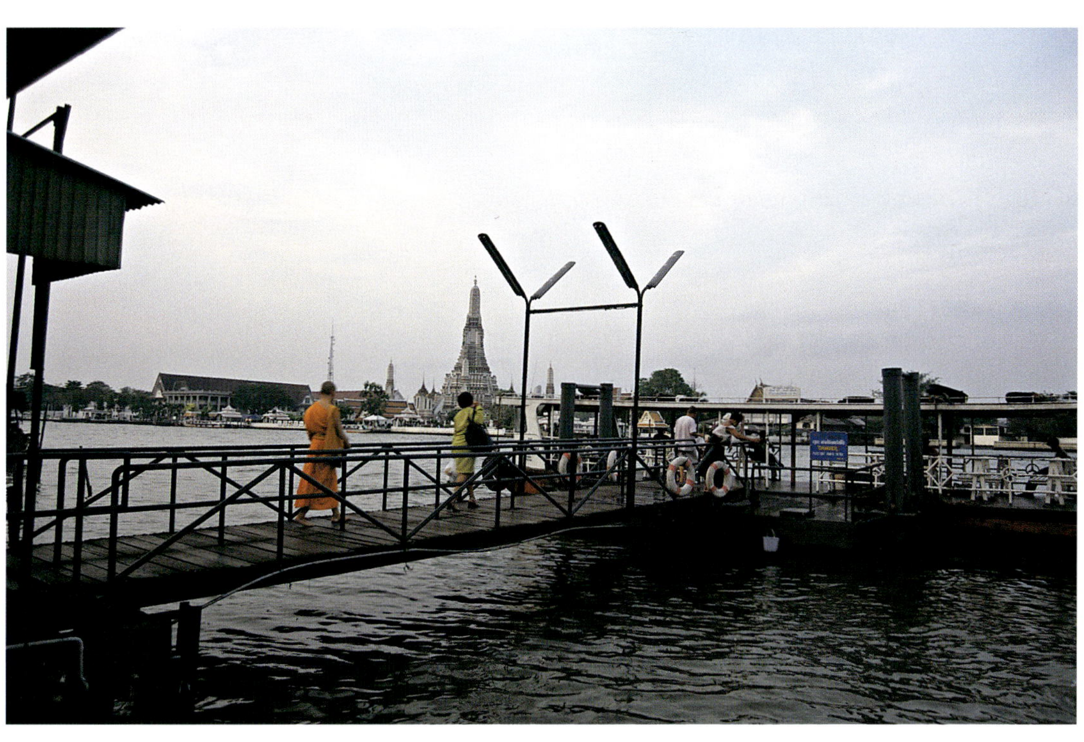

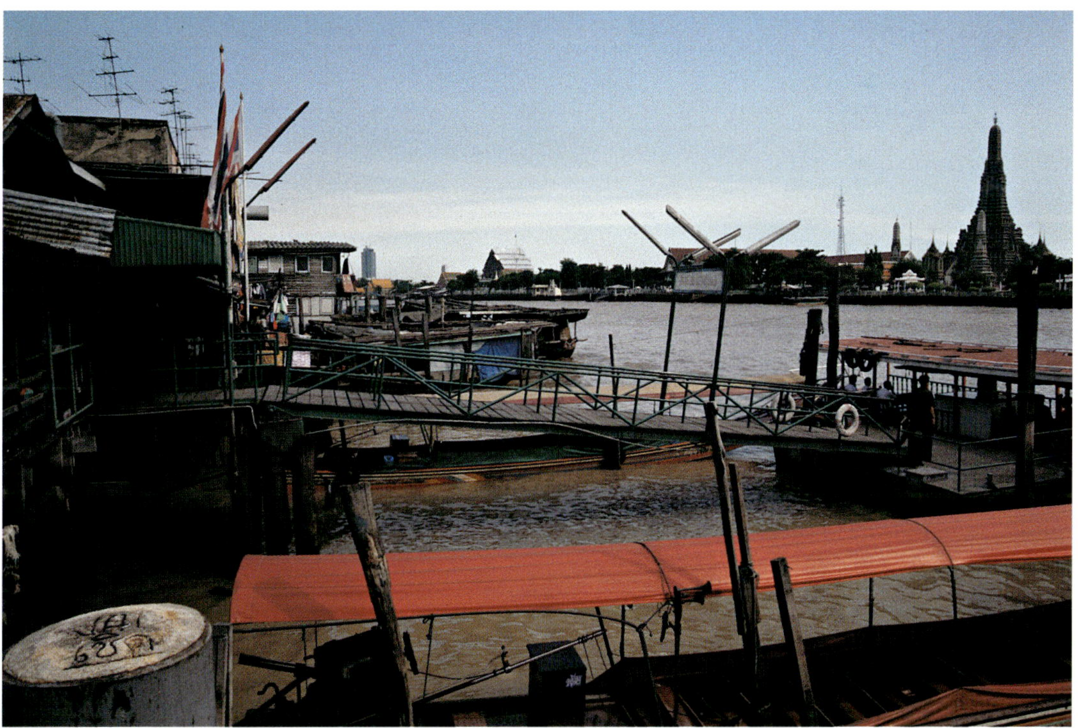

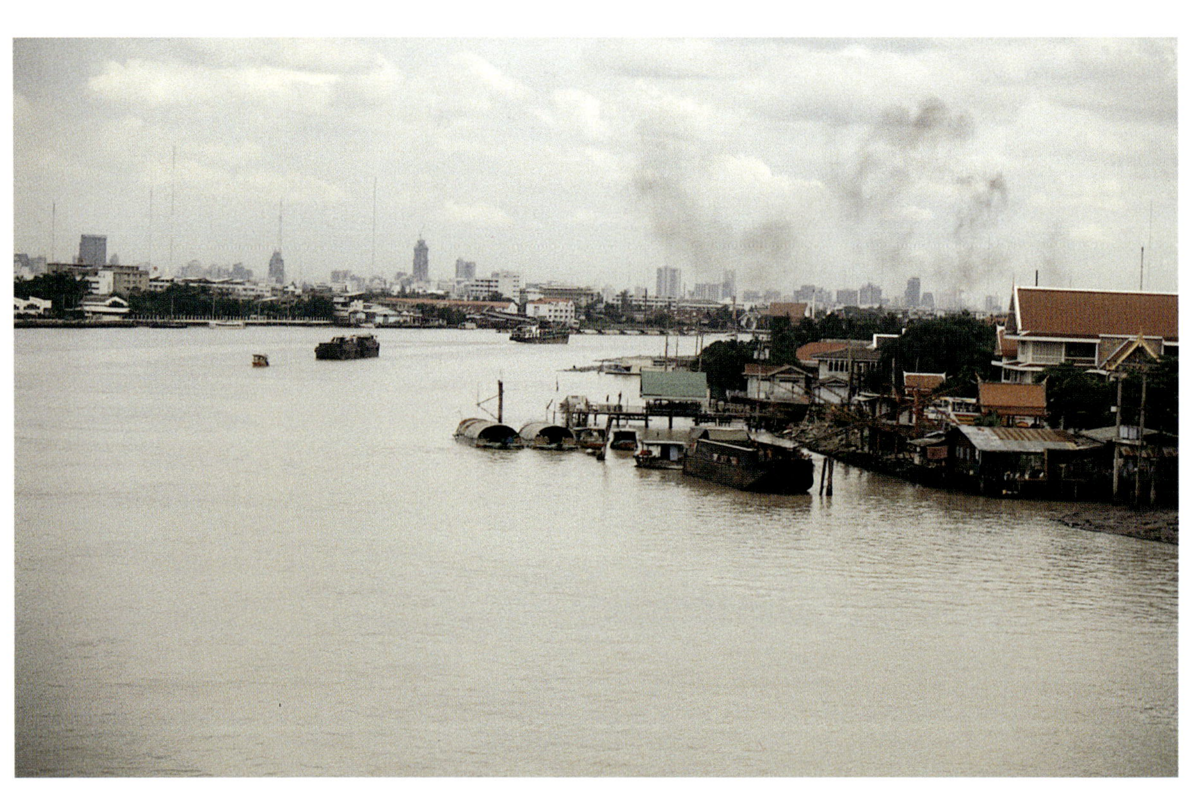

SEVEN

Land – Missing Mountains – Sea

PART ONE

Buildings on stilts, avoiding the degraded soil.

Transient, porous and unstable;

a condition to be rejected.

Escape from the ground is architecturally

celebrated; figural clarity increasing with

vertical distance. Never point your feet at

a Buddha. Landscape as absence.

Delta

Missing landscape. Adrift somewhere between the mountains and the sea, Bangkok is tenuously affixed to the Chao Phraya river delta. A flat and intangible surface, a curious ground. Small palm trees punctuate the horizon, just as patches of underbrush identify areas of barely solid earth. Water is ever present, sometimes in canals, though more often in vaguely defined pools. The rustic canals are choked with vegetal material, paralleling the industrial refuse accumulating on the land. Remnants of an older aqueous Thailand, one not yet integrated with the city, though obscured by its suburban sprawl. A once specific occupation, transformed to an urban wasteland.

The city follows the southward flow of the river, further losing its shape as it meanders towards the sea. Recognizable order is sacrificed. All that can be urbanistically noted are the relative positions of figures in fluid conversation. Industrial buildings, shrimp farms and forgotten condominium towers interact within the strange terrain. Vague foundations for a city; curious conditions in experience. A dense mix of land, water and building, with any remaining legible differences awaiting dissolution. As the river reaches the sea, the delta blurs the final distinctions between water and land. Ambiguous in both plan and section, this aqueous

condition adds to the mental uncertainty essential
to Bangkok's existence.

Closer to the city the built density increases,
though with few discernible principles of
organization. Greater industrial activity collides
with traditional *wats* and houses. Bangkok gradually
appears; the truncated end of an elevated expressway
floats in the sky to mark the intensification of traffic.
Buildings become larger and closer together, and
then – abruptly – the towers of Silom Road. A
version of the modern commercial city, presented
with no legible boundary or formal preparation
from the murky land outside.

The delta is flat and grey, a landscape of industrial
and urban refuse. The river's destination creates a
new home for the transient remains from the north.
The city spreads thinly over the flat terrain. A city
with no southern edge, an amorphous form sliding
into the sea along with the disappearing river. Lost
and aimless; urban flotsam, adrift. Form is discarded,
like the memory of one's sins at the festival of Loy
Krathong. The delta, a destination for sedimented
remains and impure thoughts. Barely earth. A land
of questionable value and questionable sensibilities.
This dissolution of form creates a special kind of
earthly hell. Exponential city; Bangkok's faults are
rendered extreme.

The Unloved Earth

Bangkok's foundations within this delta condition are
formed of a curious mix of water and earth. A land so
malleable that it can be carved at will, so insignificant
that it barely matters. An earth of little independent
personality, but crucial to the generation of an urban
sensibility. A terrain that seemingly floods at any

time, whose only tangible forms are architectural.
Yet these constructed orders are curious. Following
the fluid land, Bangkok's infrastructure is flexible,
even unstable. It is a city of relationships and
patterns of habitation rather than secure forms and
figures. A city whose architecture manifests an agile
relation to the fluid ground, and a casual disdain
for its worth.

In a city defined by the forms and rituals of water,
land has dubious value. Unavoidable but unloved,
Bangkok's earth is indeed an unappreciated
foundation for civic life. A place for garbage.
The city's apparent tolerance for pollution supports
the sense that the land is unworthy of serious
concern: an irredeemable problem to be escaped
rather than any locus for engaged action. It is an
enduring condition. In 1910: 'The Siamese are
personally extremely cleanly, but unfortunately the
same cannot be said about their houses . . . In those
houses which border the klongs the refuse is
disposed of by pitching it into the water, but if no
klong is handy it is equally simple to throw it
through some interstice in the floor boards, and the
ground underneath is often indescribably filthy'.[1]
In 1690 (describing Ayutthaya):

> In this order we went up the river, coasting
> for some time the walls of the City, and then,
> turning in toward's the Berklam's House, where
> he gives publick audience, and appears with all
> his pomp and splendor. We went ashore on this
> side of his House, and walk'd the remaining part
> of our way thither. The Court was dirty and nasty
> enough, but however in somewhat better a
> condition, than that of his other House, where
> we had had a private audience of him some Days

before. Entring the Court we took notice to the left of an open House or Room, almost square, without walls, the floor of which was cover'd with boards and full of people, some sitting, some walking and conversing together.[2]

Mai pen rai, a popular Thai phrase. 'Never you mind'. The neglected land is an issue to confront and confuse the visitor: an insignificant reality, unworthy of attention for the citizen.

Buildings, originally on stilts, replace this ground with floor planes of increasing value. Levels are established, a layered terrain created to progressively remove one from the literal earth. In the *bots*, monks rest on raised platforms, the floors themselves elevated from their exterior precincts by steps. Significant thresholds prevent any horizontal connection between the ground and the more celebrated interiors. Contaminated shoes are left behind, the carefully delineated floors protected from the debased exterior terrain. This polluted earth is viewed in dramatic contrast to the highly articulated roofs of the city's architecture. Different destinations; clear hierarchies of value. Just as the head is the most sacred part of the body and one's feet should never point at an image of the Buddha, the roofs are the city's most significant forms, validating the practical buildings active beneath.

Buildings on sticks, whose ground is never solid and seldom appreciated. Agriculture is the historic source of the nation's wealth. Yet rice grows from flooded fields, the earth invisible beneath the cover of nourishing water. A liquid city in a liquid terrain, where the value of the earth, and any accompanying illusions of permanent order that it might imply, hold limited appeal.

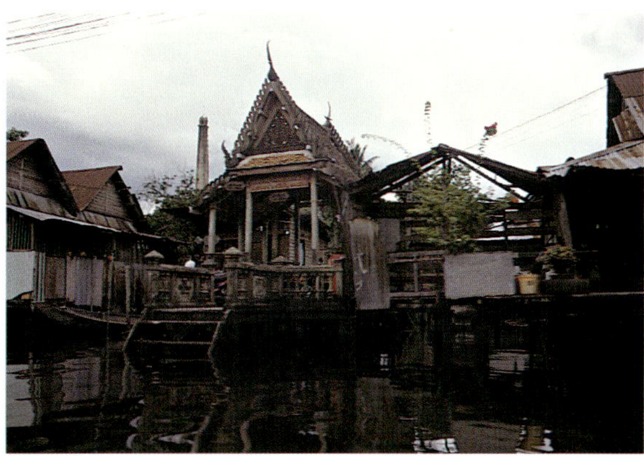

Both Rama and the Buddha act in concert with the land, but in particular ways. Rama cleanses the forest of demons, rendering it safe for hermits and holy men. It is a symbolic landscape, a dangerous place of personal trials, more raw than the comfortable city of traditional allegiances and inherited wealth. A place for personal definition. Yet the encampments and palaces set within this forest, as portrayed in Bangkok's frescoes, articulate distinct and protected enclosures. Social life, once achieved, is set apart from the exterior world of struggle. Nature, as embodied in the forest, is a place to be abandoned once the battles have been won. For the Buddha, the earth is a figure of intentional renunciation, a metaphor of all that is 'becoming' and transient rather than 'being' and eternal. The literature borrows striking physical images as narrative foils, which are all the more valuable through their necessary renunciation. Heroic actions are rendered legible through juxtaposition to a competing landscape. Mythically potent yet ideally abandoned, one interacts with the earth while simultaneously rejecting its significance. Rama returns to Ayodhya, the Buddha accedes to Nirvana. The significance of the natural earth flows away like rain once these more viable alternatives have been achieved.

Land as effective water. It is equally unstable, equally a place to challenge action. This condition provides an inverse conceptual grounding. The flat delta is really a place of absence, experientially transient and easily sacrificed.

Existential Absence

Bangkok's flat terrain suffers a narrative void. Real land, the place of struggle and renunciation, is central to the city's self definition. Real land, crucial but absent, is identified with the distant mountains. These origins and points of return integral to Bangkok's mythology, must, as a result, be re-created. Real land, temporarily displaced, is mimetically remembered through architecture.

Life is elsewhere. The stone model of Angkor Wat, located within Wat Phra Kaeo, references this missing landscape, twice removed. Hindu (and subsequently Buddhist) cosmology, centred around the image of Mount Meru, is clearly articulated in the architecture of the Khmer monument at Angkor. This architecture, also representative of the Khmer traditions of divine kingship, is then referenced in Bangkok via the stone model. The model, further, is a type of royal trophy, a symbol of conquered lands. A remarkable grouping of architectural compressions, a conjunction of cosmological and historical ideals, intentionally set within the city's most symbolic precinct. Its fixed orders, distant in both time and place, are repositioned for reflection. Links to historic monarchic authority are maintained, the divine mountain as a guarantor of idealized order. This cosmological landscape,

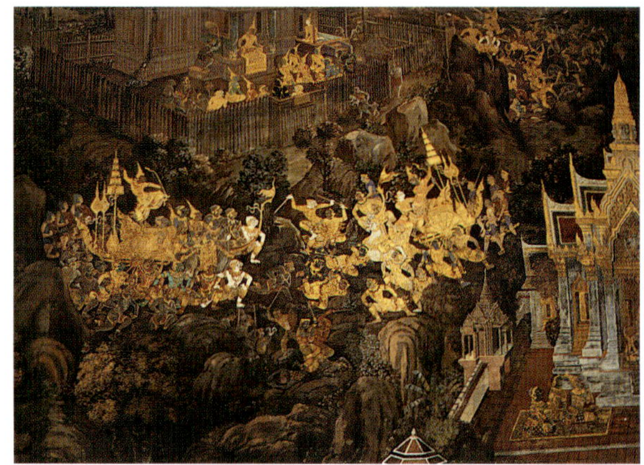

subsumed within the royal *wat*, serves to remind Bangkok of its distant origins. A figure of memory and desire, idealized and resonant in its new context.

A model as signifier of urban intent. The strong horizontal base separates the vertical figures from their immediate setting (in both the model and at Angkor). The mountainous icons act within their own world, as a visual tableau. They do not engage directly with any exterior reality, but remain comfortably aloof. A dream space; far away or lost in the past? Angkor Wat articulates an image of a distant heavenly order. Celestial forms are mapped out, the whole symbolically complete and presented for appreciation. Reference to physical context is not required. It is an ideal land: symbolic, mysterious and dense. An intact world, distant yet ready for study.

One clear message. It is not land in general that lacks value, but rather Bangkok's land in particular. Land that is really water. Transient, non-mountain land. Real land is the place of symbolic memory and mythical action, temporary land the home of intangible orders in flux. Yet Bangkok, despite its many centred temples, does not generally follow

Angkor's lead. The clear forms and ideal geometries articulated in the model (and seen in the earlier capitals of Sukhothai and Ayutthaya) are abandoned, the coherence of the inherited order rejected.

The values of solidity discarded? In contrast with this fixed ideal, Bangkok's terrain remains fluid in the extreme. Equally the traditional urbanistic role of distant, but actual, hills (as seen, for example, at Chiang Mai) is unfulfilled in Bangkok's flat terrain. A mythical city, whose requisite symbolic landscape is notable in its absence.

This valued land appears to be a missing element of the urban puzzle, a void in the rituals of monarchic order. Missing mountains, imaginary absence. Subtle remembrances may be seen in the layered floors of the *bots* and houses, established architecturally to re-create modest variations of real land over their fluid foundations. It may also be partially present in the dramatic roofs, and addressed through narrative painting. Yet more significant mountains are also re-imagined architecturally in Bangkok's terrain. Their appearance, however, takes different forms from the complete worlds referenced in Angkor. Landscape as reference or engaged experience? Bangkok's mountains are more constructed, more contextual. More participatory within the city's curious landscape.

PART TWO

Flat terrain; missing mountains.

Architecture as symbolic landscape; urban participant. Illusory stability, solidified transience. Landscape as reflection.

Missing Mountain: Meru as Memory

The flatness of Bangkok's terrain is central to its lack of appreciation. Bangkok is a consciously mythical creation, conceptually grounded within a mythical landscape. But it remains physically sited in a location with no topography. In reaction to this deterministic absence a complementary narrative landscape is required, though one at odds with Bangkok's particular reality. Architecture to the rescue of nature.

The memory of the sacred hills is arguably central to every *chedi*, if somewhat abstractly referenced. Bangkok's *chedis*, however, are generally internal to their *wats*, and subordinate to the great roofed *bots*. The formal clarity of Angkor, present in miniature stone, is perceptible only within the Wat Phra Kaeo compound. Landscape at the scale of the city? Three more literal architectural mountains have been constructed to animate this urban void. Yet these constructions reject the fixed unity of Angkor in favour of a more open and flexible relation to the city. A varied architecture of subtle hints and foreshadowed realms is presented, each opening new symbolic possibilities within the urban context.

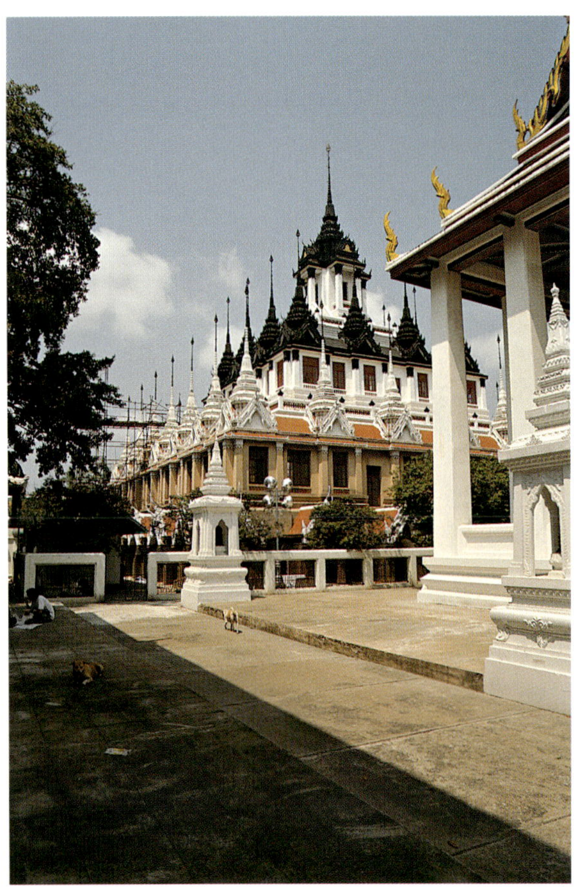

The Loha Prasat, part of Wat Rachanadaraman, re-creates Mount Meru as an experiential labyrinth. The building is a curious confection, a box with an animated roofscape. It is more clearly a construction than most of Bangkok's *chedis*, more obviously an architectural mountain. Visually it derives from the same architectural family as the cremation monuments. Yet it also constructs an internal journey. Hybrid between *chedi* and *bot*; image and interior passage. Adjacent to the Golden Mount, and close to Wat Suthat, a shadow of the funerary constructions is rendered into more permanent form. Foreshadowed futures, symbolically remembered.

The building's distinct exterior presents an enigmatic volume, surmounted by an exotic roofscape of independent figures at the summit. A terrain of complex roofs is separated from the ground by the white supporting walls. Yet it is the interior that is particularly intriguing. It narrates a unique process of architectural transformation, internalized within a single building. Elsewhere Bangkok's *wats* order a conversation of architectural possibilities, highlighted by the relation of *bot* and *chedi*. Here a synthetic summary is constructed. Bangkok's temples, and even perhaps the city itself, are mimetically internalized. Breadth is sacrificed to a remarkable distillation of passage and effect.

The ground outlines a preparatory underworld, a strange preliminary forest of concrete piers open to the sides. This dense field lurks beneath the building proper, defining an internalized labyrinth with no single focus. The centre, once discovered, is occupied by a stair. Passage as curious destination.

The first floor is composed of a series of long inter-locking corridors, each leading to a seated Buddha. The structure between the corridors is apparently unoccupied: solid blocks supporting the upper storeys, but with considerable redundant mass. From the exterior, clearly architectural. Within, a carved mountain, a work of landscape interwoven with a series of complex journeys. Life inside a *chedi*. The solid volumes define the tight passages, increasing the directional focus on the Buddha statues. The figures, however, are viewed across an open gallery, a gap. Each remains physically inaccessible. Destinations are presented and equally distanced. Accentuating their difference, the statues are lit from above, the building gradually stepping back towards its summit to expose the open galleries below.

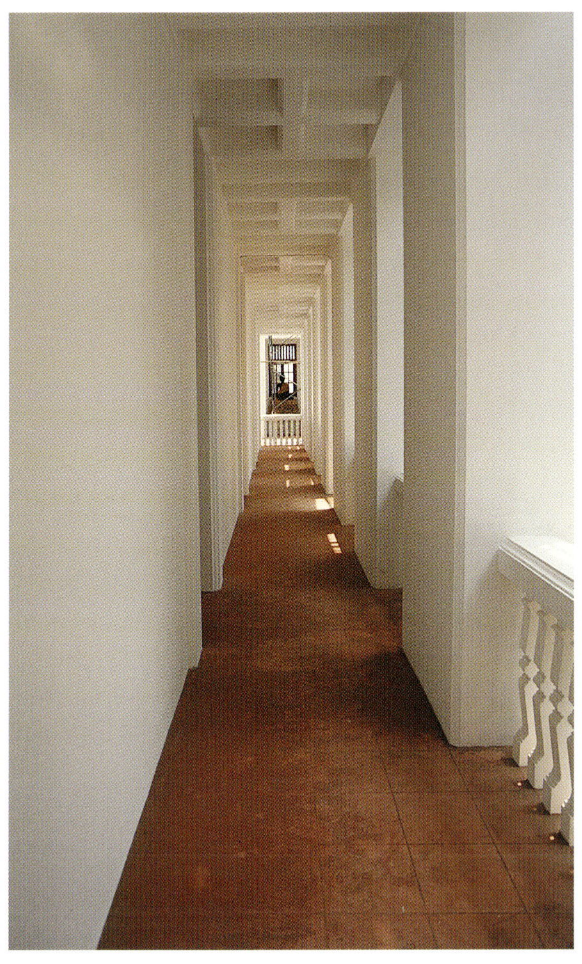

A journey from darkness to light, both symbolic and actual, is constructed through plan and section.

Clear views but broken journeys. Travel towards an imaginary, referential escape. The Buddhas create an internal facade to this labyrinthine world. The symbolic passage though the teachings replacing the view to the horizon? The figures are never clearly visible as a group. Only one or two can be seen at a time, each conceptually part of a collective though visually separate. A destination lit from above, viewed at a distance, in fragment. Yet together the figures form the outer wall of experience. Travel towards images of desire, whose accomplishment is architecturally denied.

The upper levels are composed of similar intersecting corridors. Equally defined views are created, though here they look out past the roof canopies to the city beyond. Urban contact is reintroduced after the interior journey. Attention is focused within to the Buddha, above to the urban view. A sequence of education and civic reconnection.

Passage and image; darkness to light. The constructed views present fleeting visions of perfect yet physically inaccessible order. The Loha Prasat is an anomaly in Bangkok, where the building's transformative journey is constructed as an internal spatial narrative. Yet its ideals of ascent and sequential figural replacement are perhaps fundamental to all the *wats*, though usually experienced in less explicit ways. Here the building constructs a landscape of internal reference, only to be later superseded by the reintroduction to the physical city. Like the cremation monuments (and unlike Angkor), it defines a fleeting experience, though paradoxically remembered in more permanent form. The Loha Prasat, a strange urban summary, completed late in Bangkok's history. A desperate reminder, or a precise foil to more general urban conversations?

Architectural Nature: The Golden Mount

Bangkok's two most significant hills rest immediately outside the historic city. Wat Arun, the Temple of the Dawn, is sited across the river, west of the central precincts. Phu Khao Thong, the Golden Mount, is adjacent to the city's walls to the east. Symbolic gates. Bangkok's centre is defined by its canals, but framed by these architectural mountains. An artificial landscape as existential urban boundary.

The Golden Mount adopts architecture as formalized nature. Perceptually it is natural first, architectural only on closer inspection. The Golden Mount, the chedi of Wat Saket, was constructed by three kings; Ramas III, IV and V. The artificial mountain houses two important Buddha relics, the last discovered in India at Kapilavastu near the Nepalese border and presented to King Chulalongkorn by Lord Curzon, the Viceroy of India. The kings jointly built a mountain to house the significant relics, but also to celebrate special legendary events. Rama I stopped at the site to wash his hair prior to entering the city for his coronation. Kings, mountains and relics are joined to remember the ceremonial entry of Bangkok's first king (and founder of his dynasty) into the capital of his own creation.

Building masquerading as hill; a sacred spot standing in for a distant land. The Golden Mount also references a *chedi* in Ayutthaya, by name and general form. The Buddha's birthplace in Nepal, by extension the Himalayas, and Ayutthaya, are all rendered present in the flat landscape. The building constructs a synthesis of many diverse hills, all far away, all necessary to the healthy life of the city and its kings.

The Golden Mount is Bangkok's most striking feature, even if it is artificial. It is a *chedi* in its entirety, though less explicitly Meru-like than either the Loha Prasat or the funerary monuments. Its image is more geological, and easily mistaken for natural. It is not an architectural version of a mountain, but a real one. A natural image is constructed architecturally as the necessary foil to the artificial city. The great base, a construction floating on a massive raft of teak logs, is surmounted by a large gold *chedi*. Nature as a foundation for the sacred beacon, and a reminder of its essential origins. Together they control the surrounding context. The composition is sited at the primary point of symbolic terrestrial entry, but outside the walls. A mountain to the east, a place of preparation. A royal foundation, but external to the official city. A point of entry and reflection; a privileged view providing a sense of urban challenge. With his royal authority established, Rama returns to the city to regain his rightful position.

The ascent? Unlike most *chedis* the Golden Mount exists to be climbed. The promenade begins in a forested glade of shrines and tombs, spiralling around the central figure to summit eventually at the terrace of the golden *chedi*. The Buddha images viewed along the way appear almost circumstantial, a brief pause before travelling to the exposed platform above. A terrace with a remarkable golden *chedi* and a singular view of the city below. Bangkok is unveiled, to be appreciated or conquered, its narrative landscape rendered as clearly as in the wall paintings. City viewed in relation to the shimmering mountain. The descent to the ground follows a different path, the spiral passage actually a double helix with two interwoven but separate routes.

The return, a new journey leading to the city; the traveller refreshed and validated; the mission clear.

Spiral as experience; *chedi* as point. Adjacent to the city, a symbolic mountain constructs significant journeys. Mountain as mythic gate? Or perhaps a visible guardian, protecting Bangkok from the very nature symbolized in its mountainous form. The Golden Mount brings a memory of this distant and challenging terrain to visibility. A reminder of a difficult past, the heroic challenges faced by the city's founders. The context of mythical history is re-created, the dangerous land outside of the walls made immediately present. Spiral as helix, the construction celebrates the journey out and back: exile and return. A symbolic re-entry to the city after travelling to distant lands. The journey to nature remembered, the successful return a cause for celebration.

The Golden Mount was also constructed late in Bangkok's formative period. Rather than a foundational symbol, it inflects the city's previously established form and clarifies its essential orders. Intentions can be inferred by results. Here contrast is applied to sharpen the new city's principles: difference and foil. Urban coalescence leading to gradual coherence, Bangkok's histories and implicit destinies are made manifest. The Golden Mount flanks Thanon Bamrung Muang, the road that leads to the Grand Palace, and marks its junction with the wall and outer canal. Rama returns in triumph from his exile in the distant forests, the palace his temporary destination. A new urban figure, it complements the centred palace. Each an articulation of edge. Later, passage onwards, to Meru and the sea; Wat Arun and the river.

Wat Arun

The Golden Mount; architecture imitating nature. Wat Arun presents symbolic nature imagined through architecture. Wat Arun, The Temple of the Dawn. This construction floats outside the city and establishes its western focus. Mount Meru is rendered as a brooding presence, distinct in scale and orientation from its surroundings. An alien figure, it contrasts the low houses nearby to focus attention on its most significant neighbours, the Chao Phraya river and Bangkok itself. Equal characters in a figural conversation, architecture is at the perceptual scale of the city. The monument predates Bangkok's foundation, and perhaps inspired its location. Wat Arun, the only found landscape in Bangkok's reticent topography.[3] Formally Wat Arun is reminiscent of Angkor Wat, with its highly ornate Khmer-style *prang* presenting a magical landscape in the landscape-free city. It constructs an image symbolic of Meru, both icon and reference. Yet Wat Arun is tangibly and specifically physical, composed as a complex sculpted form. Its profile is highly modulated, contrasting the clear outlines of the *chedi* of the Golden Mount with a dense richness of form and articulation. These animated surfaces are clad in fragments of glazed coloured ceramics. The walls and gates are proportionally modest, the *prang* clearly taking precedence over its supporting enclosure. The *bot*, rare in Bangkok, is more modest still. These subordinate figures are compressed, and all distractions diminished, to focus the more significant conversation between tower, river and city. Passage, view and destination.

Wat Arun, viewed from across the river. It constructs a mountain, but also a curious beacon,

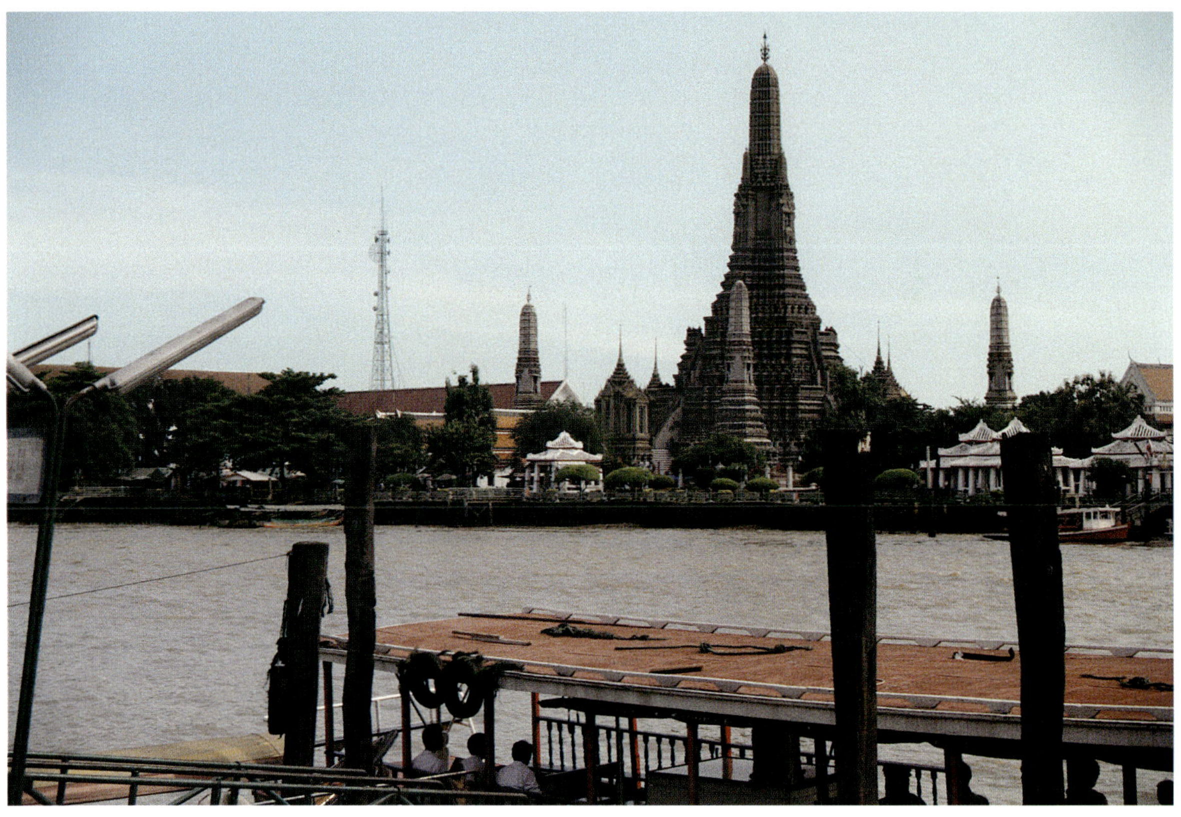

whose form changes character throughout the day. These different appearances accentuate temporal passage. A solid mass, but a fluid image, carrying out strange tricks of visual transformation. At dawn, the temple is lit by the rising sun. Its multi-faceted surface glistens in the soft morning light, the inlaid ceramics performing their reflective function. The temple greets the sun by returning the favour, sending its flickering light back across the water to the city. The colour of the ceramics is fairly subtle, the modulation of the shining forms enlivening the reflected light.

During the day Wat Arun's overall shape becomes clearer. As the sun rises, the surfaces are differently animated, form competing with surface. Later, as the sun sets behind the *wat*, the tower becomes visible only in silhouette. More enigmatic; form, mass and outline. A work of landscape, more clearly a mountain than a designed confection of parts. As the profile gradually merges with the surrounding darkness, the architectural figure is transformed into a shadowed memory, complementing Bangkok's flat terrain with a barely legible image of the mysterious, distant hills. Architecture blurring into the night, inflecting its message along the way. In each iteration, Wat Arun's brooding presence animates the river. The mountain centres the city, and narrates its different possibilities.

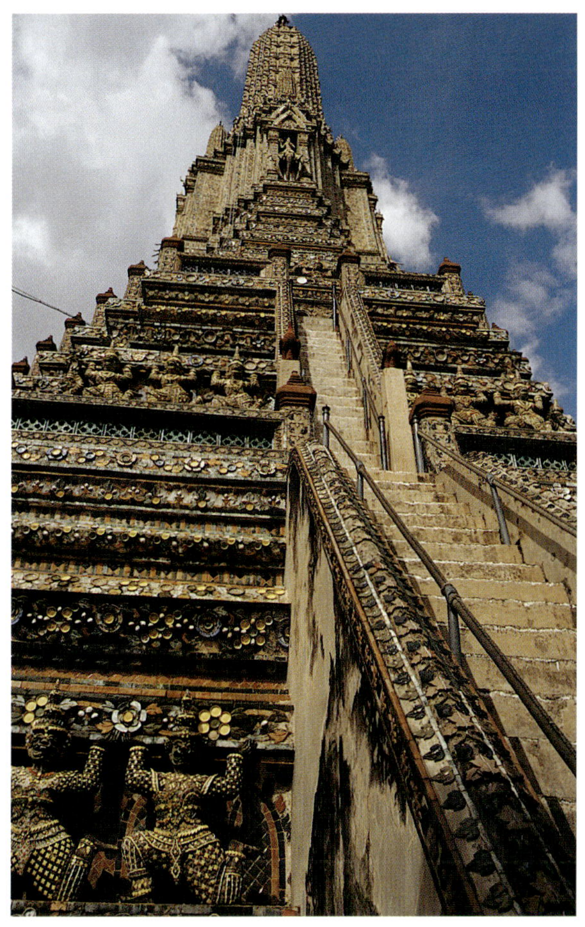

idealized within the flat landscape, the distinctive architectural mountains creating points of contrast and support. The figures relate to a larger landscape, both physically and mentally. Different Merus; mountain as mythical foundation, gate or destination. The ideal city is fulfilled by the addition of its narrative landscape. Mountain as existential boundary. The complement to the sea, a differently imagined presence within Bangkok's sensibilities.

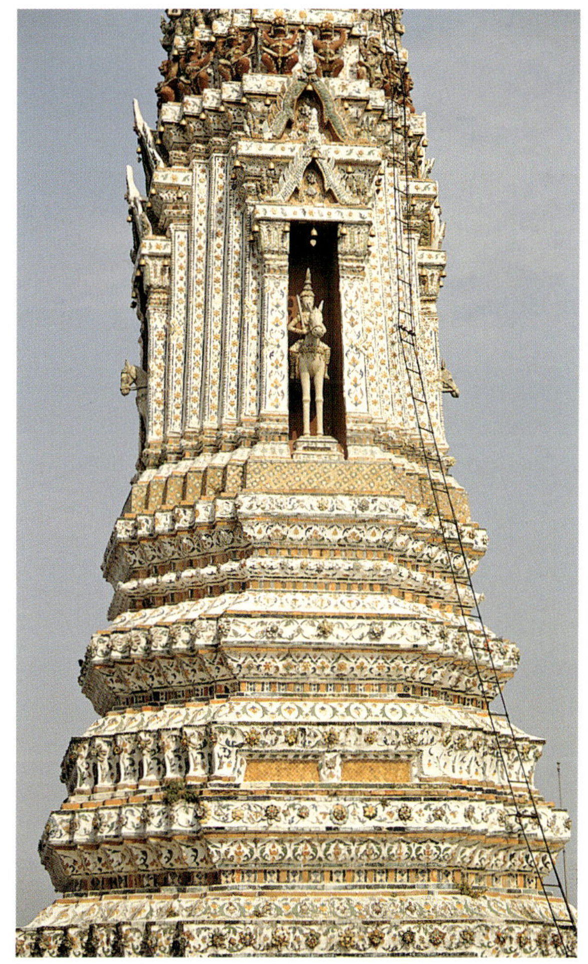

River and architectural mountain, viewed in immediate proximity. Each manifests a flow of time and energy. Values are embedded within their orientations and implied destinations. Directed travels, constructed in contrast. Up into darkness or out to the sea. The only significant figure within this scenic tableau to lack a clearly articulated orientation is Bangkok itself. A city caught between, whose personality struggles between the specificity of the natural symbols.

Each of Bangkok's mountains manifest different ideals of symbolic journey. Form and passage are

Bangkok: a port city with no recognizable port. Mouth of the river; strange delta. Place of refuse and industrial carnage; end of the land. Home of Pattaya, Bangkok's dark cousin (and possible model). The sea, a glittering destination of freedom and forgetfulness. A distracting trap or an ideal future?

The Sea: Questionable Destination

Bangkok rests on a neglected land punctuated by artificial mountains. Its images of memory and destiny float on intangible foundations. A city caught between the mountains and the sea. Contrasting figures, different destinations. The sea? Bangkok's southern neighbour and implicit future.

The Gulf of Thailand arrests Bangkok's southerly sprawl. The actual sea, however, is a new figure in the city's historic experience. Unrelated to the northern landscapes of mountains, rice fields and rivers, it brings novel qualities to Bangkok's introspective nature. The sea is a disruptive element in the psycho-logical geography of the historic capital. An alien character of compelling difference or the replication of a forgotten dream?

The sea. A destination for celebrated waters and historic cities. As the transient capital has descended from the stable north it has become increasingly aquatic, its forms increasingly ambiguous.

Confronted by the delta and the sea, historic form, and perhaps history itself, threatens to disappear. In contrast to the mountains, known through reference and memory, the sea is a symbolic destination, actually if only gradually becoming realized. It is a tangible place of worldly destiny, a foil to the symbolic journeys associated with the imaginary hills. A destination of open possibilities that simultaneously are both attractive and dangerous.

Bangkok is an extended port city, an outward focus that is key to its economic responsibilities. The descent towards the sea has provided the city with greater access and control over trade, the growing commerce a national boon. Yet it has also led to an increased exposure to the challenging outside world. International contact is a difficult balance. These open relations have financially enriched an aristocracy possessing historic commercial monopolies while simultaneously introducing forces disruptive to its cultural authority. The same voyage has rendered Bangkok peripheral to its own country. Bangkok inhabits a strange mental landscape. It is Thailand's only metropolis, its functional, economic and political centre. It is a city constructed about a historic focus, centralized and introspectively inclined. Yet the city relies on contact with the outside world for its survival, and increasingly follows the outside world's examples. A construction on the edge. Bangkok and Thailand? The capital represents the country, but it is clearly not representative. A centre, but resting on a distant and – for most – an inconceivable boundary, alien to daily concerns. A locus of author-ity and wealth, of decisions taken, Bangkok also defines a conceptual perimeter, looking out to the shrimp markets of the world.

This internal–external dialectic is central to Bangkok's experience, and perhaps to its very existence. But where do its real attentions lie? A commingling of memory, conscience and desire. The image of the sea. A foil to the symbolic land, a test of local values? Or a vision of a decadent future, perfect for an aimless commercial age?

Pattaya: Foil or Future?

The escape to the sea, to a bright and open expanse, is a compulsive attraction. Evident in its glittering mosaics, ceramic roofs and neon lights, Bangkok is attracted by bright and shimmering images. Barely tangible forms and floating destinations, specifically rendered. Yet this seems, ultimately, urbanistically impossible. Can a city dissolve into an insubstantial sensual world of earthly illusion? Impossible perhaps, but already realized. Pattaya, the resort of tawdry pleasure south of Bangkok in the Gulf of Thailand, presents one existing version of such a dream. Evil sister or the future of the City of Angels? A celebration of disappearance, in a froth of manic euphoria. A city composed of surface alone.

Pattaya, dark twin. The entire town is dedicated to the pleasures of the flesh. A modest beach, with water, sun and sand. Restaurants and bars. More distinctly, girls and boys, to watch or rent. A shopping centre for sex.

Pattaya is similar to Bangkok's Patpong in its concentration on pleasure. Yet it is even more sexually specific, more fixated, without the distracting hints of normalcy that greater Bangkok brings to Patpong. No office workers enjoying lunch, no music pubs, few markets. Here it is only pleasure of a particular kind; a sex precinct as an entire city, enlarged and exposed. Beer-bars, maintaining a pretence of courting and conversation. Go-go clubs, with beautiful but mostly listless girls imitating dancing, numbers pinned to their bikini bottoms for easy identification. Less dancers than kinetic billboards, advertisement and product conjoined. A surface glitz, deeper despair. The visible attractions are clear enough, the less-advertised late-night action likely more remarkable still. Degenerate cousin or urban essence exposed?

Pattaya hosts a considerable number of vacationing Thais, along with a surprising complement of retired Western couples. A place of meeting, the floating seaside restaurants. Discrete from the action outside, it appears a balanced resort world, with a harmonious mix of foreigners and locals. The restaurants serve mediocre food by Thai standards, yet their terraces are full of Thais hosting large dinners. And what is being celebrated? The house specialty, aside from grilled king prawns, looks to be a local version of Spanish coffee. Flames celebrate its arrival, rising up over the table in an energetic dance. Glasses are moved about like shadow puppets preparing for action. Rama and his arch rival Ravana, on fire in a curious drama. A battle or a heightened courtship? The celebrating locals seem to appreciate the show. At least most know and choose to order it. Fire and water. A taste for extremes in a context requiring utmost social tolerance. The fleeting events, unreal but intense, are viewed against the darkened sea.

Urban structure. Like Bangkok, Pattaya is composed of a combination of avenues and *sois*, though here the main avenue opens to the Gulf. This maritime facade is somewhat like Bangkok's to the

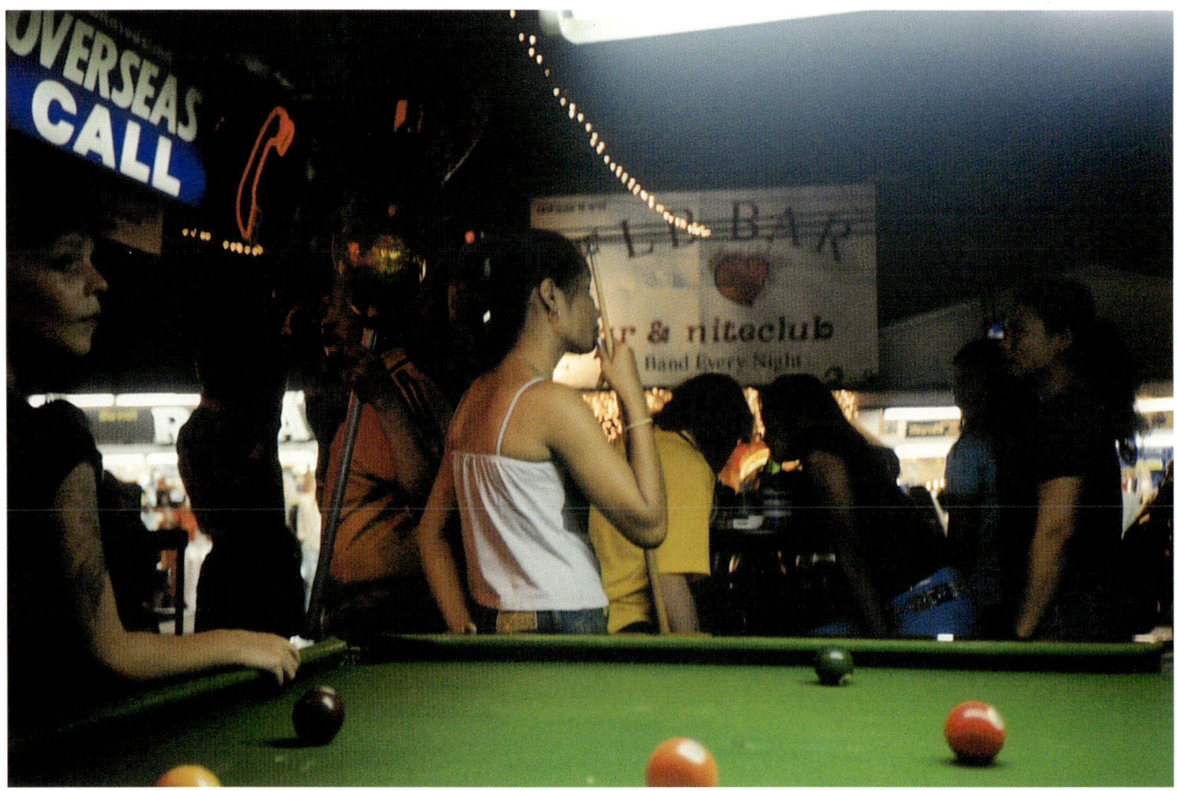

river, though more publicly accessible. The next major avenue runs parallel, creating an inland route linking the large hotels. The long *sois* between are traditional in their form, but extreme in their occupation. Shops and offices distinct through their rarity. It is a place with few redeeming qualities except, perhaps, for the fleeting beauty of the girls and boys. Pattaya, for some, a Daytona Beach with rice; pleasurable festivity more evident than pain. For others, well-documented suffering. An Asian Vegas, accepted for its own distinct culture and commercial success? A symbol of Thailand's legendary tolerance, or a recognition of the natural end of earthly desires?

The reflective sea? The sun sets over the Gulf, celebrating its surface. A strange destination, a source of reflected light. The beautiful, if somewhat melancholic, sunset is soon replaced by the neon of the bars and clubs. Pattaya consciously follows the light, memorializing its transience. As the sun disappears, celebrate its absence. Fleeting void, significant transformation and tangible replacement.

Pattaya is a companion to the sea; both are foils to the symbolic mountains. A foreshadowing of Bangkok's earthly future? Pattaya is a city with no *wats*. Bangkok's lively contrasts of its introspective nature and open horizons is missing in Pattaya's singular focus. The symbolic city, already largely submerged in contemporary Bangkok, is recognized here by its absolute absence. The distant mountains are

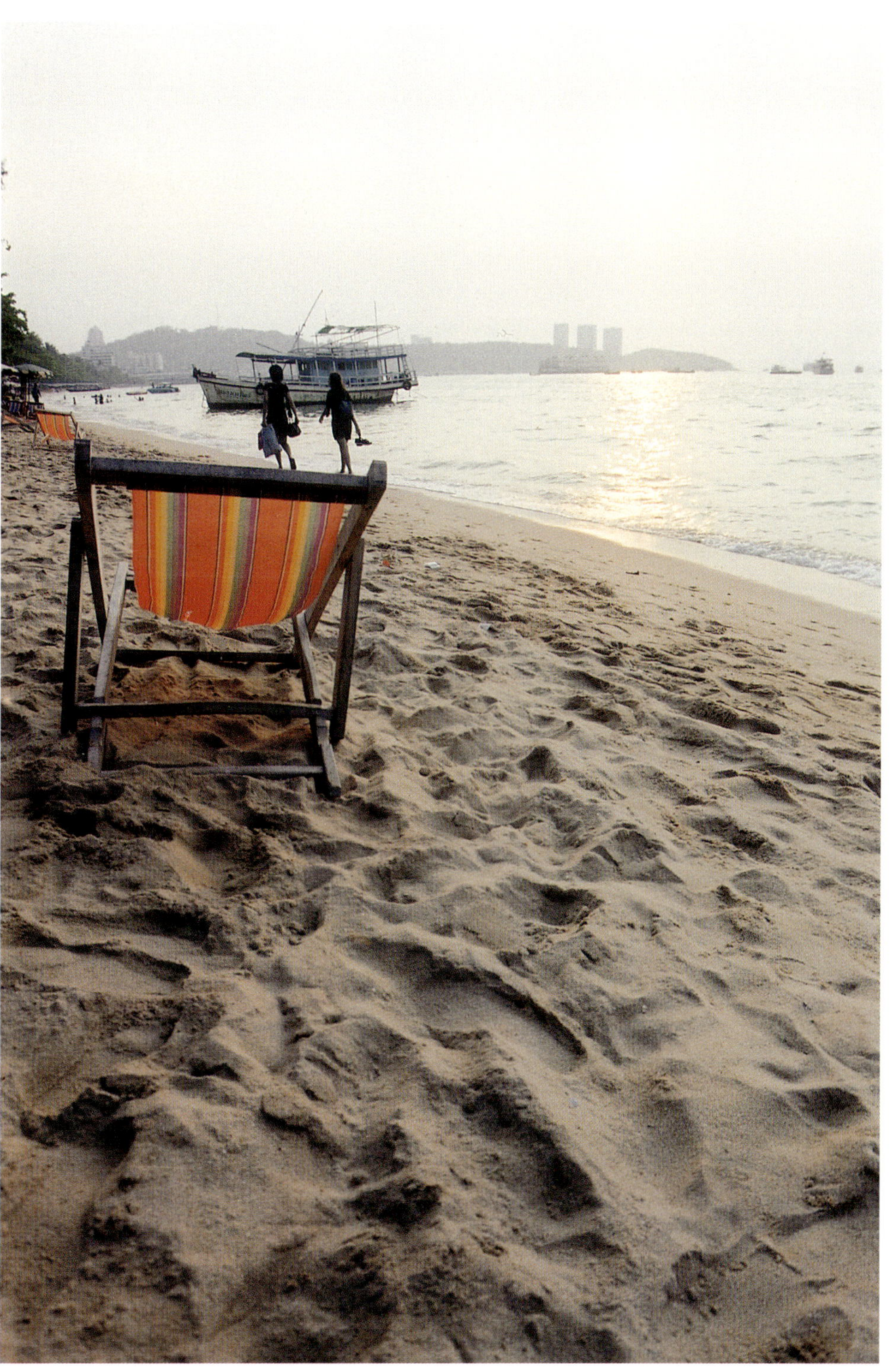

provocative by default; their final disappearance into the glittering sea complete.

Destination as Quality

Flickering in the sun, the sea belies its role as repository of Bangkok's refuse. Whatever murky depths it might contain remain hidden beneath the shiny surface. The water may be filthy, but it remains well-dressed. The sea as destination and quality. A compelling and dangerous attraction.

The sea: Bangkok's surfaces and their confusing realities are rendered metaphorically present. Tantalizing but distant, shining and dark. Fluid and unstable, but with exquisite form. Analogous qualities appear in Bangkok's most tempting attractions. The shimmering mosaics of the temples, the mysterious deep golds of the *chedis*. The polished black plaster walls of the *bot* interiors, glistening surfaces of unfathomable depth. Light reflected from darkness; a reality to be celebrated. Neon, flashes of colour in the night, the ephemera of sensual life. Similar modes of attraction are applied to remarkably different destinations.

The sea is the extreme manifestation of Bangkok's aquatic sensibilities. It is a place of destiny, but perhaps one to be guarded against. The end of earthly life and its earthly pleasures. Pattaya, a manifestation of physical desire, a pointless destination masquerading under provocative enticements. The sea, a seductive image. Light as attraction, yet like the siren's song, a dangerous lure.

The sea, a beckoning figure. Bangkok's historic destiny, earthly travel leading to an ultimate disappearance within its waters. A quality and a temptation, to be recognized, celebrated and feared.

A world that the mountains protect against. Bangkok's amorphous land is caught between the mountains and the sea, challenged by one, seduced by the other. Landscapes of memory and future disappearance. In between, an existential state most akin to floating. A condition narrated in Bangkok's most specific architecture, its angelic emissaries.

EIGHT

Angelic Emissaries

Missing mountains, dissolving forms. Curious destinations, floating ground. Desired stability? Movement as reality.

Floating Image, Intangible Surface

Wat Arun is an enigmatic destination. Both beacon and ghost, clearest when seen from afar. Wat Arun, Temple of the Dawn. One looks west to view the rising sun, faintly reflected in the fragmented ceramics. At sunset, a shadowed figure silhouetted against the darkened sky. A striking image from a distance, whose formal clarity disappears in proximity. The symbolic mountain dissolves into disconnected outlines, its surface into broken shards of cheap domestic plates. The potent figure of the day quietly subsides, a fragile reminder of the tenuous stability of earthly life. In immediate experience, a strange confection of fractured ceramics and compressed forms. A symbolic monument, necessary to Bangkok's incomplete landscape, or a mythic stage-set, with its expedient and manipulative artifice exposed? Wat Arun is a suspect construction, simultaneously articulating the power of symbolic mountains and the dissolution of their earthly significance. Insubstantial weight, security abandoned.

Wat Phra Kaeo. The altar that supports the Emerald Buddha is configured as an interior mountain. The sculpted elements combine to construct a natural image, the broad base ascending to the honoured summit. The statue, a sitting Buddha carved from a single piece of jade.

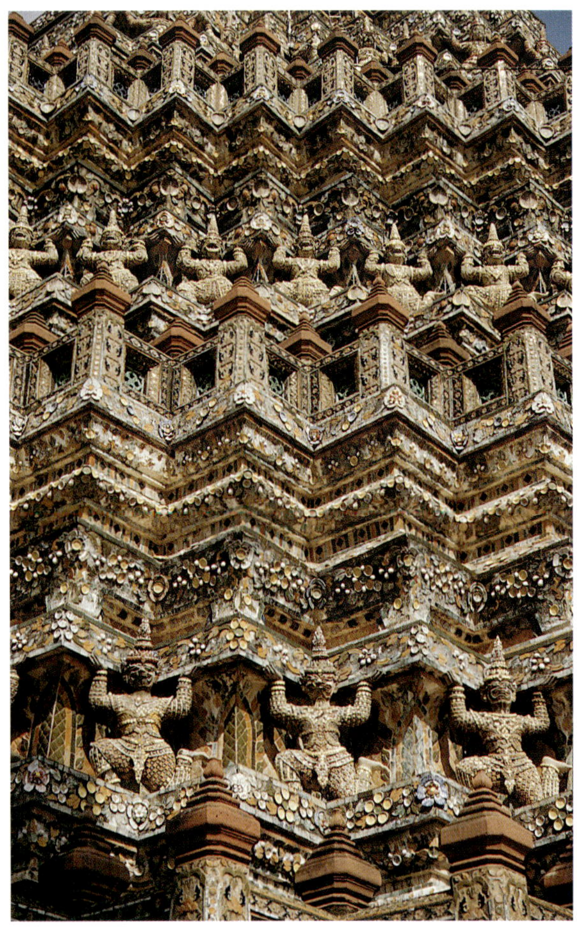

The composition is *chedi*-like, but more obviously sculptural, more fragmented and particular. The layered steps reinforce the idea of a gradual ascent, passing through each articulated level towards an ideal of represented enlightenment. Similar to the more abstract *chedis* outside, visual travel leads to a singular destination. Here, however, it is represented by a figure rather than by a disappearing point. The ascent to a pure and solitary pinnacle concludes in the figure of the translucent green Buddha. Clear value is expressed by the vertical path; a shimmering destination revealed.

Yet this simple narrative clarity is challenged by the mountain's figural complexity. Every surface is modulated, the basic conical shape fragmented into a myriad of subdivided parts. Encrusted with canopies and supporting figures, its volume dissolves into a proliferation of constituent lines and edges. The altar may represent a symbolic mountain, supporting the Emerald Buddha through mimetic form, yet this same form disappears in the effervescent froth of fragmented geometry and light. This condition is further accentuated by the composition's material reality. It is a mountain of gold, flickering in the relative darkness. Obvious physical weight is challenged by visual instability. Symbolic density, perceptually dissolution.

The Emerald Buddha is a highly honoured figure, an image central to Bangkok's claim to national predominance. The statue's travels from the north to Thonburi (there housed at Wat Arun), and eventually to Bangkok parallel and even justify the creation of the city itself. The green figure: ethereal and distant; small in the context of the *bot* and its supporting mountain, venerated and worthy of a solid foundation. Its support, a glistening, fragmented landscape. Through its formal articulation and material presence the referential mountain is experientially insubstantial. Like the emerald image it is solid and immaterial simultaneously. Necessary metaphors, necessarily abandoned. 'He who knows that his body is the foam of a wave, the shadow of a mirage, he breaks the sharp arrows of MARA, concealed in the flowers of sensuous passions . . .'.[1] In the canonic Buddhist texts, vivid images are used to argue for their own replacement. Architecturally, Bangkok's symbolic centre, its most solid core, is constructed as an ephemeral figure. The impression?

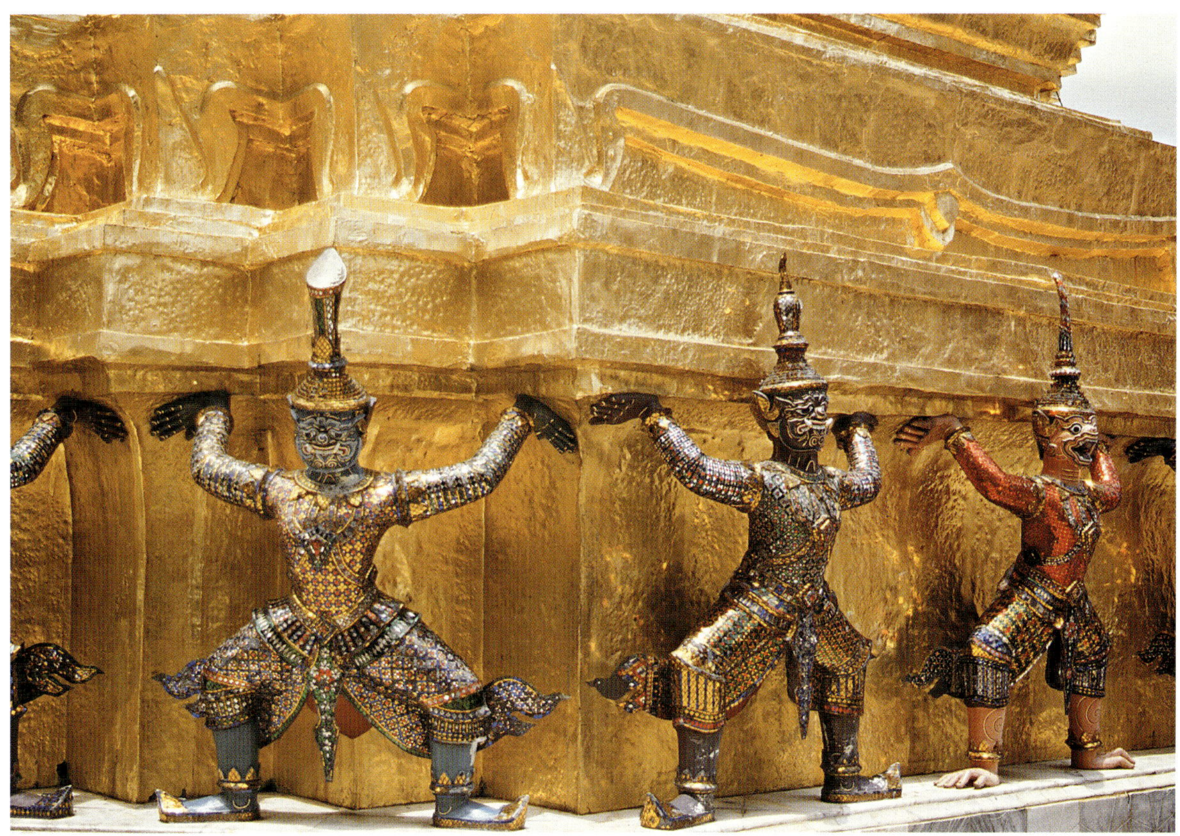

As solid and fleeting as the transient shadow remaining in one's eyes after gazing too directly at the sun.

Travel towards the Buddha, with the sun implicitly at your back. Travel towards the reflected light, the honoured figure an illuminated glow. The statue on its mountain identifies a bright destination, but it isn't the source of light itself. The Buddha's sculpted images reflect the truth, metaphorically understood. The Buddha is not a god, but a guide, his teachings outlining a path. A figure clearly worthy of respect, but not, strictly speaking, worship. The deep golds and jade of the sculpted mountain capture light prior to its retransmission. Transformed into a more mysterious glow,

light is reflected but also possessed by the sculptural figures. Perceptually – reflection and source simultaneously. Attraction and essential absence glitter in the darkness. The compelling but curious figure, mysterious and beautiful, is a temporary pause in the search for more secure meaning.

The value of shiny objects. Reflected light is used to create compelling but ambiguous destinations. Figures are idealized, but the clarity of the forms dissipates under closer inspection. Valuable reference is rendered as intangible experience. The manipulation of reflected light is a key aspect of these illusionary constructions. Materials are apparently solid yet visually fragile. Weight is conjoined with

glistening reflection. Gold, the ultimately ambiguous
medium. Heavy and expensive, it visually maintains
a sensation of volumetric depth and retained light.
Yet its surface is largely sacrificed to reflection.
Weight, depth and glittering surface simultaneously.
Dissolving form, floating experience. The sea's
quality is intuited through architectural experience;
the parallel dissolution of form created as an
intentional architectural effect.

Floating Realms, Intangible Ground

Floating destinations, unstable landscapes. This
groundless sensibility is subtly rendered in Bangkok's
wats. Their architecture: angelic emissaries revealing
urban truths. Image as reality, form as embodied
message. In Bangkok, ground is understood as water,
the sea an existential foundation. Enigmatic orders.
This fluid instability is paradoxically celebrated in the
city's monuments of symbolic order.

Wat Suthat, adjacent to the Golden Mount and
the Loha Prasat, renders Bangkok's aquatic
sensibilities materially vivid. It is a classic *wat*, large
and ordered. Most famous for its long *bot*, it is also
distinct for its missing *chedi*. Absent landscape. The
lengthy *bot* is paired with a large centralized *viharn*
to the south. This figure takes on the conversational
responsibilities of the *chedi*, though in a different
location. Missing mountain. The absence of this
historic grounding is heightened by Wat Suthat's
remarkable courtyard. The floor is constructed of
highly polished marble, bright in the sun, glistening
in the rain. A ground that assumes the appearance of
the shimmering sea. The floating temple, an idealized
land poised over the architectural water. The *bot* is
both figure and reflection, its ghostly image

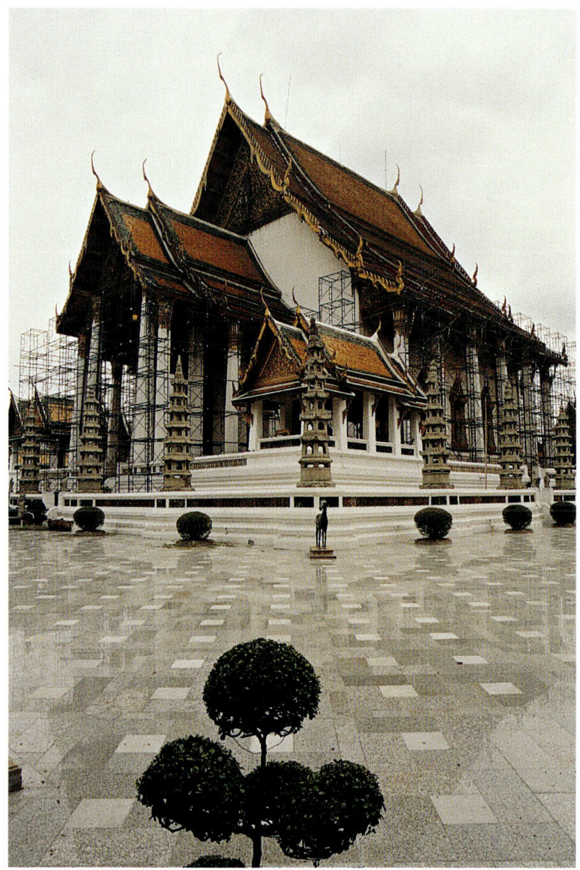

animating the geometric court by contrast. Bangkok's
aquatic sensibility is carefully articulated in the
polished marble surface, its mysterious foundations
visible in material form.

A lengthy arcade borders the court, providing
places of shaded protection. Small pavilions inhabit
the edge: islands raised above the unstable terrain
and held in place by the surrounding walls. Within,
floating figures. These clear edges create a dramatic
spatial theatre. Architecture versus water, the *bot* a
leading protagonist within the challenging realm.
Whether in struggle or conciliation, the *bot* appears
as a large vessel, a travelling roof centred on the

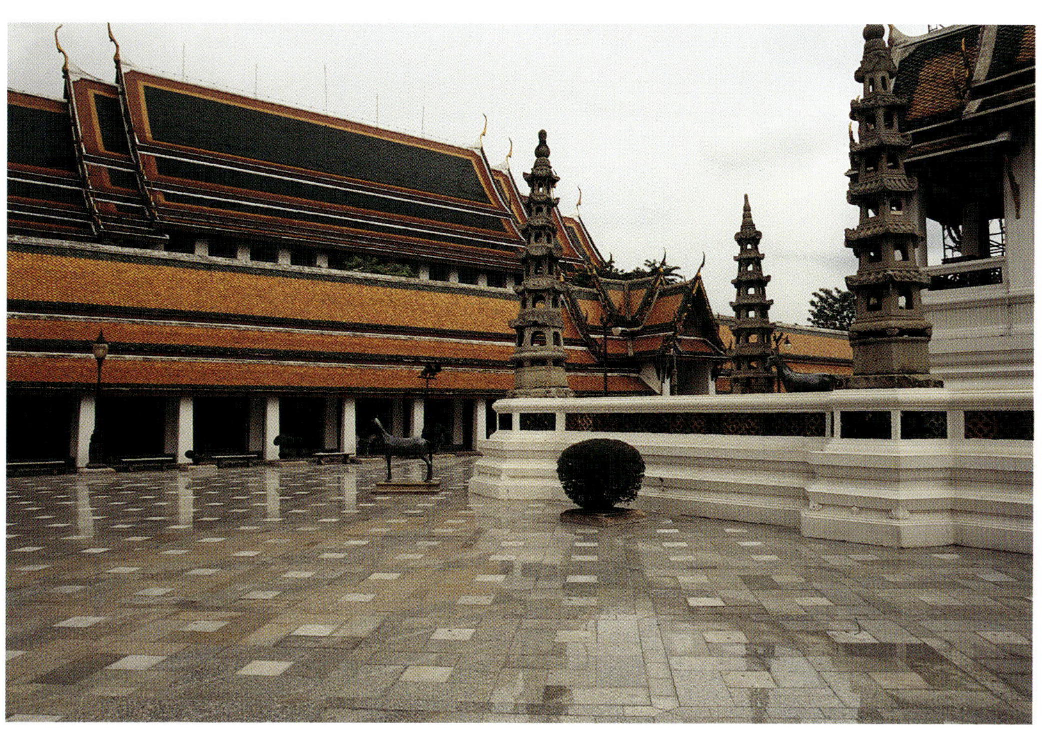

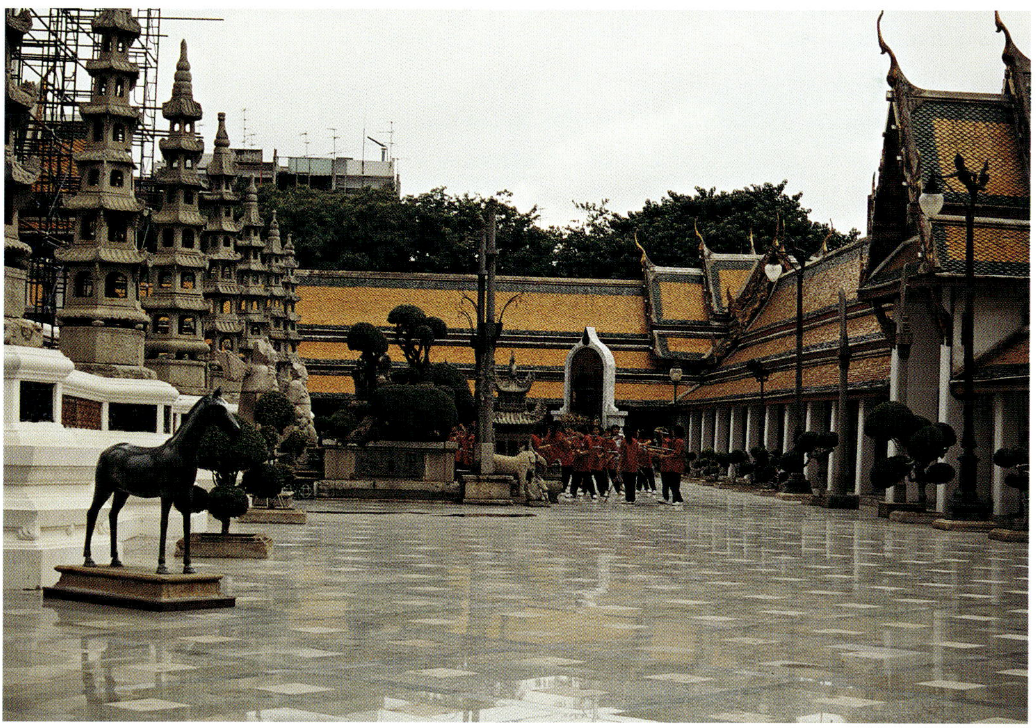

symbolic sea. In abstraction, the figures of *bot* and *viharn* carry out their own conversation of shifting orientations on the fragile surface. A condition remarkably like Bangkok.

The sea is a strange and dangerous destination. Yet it is also compelling, like all manifestations of earthly desire. Surface as summation; glitter as future. A state of longing. Bangkok's desire for a distant landscape, and its ultimate disappearance, is clarified by the flickering water. Intuitions of this existential challenge appear architecturally, perhaps even predating the experience of the actual sea. Wat Suthat, by example, articulates the city's essential concerns. A figured, though directed, centre, celebrating disappearance, must be accessed by crossing a shimmering ground of material value. Exterior delight or interior submission? Both options are made attractive, perhaps challenging original intent. An even choice? Bangkok's temples manifest sensory temptations and provide glimpses of their proper replacement, often within the same image.

Floating Destinations

Bangkok's ground is an ever-present challenge. Living on its intangible foundations provokes an understandable desire for stability. Idealized in the social worlds of the urban precincts and the superstitious boundaries defined by the spirit houses, Bangkok's desire for grounded order finds articulation. At a different scale, more figurally specific, the city's *wats* create tangible narrative journeys, leading towards symbolic destinations. Foreshadowed conclusions offer purpose within a fluid existence. Indeed, a sense of a secure destination might make one's earthly travels more

endurable. Ceaseless movement can be tolerable if understood as a necessary prerequisite to a more comfortable and enduring stability. The representation of this message is a suitable task for architectural order.

The composite structures of Bangkok's *wats* demand different forms of travel. Movement is determined by their dense architectural landscapes, negotiation within and around the principal figures a consistent condition of their experience. Each different route hypothetically provides a fragmented variation of the more general theme of resolved destinations. Travel directs us from an unstable ground towards a more secure future. Journeys through layers of defensive arcades lead to protected zones of narrative purpose. Fields of symbolic value are discovered, all with potent possibilities. Within the *bots* the Buddha images rest at the end of lengthy horizontal travels. Circumnavigations of the *chedis* focus directed views towards their perfect, invisible summits. Different versions of travel, each leading towards a defined point. The destination, a freedom from movement. Stasis as ambition. Temporary confusion and spatial complexity endured become palatable when viewed back from this more conclusive end.

Yet Bangkok's *wats* do not ultimately fulfil this purpose. The role of movement within their composed forms remains more curious. Destinations are celebrated but also obscured, ordered values presented then seemingly invalidated. Coherent in fragmentary parts, the *wats* remain perplexing in their overall realities. *Chedis* compete with *bots*. Forms align around major axes that remain divorced from direct experience. Distinct architectural guides are presented, then abandoned. Paths previously thought important are diverted, their continuation blocked. Directions are reconsidered, imaginary orders implied then dislocated. Even in the calmer, more axial constructions, the final resolution is often architecturally anti-climactic. Within the *bots*, behind the Buddha statues, places for storage. Constructed passages lead to disappointing destinations.

Bangkok's *wats*, though seemingly presenting ideal models for urban order, actually manifest multiple variations on the theme of unfulfilled journey. Within these apparently structured spaces, strange axialities lead to unresolved ends. Formal resolution is left incomplete. Precisely unresolved, the architecture provokes respect and perplexity simultaneously. Buddhas and internal mountains, *chedis* and relics. Flickering grounds. Partial journeys, dissolving forms. Sequential experience, oddly incomplete. Bangkok's angelic emissaries bring cryptic lessons. Like the city's intangible ground, the question of precise architectural meaning remains unresolved. A general condition to be specifically investigated.

PART TWO

Wat as microcosm, wat as model.

Urban exemplar, analogous lessons. Wat

Po, key to Bangkok's curious orders?

Specific experience, intriguing lessons.

Knowledge as Programme

Wat Po, one of Bangkok's oldest foundations, is the city's most significant monastic compound. While Wat Bowonniwet, the site of the initiation ceremonies observed earlier, may house a more vibrant society, and Wat Arun express a more dramatic image, Wat Po, properly Wat Phra Chetuphon, presents a greater and more complete world. It is a construction to be studied for its messages: a metaphoric city with latent urban lessons.

Wat Po, like Wat Mahatat to the north, predates the Grand Palace and its figural centring of the new capital. Their prior existence assisted in framing, and perhaps even identifying, the palace's symbolic location. Yet both *wats* were also transformed by this new reality of royal adjacency. Both were given specific roles within the monarchic city, based on their historic and geographic prominence. Wat Mahatat hosted the conference responsible for revising the *Tipitaka*, the sacred scriptures restored under Rama I's programme of cultural renaissance. The *wat* remains a major Buddhist meditation centre and the site of monastic examinations. Wat Po's role was also deemed educationally valuable and reconfigured as a repository of knowledge for the

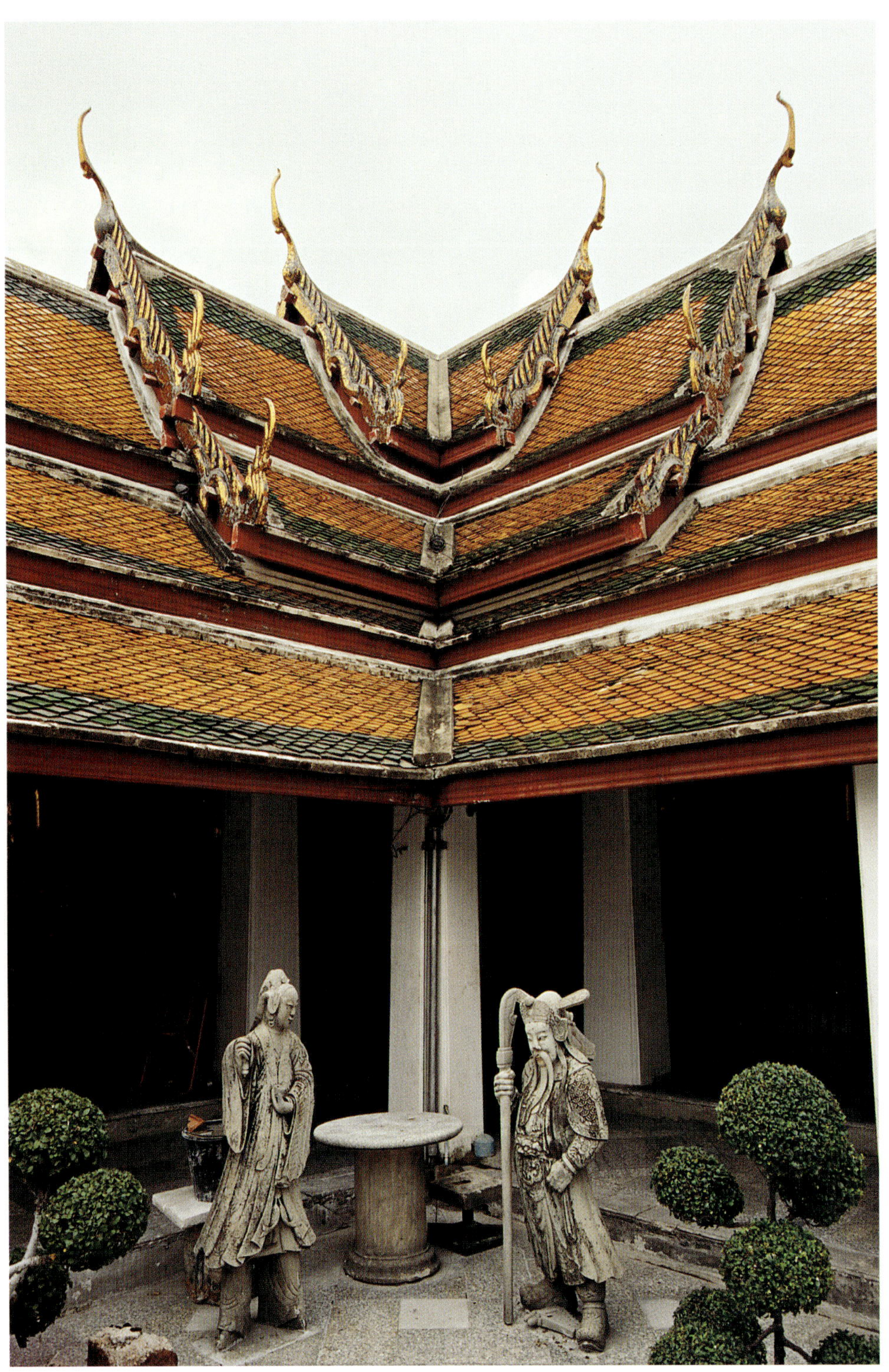

nation. This purpose has captured the attention of the Chakri dynasty, and directed their continued participation within the *wat* and its form. Indeed, Wat Po holds a special position among Bangkok's temples. Originally built in the sixteenth century, it was refounded by Rama I as a royal institution, and subsequently by Rama III as a living university. Throughout its history it has been dedicated to the preservation of Thai culture and its treasures. Under Rama I, Buddha images were rescued from Ayutthaya to be protected within the *wat* and its galleries. Wat Po's restoration under Rama III extended these priorities, redefining the foundation as a school of universal learning. Wat Po is a place dedicated to knowledge and its transmission, most notably in the arts, Buddhist philosophy, astrology and medicine.

Buddhist practice. Monastic classes occupy the many rooms of the sheltered arcades, the monks drawn from across Thailand to further their education. Pavilions dedicated to traditional medicine rest just north of the principal *bot* precinct. A centre for therapeutic massage, physically noted on the grounds by statues of contorted bodies, is located slightly further outside. Buddhist literature. A scripture library, the Ho Trai, is the home of Wat Po's sacred texts. A repository of historic treasure, it is constructed as a special figure: knowledge as focus. The arts. The scenes of Buddhist iconography are painted on walls, as are depictions of astronomy and astrology. Statues are enshrined, the *wat*'s arcade an early form of national museum. More distinctly, the low precinct wall encompassing the *bot* is covered by marble panels narrating the story of the *Ramakien* in sculpted relief. The carvings, taking clues from the shadow puppets of popular

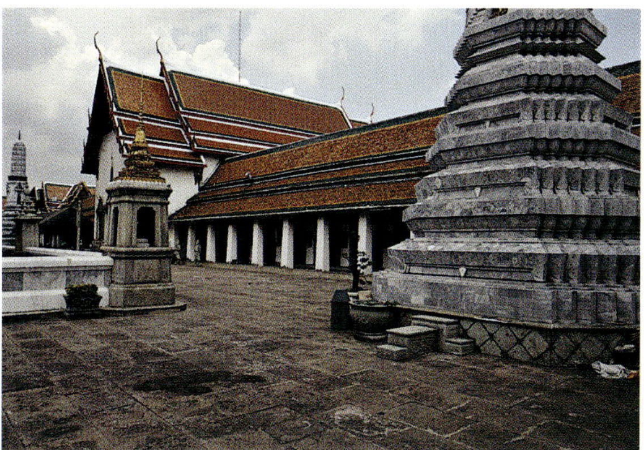

drama, enshrine Bangkok's mythical foundations in outlined stone. Narrative history is made explicit, transmitted in a place of sanctioned knowledge.

But the building proper, what does it teach? Does Wat Po's form accept similar responsibilities of artistic revelation? The transmission of knowledge – Wat Po's pedagogic function – is observed most obviously in its programmes and applied symbols. Can an equivalent educational structure be perceived within its architecture?

Temple as Landscape

Wat Po. Its civic position is central, its mission one of social accommodation and cultural demonstration. It is metaphorically complete. Monastic housing rests to the south. The major school, its places of dining and celebration, are housed within the cloistered figure. Socially diverse, educationally active. Wat Po's architectural lessons are equally dense, as vivid and complex as its host city. A place of travel, spatial revelation and enduring perplexities.

Wat Po's present entry along its north facade is anomalous, based on providing immediate tourist access to the Reclining Buddha, a major statue sited at the north-west corner of the precinct. Properly one enters from the east, though a centred gate pavilion. This entry leads first towards the *bot*, which,however, remains sheltered by its surrounding cloisters. The gate is a significant figure, one of a cardinal four that stabilize the concentric arcades. These galleries extend the entry process, thickening the threshold between city and shrine. Sequential layers, boundaries upon boundaries. The realities of horizontal travel are essential to the plan. One moves gradually through defining limits, the gates and thresholds articulated as key episodes along the journey.

The gallery cloister is typical in its form, but distinct through its density and scale. Its long covered arcades are populated with statues of the seated Buddha. Their value, if not their spatial presence, is accentuated by their position behind glass screens. The numerous Buddhas? It is a familiar image, the lengthy galleries replete with the repetitive figures. The dense lines of conscience and example provide company for the praying and studying monks. The Buddha statues surround the *bot*, facing inwards. The populated rings help the architecture to frame the inner precinct. An ideal audience? The arcades are experienced externally as barriers, protecting their enshrined world. Internally, they shelter and condense the Buddhas' directed gaze. The courtyard: a protected world whose ordered geometry is defined by the arcades and sharpened by the axial clarity of the gates.

Once past the inner gallery the highly centred composition becomes fully visible. Unlike the more traditional pairing of *bot* and *chedi*, closely juxtaposed in immediate proximity, here the *bot* rests in figural solitude. It controls its precinct as a sole centred authority. The final concentric layer, support-

ing the raised platform on which the *bot* rests, is a low wall adorned with the Rama frieze. A line of marble reliefs, illustrating the scenes from the *Ramakien*, separates the *bot* from its court. A version of the Bai Sema, a new sacred boundary is created through image. Carved panels on light coloured stone, stories as protection and foundation. The symbolic defender, Rama, makes the terrain safe for the Buddhist rituals practised within. Rama and the Buddha, joined in a shared space. The *chedi* and its referential nature is displaced by the narration of Rama's heroic actions.

The great *bot*: a framed island. It is directional in its form and use, though centred by location and the articulated boundary. Solitary, yet part of a greater whole. In plan, a coherent figure, Angkor-like in its concentric order. In image, a great roof, oriented horizontally. Planes of coloured tiles rest above the columned frame, the sinuous ridge floating over the precinct below. Within, a large Buddha, home to the ashes of Rama I, founder of Bangkok. The *bot*, framed by its arcade, is a protected totality, centred in its own symbolic landscape.

Yet this ordered world is deemed insufficient. Although formally complete and geometrically pure, the *bot* and its precinct are inflected by the *wat*'s other elements. Required by its greater narrative responsibilities, Wat Po complements the seemingly perfect *bot* complex with a set of additional architectural characters. The result creates a more complex set of geometries, images and relationships.

Chedis are typically located adjacent to their *bots*, slightly to the west. Here the arrangement is distinct in a number of ways. The symbolic mountain is situated outside the precinct, visible only as a disconnected fragment from within the protected

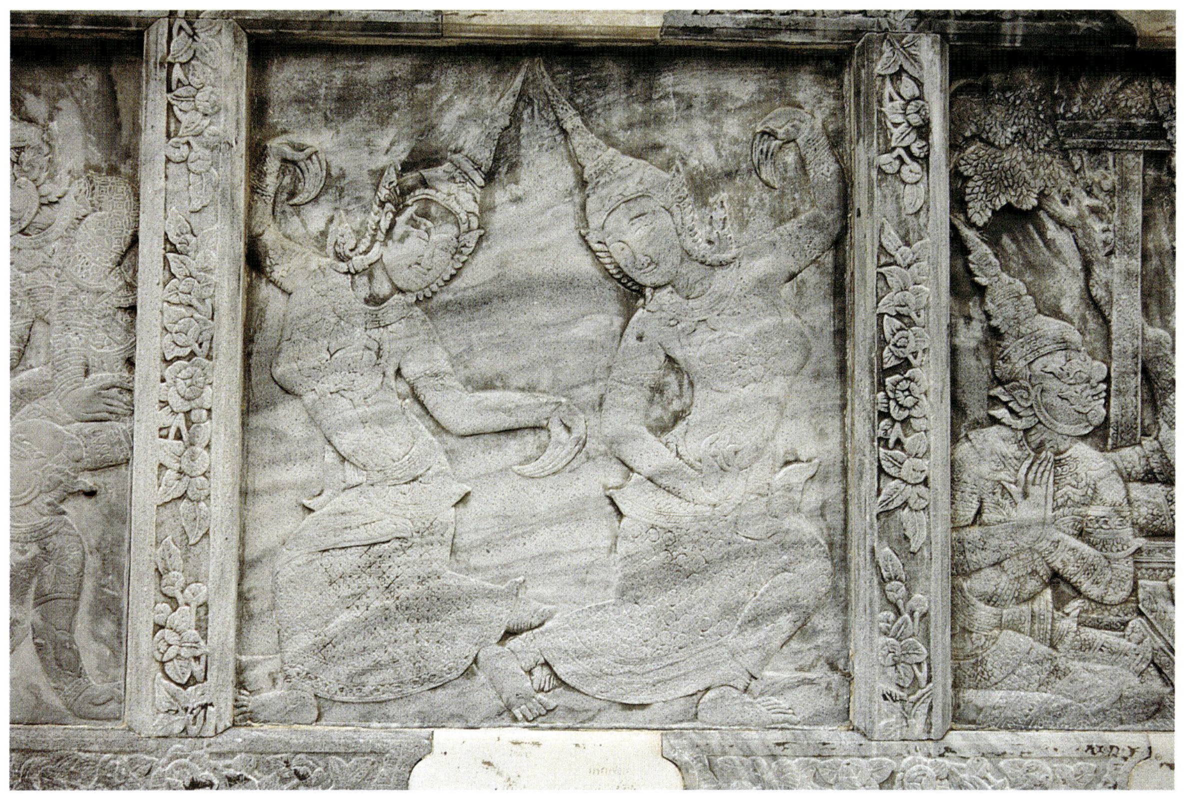

interior. A displaced destination. Even more curiously, the *chedi* is not a single, axially related figure, but one of a row, part of a range of celebratory hills. The passage through the western gate, on axis with the *bot*, leads to an architectural landscape. Three *chedis* are arranged in a transverse line, surmounted by a fourth, further to the west. A grouping of vertical destinations, the composition articulates a wall, vertical image and further horizontal travels at once. Also unique, the axis centring their arrangement inflects slightly to the south, inclining away from the virtual spine that orders the *bot* and its precinct. This creates a further dislocation between the *bot* and its *chedis*, a slight break in the tradition of sequential order.

The figures are named The Chedis of the Four Kings, referencing Ramas I to IV. In form they are highly vegetal Khmer-style *prangs*, clad, like Wat Arun, in coloured ceramics. Through subtle variations in colour, their similar forms are rendered distinct. The reference? The figures are clearly Angkor- or Meru-like, replicating the image of the symbolic mountain as historically understood. The royal legacy is constructed as a group of architectural hills, the culminating figures in a significant composition. The Chedis of the Four Kings. Acts of devotion or self-aggrandizement? They create both a destination and barrier, an architectural mountain range as visual backdrop to the *bot*. This composed landscape is framed within

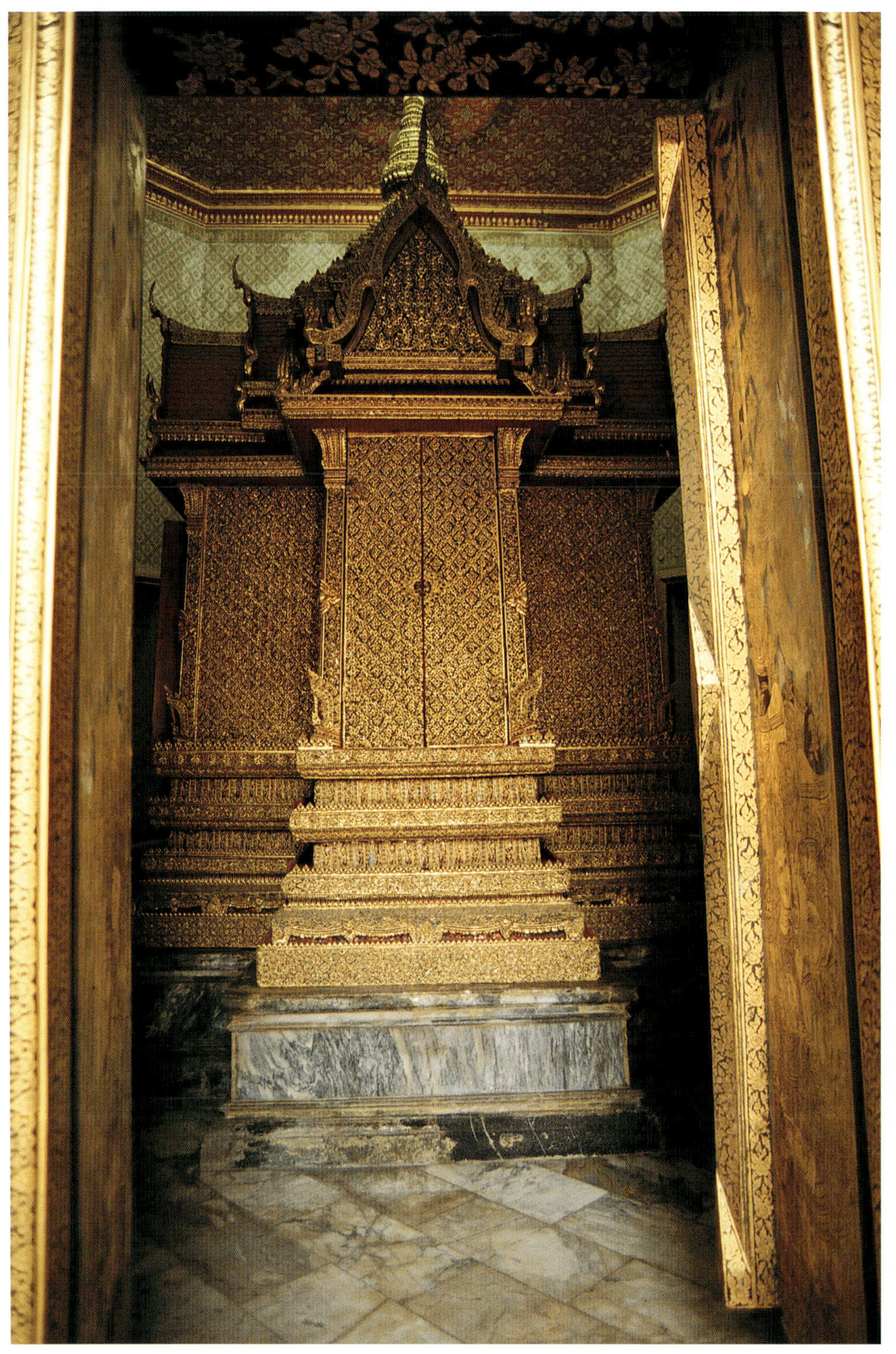

its own perspectival cloister; open to the east, focused to the west. It is more directional than the arcade surrounding the *bot*, and leads to a stronger sense of figural conclusion. *Chedis* as pointer and completion, grouped to identify further the end of a complex narrative passage.

The *chedis* are grounded figures that halt the horizontal thrust of the *bot*. A wall of vegetal hills. A landscape at the end of travel, transforming a literal horizontal motion to an imaginary vertical journey, reminiscent of the funerary rituals returning the deceased kings to Mount Meru. This mythic destination is foreshadowed in Wat Po's symbolic expression. Yet a semblance of horizontal travel is still maintained, the fourth *chedi* extending the composition further to the west.

Outside the arcade, the Ho Trai. The scripture pavilion is positioned axially with the summiting *chedi*: an additional conclusion to the oriented passage. The Ho Trai is a vertically oriented pavilion, located within its own exceptionally tight cloister. It is a complement to the *chedis*, as well as to their experiential replacement. A backdrop to the visual journeys implied in the symbolic mountains, and the means to further travel through directed meditation. Traditionally, the architectural landscape embodied in the *chedi* is the temporal culmination of the *wat*. Here the scripture pavilion provides a new and complementary version of the *wat*'s message. The internalized voyages embodied in the texts are carefully protected by the arcade and building. Within, by the highly decorated scripture cabinets. The cabinets, like the pavilion, are constructed as miniature figures of architectural order, also internally complete.

North of the scripture pavilion, the Viharn of the Reclining Buddha. Equally distinct, but shocking in scale. An architectural figure that internalizes one's travels once again, and eliminates any lingering sense of their ordered completion.

Floating World

With a general orientation to the west, the *bot* complex is juxtaposed against a collection of *chedis*. A built landscape, a symbolic mountain range. Sequential boundaries, complementary figures and illusory completions. The architecture constructs a symbolic landscape, in its parts and their composite whole. A topography of vessels and hills that requires travel for their appreciation. The architectural elements are organized along compositional axes, but human passage moves around them, personal routes constructed in more labyrinthine ways. The fluid terrain of the courtyards creates strong architectonic images and more ambiguous experiences.

The *bot* is most clearly perceived as a figure negotiating with this world. It presents an image of directed travel, leading towards the symbolic mountains. Yet it may also embody an implied landscape too. Movement and terrain become simultaneously present.

Centred in its form and location, the *bot* manifests a vertical quality through the strength of its columns and the slight inward inclination of its main elements. Doors, windows, walls: all inflect towards the centre, creating a dynamic vertical focus. These inflections lead upwards, to be set in contrast to the powerful roof. Distinguished by its striking form and colour, the horizontal figure extends over its tilted supports, its independence increased. The roof

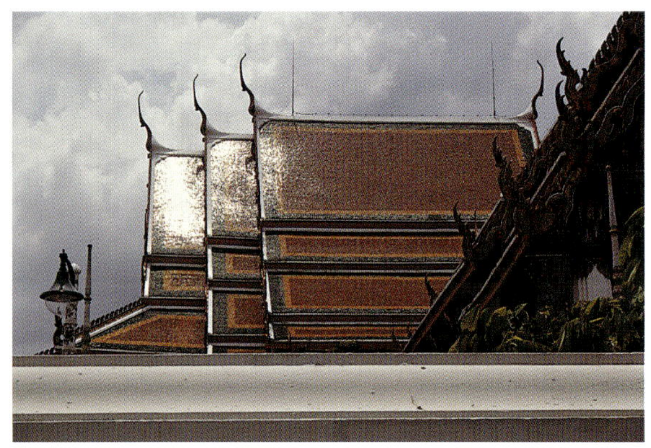

appears to lift off, to separate itself from these grounded links. Sequentially layered, each set further back, each end upturned, the roof is ready to depart. Yet it doesn't attempt to imitate the sky, to make its vertical destination explicit. Unlike the *chedis*, whose dissolution into a point establishes an identity with the air, the *bot*'s roof creates a distinct profile, a powerful contrast to its aerial setting. This sets up an interesting dialogue. The columns and walls point up and away, to support and celebrate the roof as a distinct figure in conversation with the sky. Yet the roof doesn't presume to belong to this pre-celestial realm. In fact it stresses its own independent identity through form and material, clearly belonging to the world of earthly craft. Human construction is juxtaposed against the ineffable air.

Feats of carpentry, subtleties of inclination. The roof's form is dynamic, distinct from the stable foundations articulated in the court. More floating, more aquatic, more like a vessel. Indeed, the constructed image resonates with the boats and chariots of the city of royal ritual. Crafted shelters, travelling the intangible land. Like the royal barges, Wat Po's roof is a character in motion, acting in the world. Its skin, coloured scales. At Wat Po, the *bot* travels towards the symbolic landscape articulated in the *chedis* of the Four Kings. Or perhaps the messages from the sacred hills are brought to us, an inversion of the architectural journey. Horizontal movement links the mythical destination with its recipients.

The summit is a sinuous line, an articulation of a special edge. A line rendered with exquisite sensitivity. Its elegant curves etch a striking profile against the sky. Degrees of partial aerial participation are identified, yet ultimately constrained within their own form. Earthly life celebrated at its highest point, the junction with its opposite. Is the line of the roof analogous to the river's surface? Temples and rivers. The directional figure is powerfully summarized through the elegant edge. A threshold articulated, a destination and point of contact appreciated through beautiful form. Articulation of ideal travels. The path of the waters from the sacred mountain, travelling along the back of the mythic serpent Naga, link Mount Meru with the sea.

PART THREE

*Controlled movement; resolutions
strangely unfulfilled. Illusory axialities,
architectural anticlimax. Passage more
significant than destination; surreal
spaces resisting completion. Formlessness
as intent. Relax and wonder.*

Unresolved Destinations

Replicated boundaries, symbolic landscapes. An architecture of edges is reproduced and restated in different ways. Layers of passage; replicated thresholds. These strange dislocations are reinforced by the practice of repetition. The countless statues lining Wat Po's arcades are highly similar, each a reminder of the Buddha's singular importance. Their repetition, however, serves to render their shared essence more vivid than any individual physical traits. With so many equivalent examples of the Buddha on collective view, there is less tendency to venerate any particular one. Multiple variations, each becomes a fragmentary representative of a more mysterious message. They are collectively necessary to support the concentric arcades and define the image of travel, but their formal particularity is subordinate to the less tangible truths embodied within.

A similar condition is created by architectural projection. The compression of layered figures serves first to densify, and then ultimately diminish the formal clarity of Bangkok's significant constructions.

Through reverse perspective an image of rapid passage is made legible through the superimposed figures. Most obvious in the stepped roofs of the *bots*, other compositions, such as the articulated portal of Wat Arun, demonstrate the same tendency. A visual journey is articulated, the figure of the gate replicated and compressed. Linear passage becomes image, compacted to a single facade. The solid block ultimately dissolves into a profusion of lines and shapes. Formal dissolution, created through formal overabundance. Through densification and repetition a greater, if more ambiguous, sensibility is created. Repetition: a curious use of form that first accentuates and then ultimately negates formal value. The limitations of symbol become evident. It is a melancholic realization perhaps, where a desire for formal resolution must be necessarily abandoned. Yet it also leads to intriguing possibilities, both more enigmatic and primary than those supplied by clear outlines or legible symbols alone. A sensibility that underlies Wat Po's ambiguous journeys.

Each route is carefully constructed to celebrate a focus. Yet paths are diverted or extended as one approaches the final conclusion. Destinations are replaced. The Buddha image within the *bot*, visually respected but architecturally unfulfilled. The *bot* in its cloistered arcade, perfect in its figural centrality yet inflected by the *chedis* hovering outside. The Chedis of the Four Kings, landscape as backdrop, horizontal travel vertically transformed. Multiple destinations, four almost equal figures. A single conclusion avoided. Around and behind, the scripture pavilion, movement internalized towards the sacred texts. Awaiting beside, the Reclining Buddha.

Through spatial and experiential repetition, both centre and destination are sequentially deferred.

Numerous figures and multiple paths are presented with no single formal resolution. Shifting figures of attention. Partial journeys, unresolved destinations. Travel is more important than arrival. Wat Po's various forms articulate journeys that, physically, can proceed no further. They remind us of the value of earthly action while simultaneously demonstrating its limits. Tangible links are broken, replaced by necessary imaginative leaps. The ultimate focus of concern lies somewhere between the figures, independent from their formal values. The narrative paths are continued by other means.

Wat Po may present a version of the utopic city, but it remains intentionally incomplete. Its formal messages are never figurally resolved. Ultimately, it constructs a sensibility rather than an image. The broken journeys lead to a state of mental realization: clarity in apparent confusion. A sense of impossibility is made perceptually present. The architecture, a strange pointer. A longing for a more ideal path to a distant landscape is clear. Yet in this desire there is no acceptance of any artificial closure. The appeal of firmly grounded or fixed conclusions is, perhaps reluctantly, rejected.

The Reclining Buddha

The Viharn of the Reclining Buddha is an irregular, unexpected conclusion to Wat Po's directed travels. A stunning event, even within Wat Po's complex topography. A unique provocation. A reclining Buddha, stretched out to the full length of its home. A massive statue, a vast expanse of gold. Figure as architecture.

The sheer scale of the statue is remarkable. A body barely fitting inside the building, the figural sculpture verges on the surreal. It defies any clear comprehension, its size and surface combining to create an other-worldly quality. Set off by contrast with the dark patterned walls, its material serves to further accentuate the mysterious presence. Gold, unfathomable gold. The statue may represent a historic person, but a considerable distance rests between his perceptions and ours. Walk around and wonder, dropping small coins in the line of bronze buckets so that you maintain a fragile grasp on strange reality.

The massive figure is seemingly comfortable. A calm face and relaxed posture. The image, however, is only ever partly visible (with one significant exception). Its sheer size challenges any frontal view, the longitudinal viewing arcade constructed adjacent to the statue. The building's inner colonnade defines a screen that further distorts the view to the figure within. The Buddha's remarkable scale and perceptual inconclusiveness are reinforced by this experiential fragmentation. Its figural clarity further diminished. Partial glimpses appear through the spaces defined by the columns, the statue visible in barely legible moments.

Framed visions. Small ensembles of altars and offerings are set within the piers. These compilations appear as set-pieces, little *mise-en-scènes* viewed against the barely recognizable gold monolith. The focused shrines create a rhythm of familiar settings along the longitudinal axis of the temple. Candles, incense, gifts of money, gold leaf, flowers. Places of tangible participation as personal grounding. Almost trivial in scale, they humanize the whole with scenes of familiarity in the face of absolute strangeness. Human foibles, a domestic level of contact, provided for our benefit.

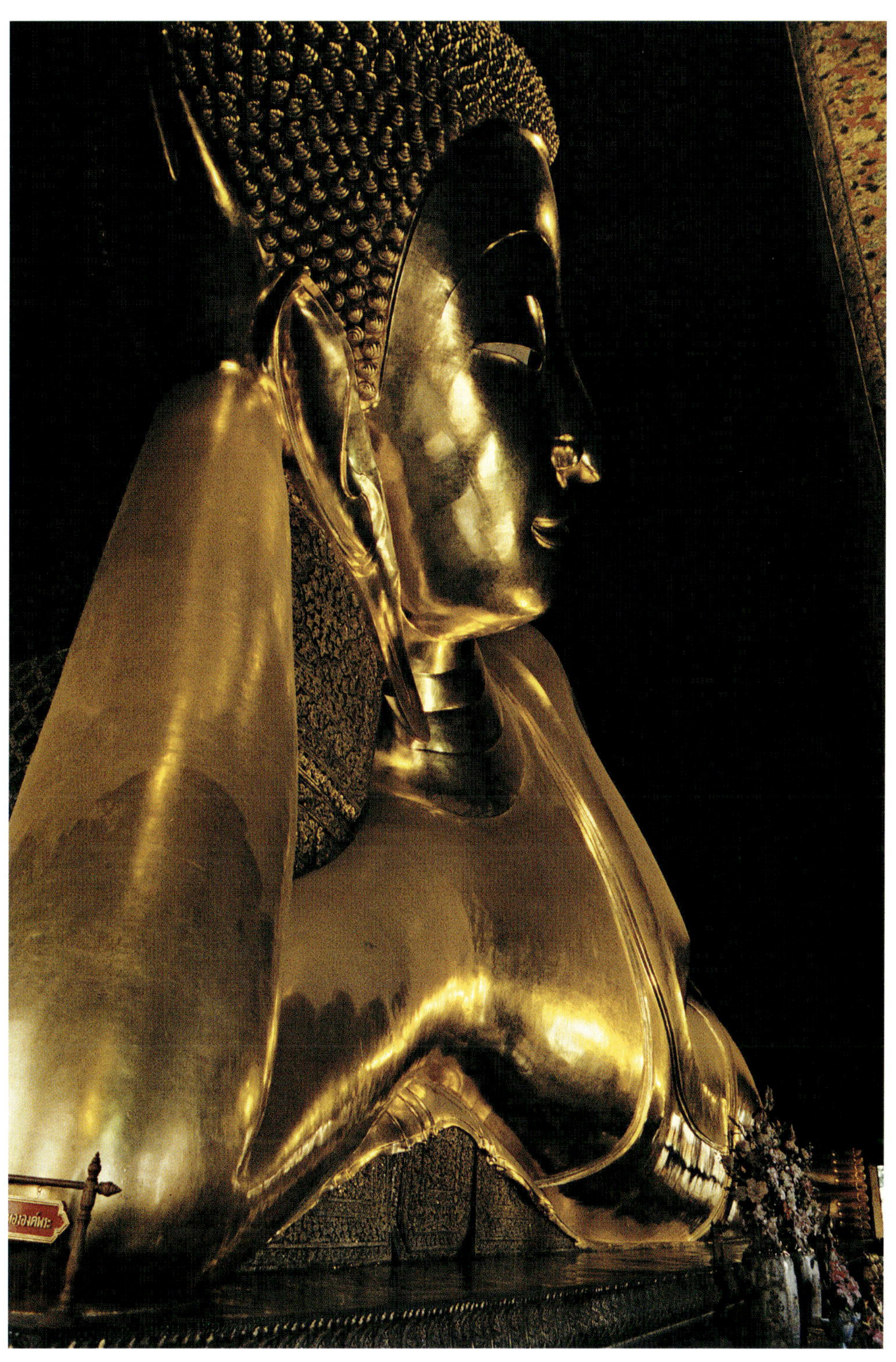

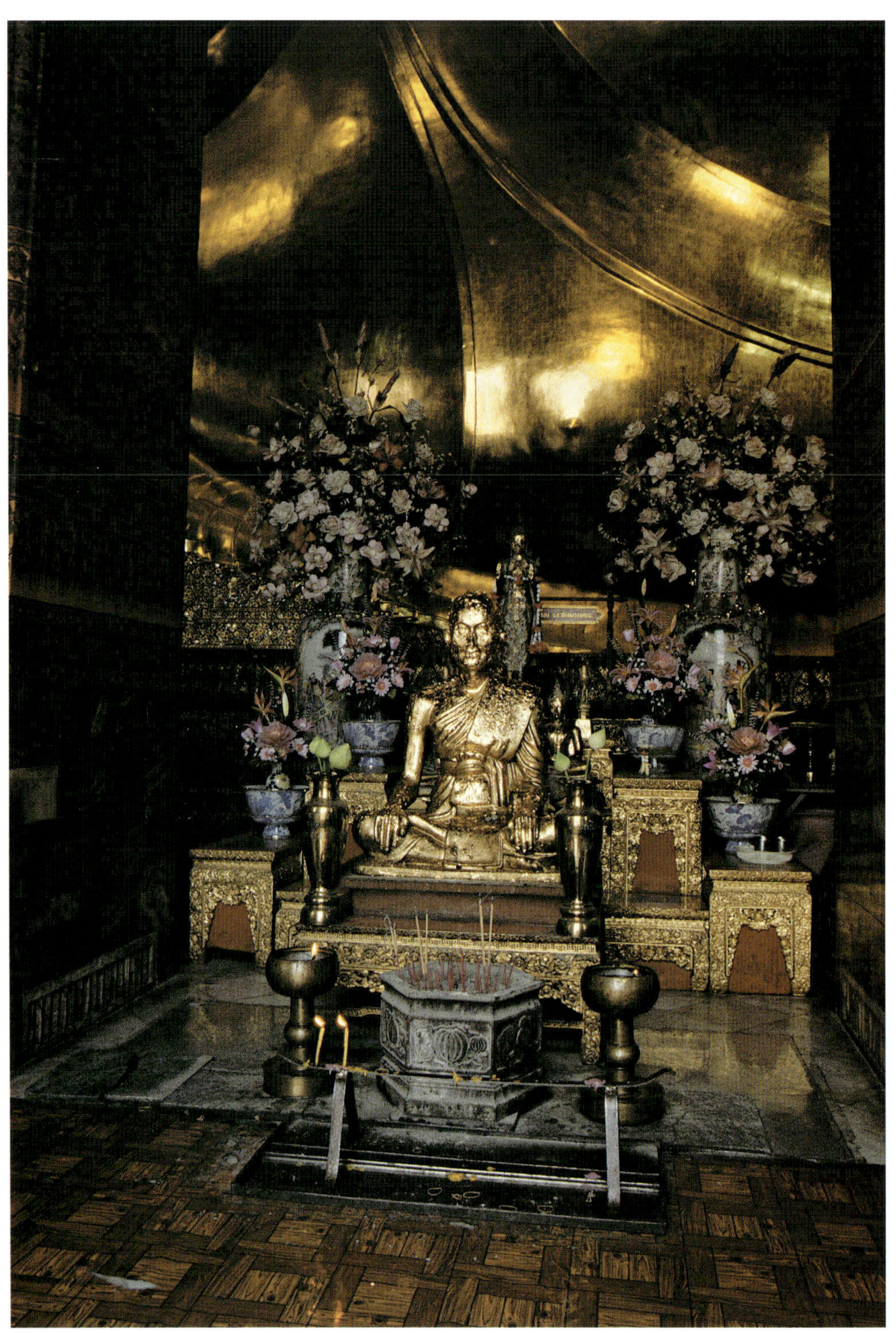

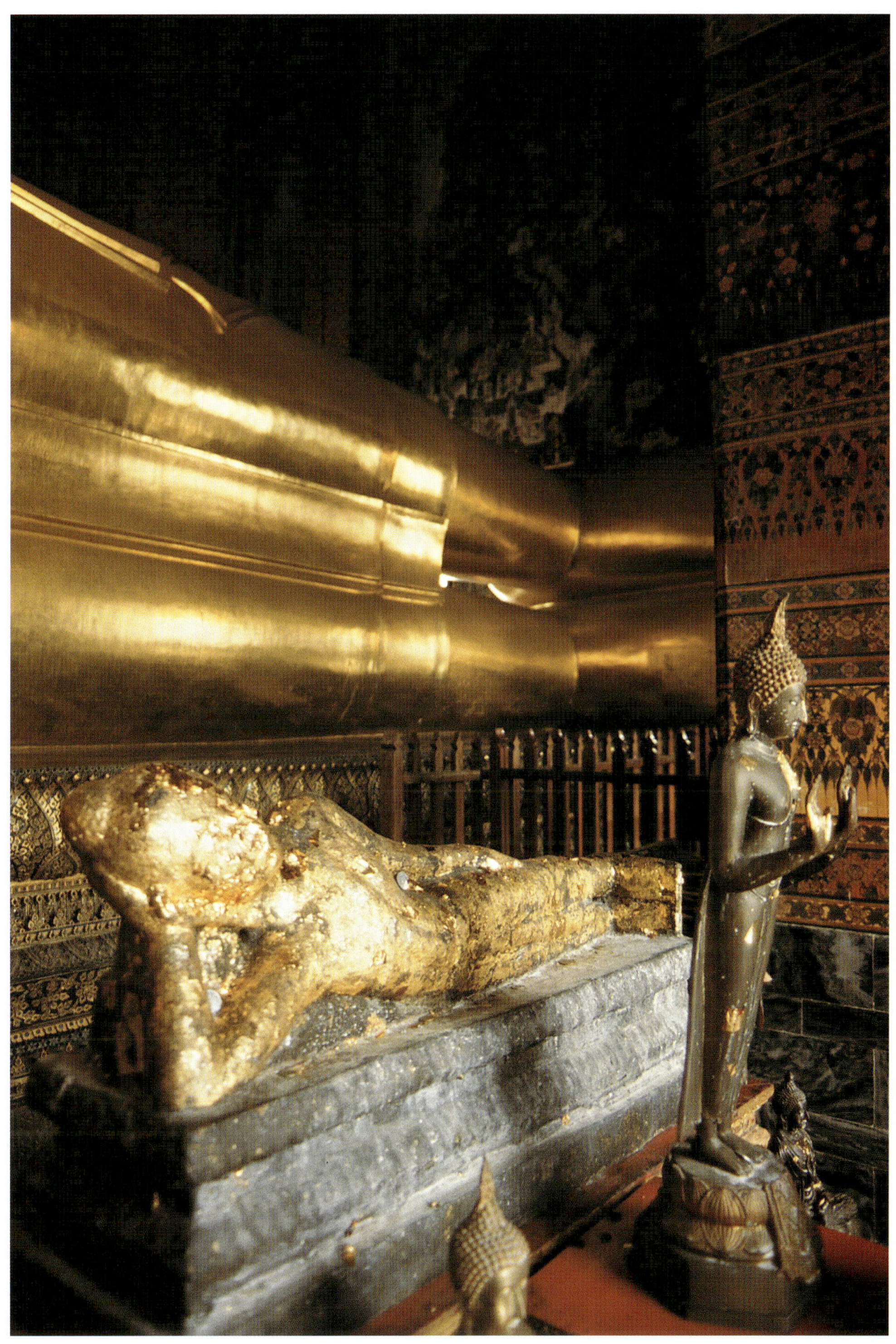

Visually the shrines, juxtaposed against the cryptic gold backdrop, construct material links with the statue. Figure to figure, gold to gold. Through created affinities, possible relations are constructed. The straightforward and symmetrical arrangements of the altars and figures provide access, and perhaps even comic relief to the mysterious whole. Hypothetical connections are attempted. But the contrast between them is so great that it renders the Reclining Buddha even stranger by comparison. The intentions are clear, but the distance to be bridged is almost impossibly large.

The building's strong and simple (though finely decorated) piers frame these personal moments. The expanse of gold is viewed through the black structure. Both are materially dense, both paradoxical in their simultaneous celebration of surface and depth. Reflection and disappearance. These piers, sharpening the individuality of the figure behind, also contrast with the floor, their mute darkness offsetting its shiny reflective surface. Figures float above the slippery and mysterious ground, an aqueous foundation for the massive body shimmering above.

The Reclining Buddha: a figure of gold at the scale of a building. One gets lost staring into the engulfing colour, its subtleties and varieties surprising. Original simplicity disappears into phenomenal complexity. Attention is drawn to the head, the only place of real sculptural articulation. Although subtle in its expression, there is a personality, a faint smile and a strange helmet of hair. Friendly but slightly aloof. The remainder of the body verges on being a horizontally striated graphic. The body provides the mute backdrop, both to its own more articulated parts (head, feet) and the smaller-scale shrines to the side.

Viewing from the feet (the only place to achieve an uninterrupted view of the entire figure), the body is a long horizontal expanse, unhindered by breaks or architectural rhythm. A version of clarity, but the distance to the head is extreme. The lines of the legs and the draperies of the cloth accentuate this distance, further reinforced by the low horizontal perspective. At the end, a slight lift to his head and the flip of a shoulder poignantly mark the Buddha's alertness. The space inflects vertically, an upward shift contrasting the relentless horizontality. The terrestrial journey, clearly visible only at the point of its greatest length, is transformed at its conclusion. Distance is reinforced, but the route ahead seemingly clarified.

The soles of the feet, viewed from the west, are treated as narrative fields. A surprise discovery: dense inlays of mother of pearl. Compositions of pink, white and black, shining in the relative darkness. Telling stories. Cosmological footprints. The Buddha's feet record his travels as episodes arrayed around a mandala, the scenes from his life set outside the cosmological image. The symbolic structures intercept, each adjacent, both glittering against the shimmering black background. His actions and the ordered world of the cosmic image articulate the means of transcendence from this abyss. And the foot itself? The point of meeting between the enlightened spirit and the tangible, degraded ground. We, who are not permitted to point our feet at a Buddha statue, study the order of the world and its most idealized life through the images recorded on his soles. What would normally be a figure of disrespect becomes a pedagogic tool. Unlike the somewhat surreal statue, whose lessons remain allusive, the footprints tell more explicit

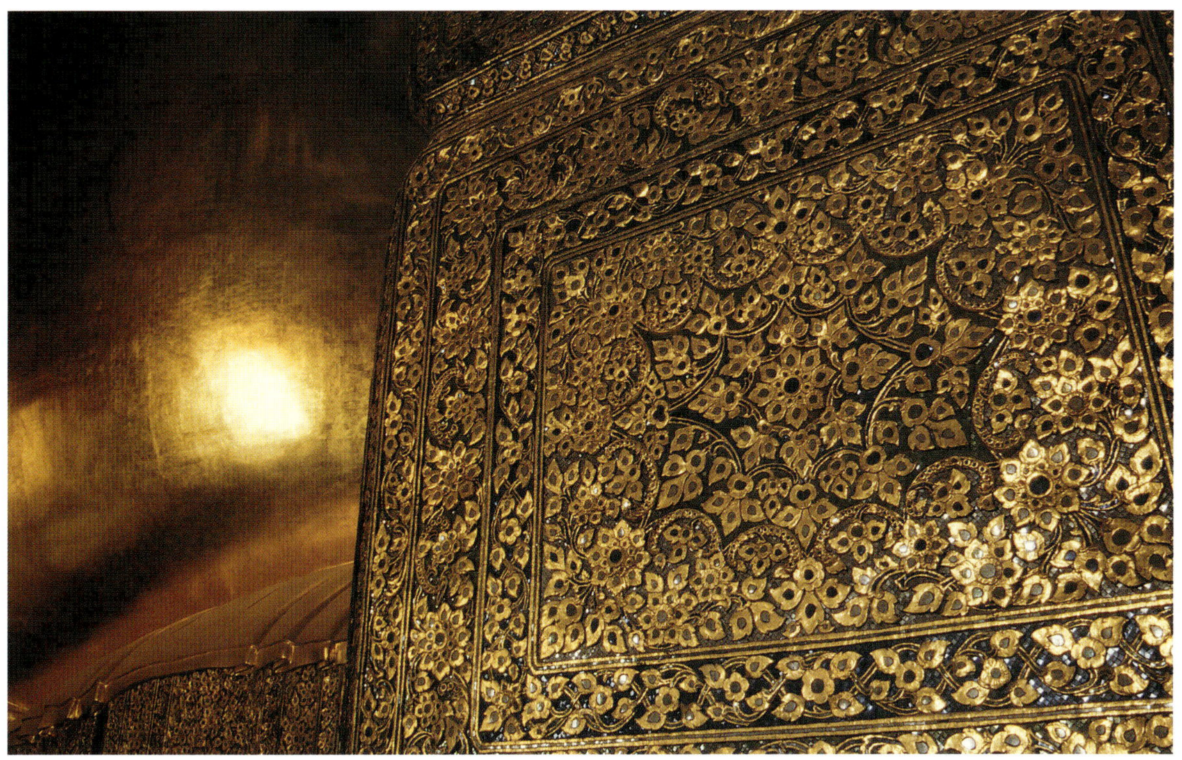

stories and demonstrate worldly orders. They pattern their lessons on the material of the physical world. Recognizable motifs are used to communicate the more cryptic message that rests ambiguously present in the figure itself.

Spiral toes and figural soles. The toes, the part of the foot that initiates or propels movement, are decorated with spiral lines: a grouping of strange centralities. The digits responsible for directing physical motion are defined as images of circular stasis. Earthly movement is inverted. So often mistaken for progress, motion is presented as pointless and cyclical. This separation of the toes from the more explicit narrative images allows the feet to present a more centred frame, a square field that outlines the events, highlights and settings of the Buddha's life. The toes, disrespected in their function of directing movement, are divorced from the more significant lessons represented in the images.

Figures in Balance

The issue of implied departure versus enclosure is present even in the strange figure of the Reclining Buddha. The head, a partial transformation of the horizontal flow, inflects attention upwards. More physically? The statue implies a greater context: his house is clearly too small for comfort. It is enclosed by dense walls, its perimeter solidified by narrative paintings. The circumscribed boundaries, animated by the numerous shrines, hold the statue in place. Yet if the Buddha was to stand up, or even stretch, the building would shatter. His awakening to an active state would destroy the world of culture surrounding him, the world that provides our perceptual accessibility. The statue is voluntarily imprisoned in bodily form, allowing the close, if cryptic, spatial conversation. Awe through temporary proximity, and a recognition of the distance that remains to be bridged. Cognitive dislocation through mysterious presence. The tension between the statue's immediacy and its ultimate unfathomability is dramatic, the sense of impending architectural dissolution adding to the spatial intensity. The tension between the figure and his temporary home? Even reclining and relaxed, the embodied force of destructive enlightenment makes the hall quiver in fear and anticipation.

The Reclining Buddha. Located outside, and west of the four *chedis*, his head points to the east. Facing to the north, the statue inverts the previously observed practices of orientation. Even those fragile assurances of conventional order are overturned. Ambiguous directions. Wat Po is a conversation of parts, arranged on a floating terrain. The *chedis*, a displaced mountain range. The *bot* as boat. The ability to travel across a shimmering ground, a literal metaphor of travel, abstracted in the form of the buildings. Roofs, scaled like the water serpent Naga, reflective like the sea. A place of negotiation, each part rendered as vividly as possible. Conversations of heightened personalities. The Reclining Buddha is there to remind us that any sense of their ordered resolution is transient.

Floating architecture. In plan, a gentle inflection towards the south. The shift in orientation defined by the *chedis* is picked up in the Sleeping Buddha's feet. Feet, pointing towards the river. The sleeping

Buddha: body as building. From outside the Viharn of the Reclining Buddha, the river. And further: Wat Arun. On the far side of the river, a distant mountain viewed against the setting sun. Seen at a distance, foreshadowing the challenging ascent. Wat Po's sequences of partial arrivals, partial completions, and newly introduced destinations, continue out towards the greater city.

NINE

Floating City

PART ONE

Avoidance of conflict; movement as survival.

Fluidity as flexibility; adaptation without

undue sacrifice. Formlessness as desire?

Stability submerged. Important journeys to

ambiguous destinations. Life floats between.

Figure and Transformation

Wat Po aligns an inward focus with a concern for Bangkok's external realities. A composition that teases with its moments of formal power and their perceptual incompletion. Its tenuous conclusion: the Reclining Buddha. A figure so recognizable, so stylized and so strange. The specific head and complex feet; a body too big for its space. It is a compelling figure. Powerful in its visually dramatic impact, yet also visually challenged. It is difficult to view the statue in its entirety. Nor is there any demonstrated inclination to fix a preferential centre. Like Wat Po itself, one is always displaced from positions of perceptual security. It is difficult to know where to stand, striving in vain for a stable moment to assist comprehension. In its composite appreciation, the Reclining Buddha is simultaneously inspiring and chastening. Part of its message: a sense or recognition that other larger issues exist. A reminder that the city is not for us alone. Wat Po's culmination leaves the visitor in a state of awe, attempting to fathom the implications of the partially glimpsed message. In all its wonderful and frightening potential, the intended effects of a floating world are made vividly immediate.

Buddhas of gold. The figures dedicated to rejecting Bangkok's temptations are presented in the most opulent ways. Symbolic ideals, materially

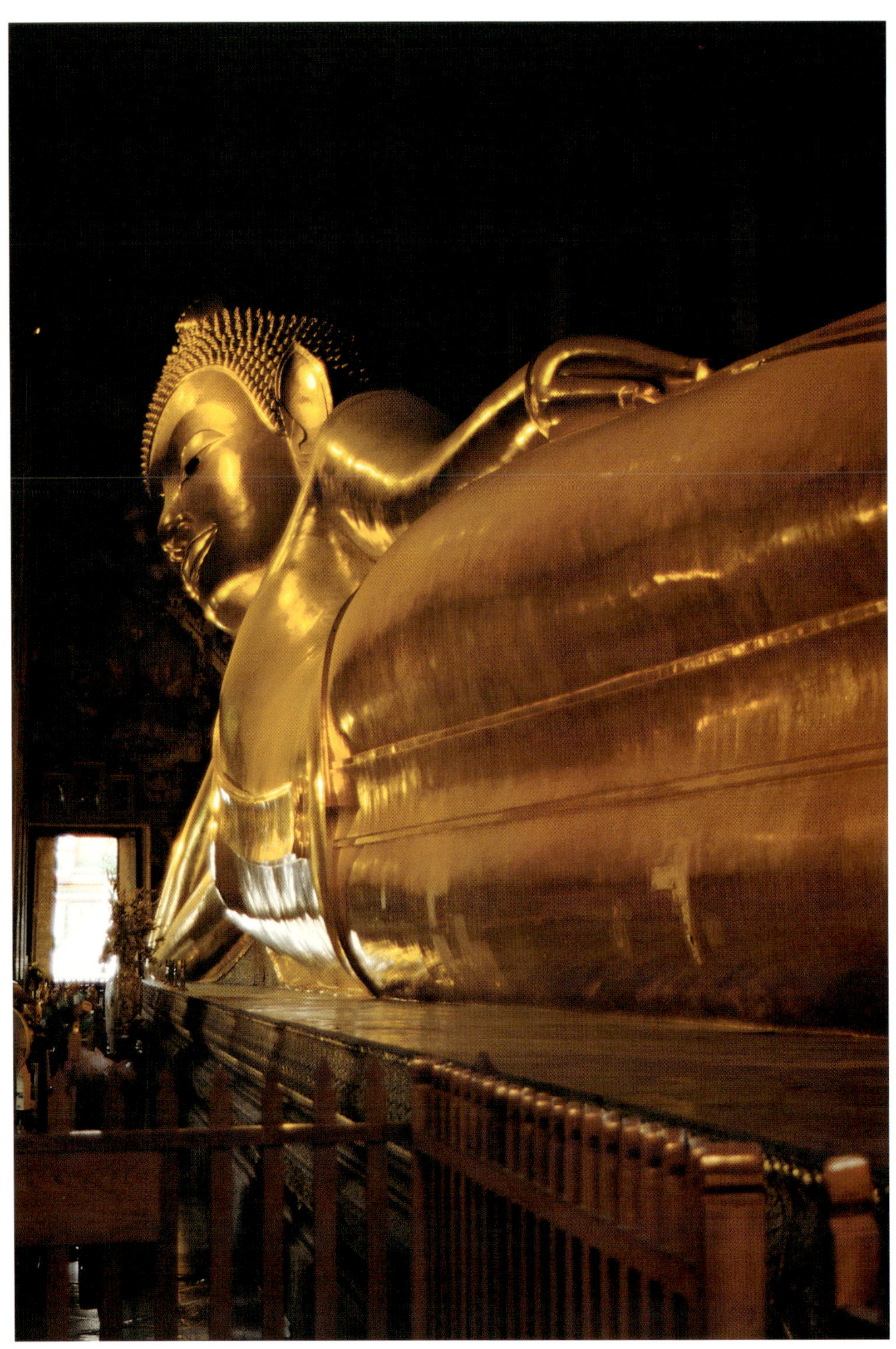

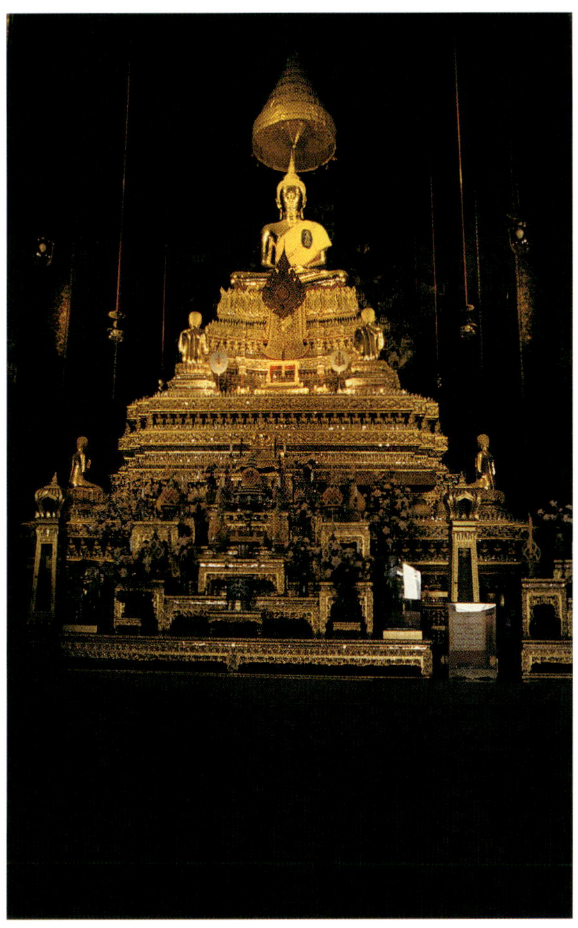

of disappearance. Survival is achieved through avoidance, anticipation and endurance rather than material confrontation. A city that celebrates the point where the land and its river meet the sea. The powerful but dissolving earth joins the bottomless, mysterious depths. The sea, the place of ultimate disappearance, is ultimately more stable than the transient ground. Curious inversions of form, always in motion. Ambiguous strength; unstable realities.

Flexible Physicalities

The *Ramakien* is a prime example of Bangkok's traditions of absorption and transformation. Diverse ideas and practices, in this case a Hindu epic, are imported from the outside world and then rendered specific to their new context. Inherited traditions support new constructions. Original historical similarities become transformed through shifts in tone and implication.

In the Indian original, Lakshmana (Rama's brother) accompanies his sibling as a faithful subordinate. He plays a major, if somewhat thankless, role as foil to Rama's greater status and destiny. A solid figure at home with earthly knowledge, fluent in the arts of hunting, building and warfare, Lakshmana grounds Rama's actions in a worldly tangibility. In the *Ramakien*, Lakshmana is still present. Yet in narrative significance he is largely displaced by Hanuman. Hanuman the monkey hero, the greatest supporting actor, and the most 'Thai' character of the new composition.

Hanuman changes shape at will, a god born of the wind. Hermit, warrior, seer, faithful servant, ambitious lover – he is a versatile character.

honoured with the earthly authority of weight and wealth. Physical resemblance; non-bodily experience. Water and gold: powerful surfaces and inner depths. Bangkok's images articulate mysterious truths. Compelling, if disorienting, pointers, these confusing indications make it easy to lose one's way. Bangkok's forms? Ambiguous enticements, constructed to draw the curious rather than articulate clear meanings. Obscuring and alluring. Form as seduction rather than didactic statement.

A city with qualities of a supple and subtle strength. Beauty in tension, revealed in its moments

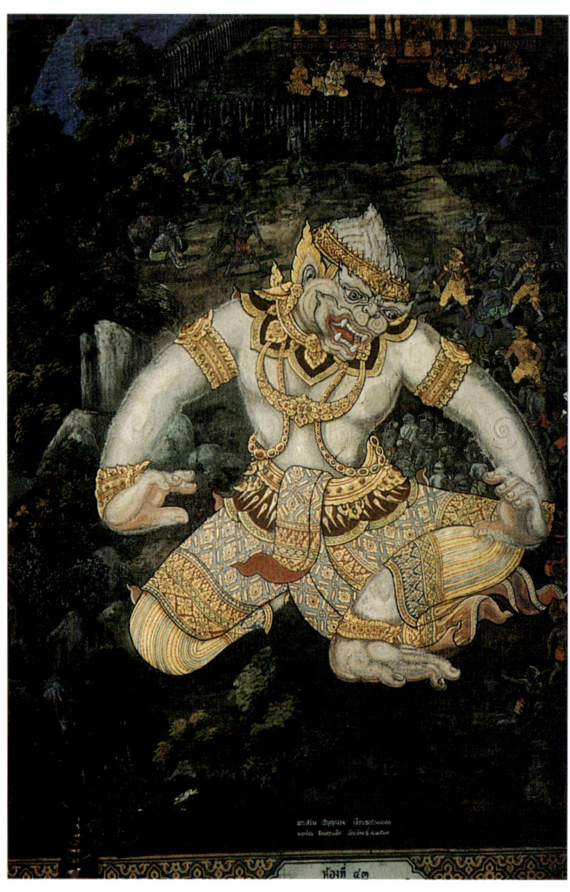

Hanuman's exploits in these different roles provide much of the delight in the transformed story. Rama, though still clearly central, is somewhat of a dour cipher by contrast. Burdened by his responsibilities, he fulfils his fated destiny. Hanuman, though equally dedicated and fearless, is more easily distracted. He complements his duties as Rama's vassal with a dedication to his own interests. 'The close touch and the warmth of her body ignited Hanumans's desire for love. We say in Thai that ants cannot get near to sugar without eating it, so Hanuman courted Benjaki [Hanuman being her assigned escort], won her love and slept with her before she was sent off to Lanka.'[1]

Although it is difficult to make any definitive comparisons, given the many versions of both texts, the *Ramakien* generally appears to be more sensual, sexier even, than the *Ramayana*. Its expositions of social order are perhaps less explicit, its parenthetical stories less educationally didactic. In contrast, its personal side becomes more significant. Passions and jealousies; beauty, illusion and revenge are common to both, but they appear accentuated in the Thai versions. This may be due to a change in function, the lengthy oration transformed for use as court entertainment. But the narrative elevation of Hanuman implies a shift in values too. Hanuman is a figure of humour and magic who changes shape as required. He is strong and flexible; sensually attuned. Consistent in his attitude, varied in his image and behaviour.

A taste for transformation and personal reinvention is equally evident in Bangkok's social worlds. Urban vitality through flexibility. Life is defined through the possibility of change, and its focus on fluid pleasures. The most extreme example: the oft noted prevalence of *katoeys* ('lady-boys' in the vernacular translation). Surgical girls. Newly female singers populate the numerous transvestite cabarets, masterpieces of will and focus. Yet this popular phenomenon is evident across the broader range of society as well, and is highly visible on the city's streets. Social tolerance and a taste for change. A desire for beauty. In appearance, the newly constructed women are often monuments to medical artifice. A physical transformation that has caught many a bewitched foreigner unaware. In spirit, manifestations of flexibility and earthly dedication. All can be rendered anew, and time is fleeting.

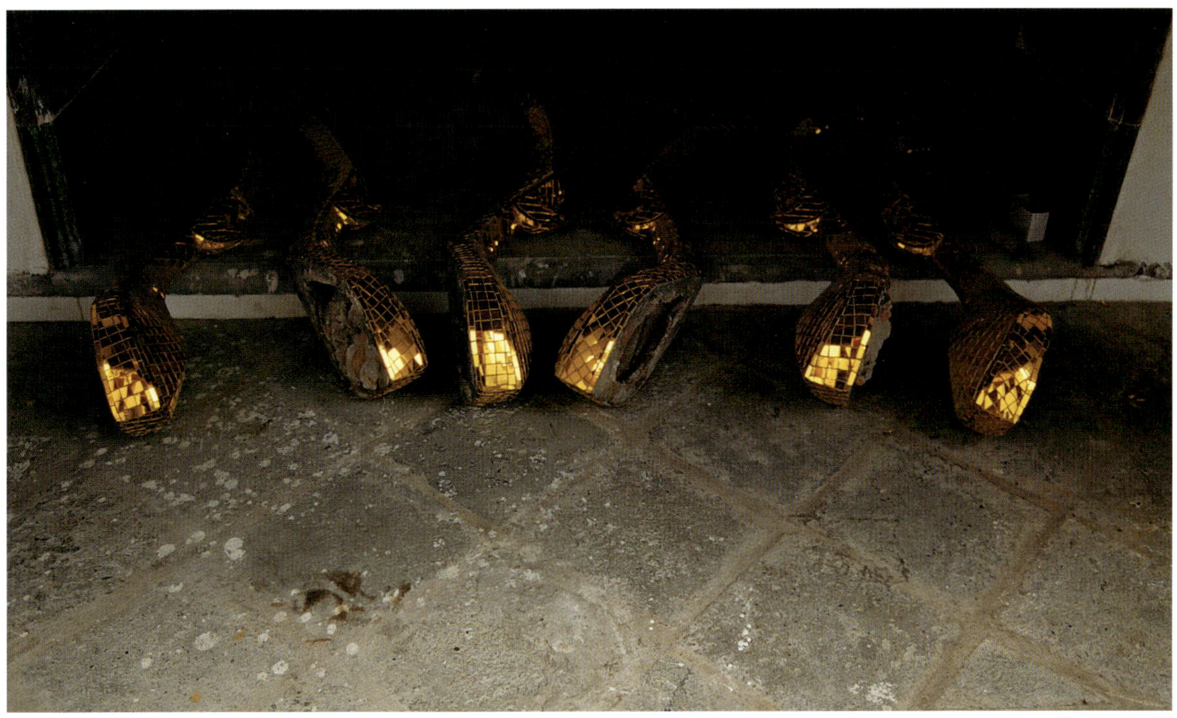

Bangkok's *bots* deteriorate rapidly in its tropical climate. Their wood and tile roofs, the gilt and ceramic mosaics, are fragile. Buildings return to their natural state. Yet this isn't for any lack of resources. Alongside the crumbling originals, new constructions rise. Why restore to historic perfection when one can build anew? Value lies in the act of construction at least as much as it does in construction's results. Like the vegetal boats built for an imminent disappearance at the Loy Krathong festival, beauty is most powerful when fleeting. Ritual dedications and honorary constructions; value in the sacrificial act. Unlike the more spatially stable, museum-oriented cultures of contemporary Europe and North America, Bangkok's physical artefacts take on greater value through their actual or perceptual disappearance.

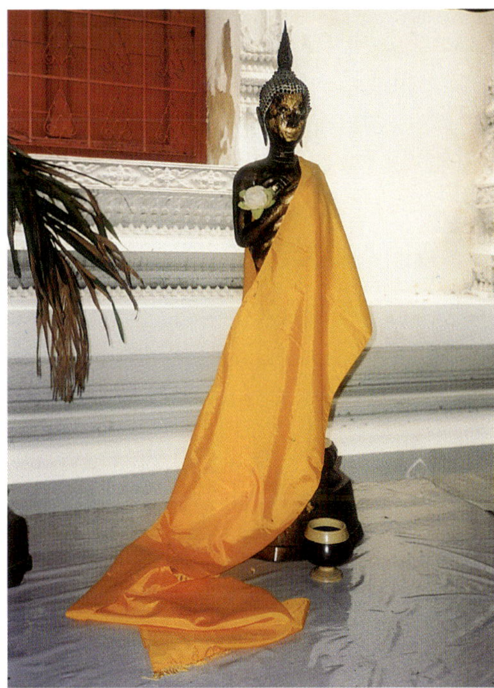

The general belief in change manifests a sense that earthly reality is ultimately transient and therefore to be sensually celebrated. Bangkok's arts are dedicated to fleeting experience. Food and textiles, silk and dance. Moments of vitality and vigour, bright colours and vivid experience. Festival and ritual. Malleable form provides the celebratory means, both important and casual. Acceptance of lifestyle freedom, tolerance as a social virtue. Perhaps simple acceptance for its own sake? A recognition of cyclical transformation and formal transience, related to the seasons and the rain, the land, rivers and canals. Ritual celebrations; the recognition of these ever-changing forms, and reminders of their possible transcendence.

And for the city – what is being remade in its various reconstructions? Bangkok, like its temples and citizens, lives in a process of constant change and redefinition. Yet these transformations define its essential spirit rather than attempt to create any future stability. In Bangkok, changes manifest a secure, if cryptic, sensibility, legible in the fluid experience of its principal elements.

Unstable Realities, Hidden Patterns

Bangkok is a liquid city, constructed of fickle forms. Change as existential model. A city whose shape dissipates when directly approached. Shades of Narcissus, tantalized by his own reflection on the water's beguiling surface. Bangkok is a mirror whose forms are visually potent yet fragile. Ungraspable but tantalizing and provocative. The unfathomable nature of the reclining Buddha, the soft rustle of coloured silk, the fleeting pleasures of highly spiced soup. Imperceptible orders, sensory and sensual

attractions. Challenging, and highly dangerous in excess. A place in which to lose one's wits.

Bangkok Post, 8 November 2001: An 'elderly (62)' Japanese man burns himself to death after shooting his Thai wife, aged thirty-two, and her alleged lesbian lover. His wife had moved in with their next-door neighbour, living openly in her new relationship. 16 January 2002: Police officer identified by a twelve-year-old girl as the man who paid her for sex. Other officers were involved as well.

It is easy to get lost on Bangkok's challenging terrain, trapped by its surfaces. Its lessons? The patterns that do exist are subtle. *Bangkok Post*, 8 October 2001 ('Kat's Window on Thailand')': 'Laundry Time' describes the unexpected difficulties that lurk in the simplest, most unexpected places. In this case, the unspoken rules for properly doing laundry. Clothes must be sorted based on the parts of the body they cover. Head to toe, a distinct hierarchy. Underwear, trousers, shirts, anything for the head; all are treated differently. Ideally, male and female garments are separated. Special taboos are applied to washing undergarments, governing both by whom and how. This ranking also directs how clothes are hung to dry. Buddhist amulets must never pass beneath female underwear. Submerged under Bangkok's apparent formlessness is a conscious culture full of unstated but necessary rules of conduct. Its patterns of order are celebrated in social practices and social rituals, its transient life the sources of artistic inspiration.

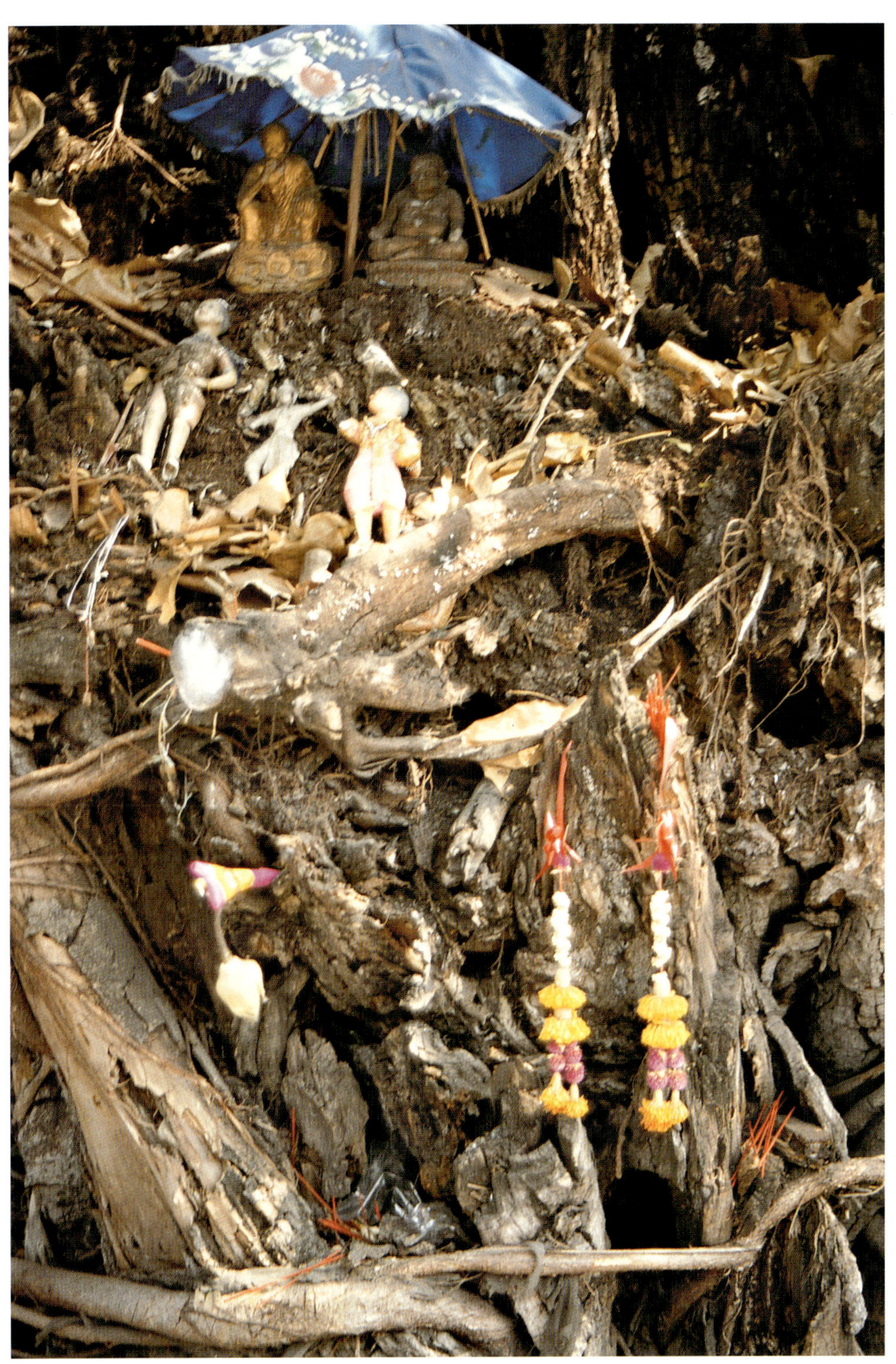

Formlessness as setting? Personal challenges. A path towards dissolution; a subconscious Bangkok.

Celebratory Flux

The major challenges of living in Bangkok are made simpler by the proliferation of its personal spirits. Underlying the official – and, for some, abstract – Buddhism, the city is a populated and animistic realm. Its streets and rivers are occupied by beings who best remain invisible. Spirit houses and charms are applied to ward off evil. The dangerous terrain is rendered safe by paying attention to its details.

This desire for greater spiritual tangibility is also fulfilled by the figures and stories of the *Ramakien*. It is interesting that the non-Rama Buddhist countries, such as Nepal, construct symbolic order through variations on representational cosmology. Kathmandu's Swayambathu Temple, for example, articulates a clear cosmological mountain, the stupa centred within its precinct. The superimposition of the smiling face on the architecture creates a more integrated composition than the paired conversations described by Bangkok's *wats*. Mandalas, the variations of the 'Wheel of Life' depicting earthly activity as a whirlwind of pain, and the portraits of the Buddha, appear as striking compositions, painted on portable canvases and temple walls. They locate perceptual and narrative realities within the forms of idealized universal order. Yet these clear articulations of cosmological symbol are rarely found in Bangkok.

Bangkok's symbolic orders remain less tangible and complete, its vivid images more attuned to earthly narratives than their celestial model. Communicative symbols are clearly still required, but they act in more varied ways.

In Bangkok the vividness of the transformed *Ramayana*, consciously installed by the city's founders, creates the link between personal belief, so tangibly evident in the talismans and charms, and the more abstract Buddhist principles embodied in the *wats*. The earthly struggle between good and evil (and Hanuman's fun) form its core rather than any abstract celestial framework. Its cosmology is more personal, and more crowded, its events grounded within the landscape of action. The narrative and its symbols act as intermediary. Rama is both a man and an avatar of Vishnu. More comprehensible in his passions and responsibilities, distant through his divinity. The value of this link underlies Bangkok's official celebrations. Masterpieces of choreographed order, ritual belief is re-created at the scale of the city. The Brahmanic symbols celebrating the divine kings

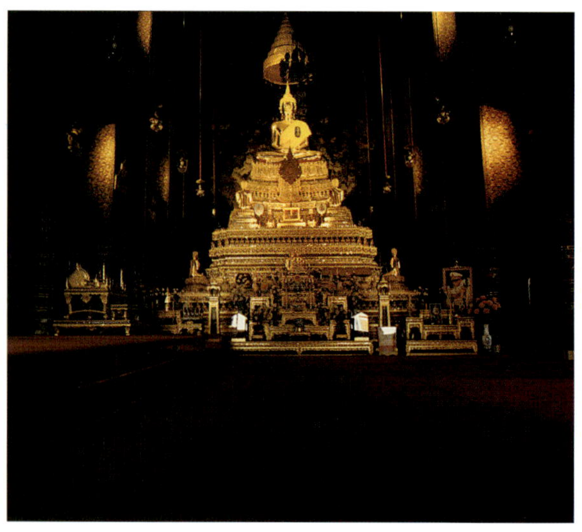

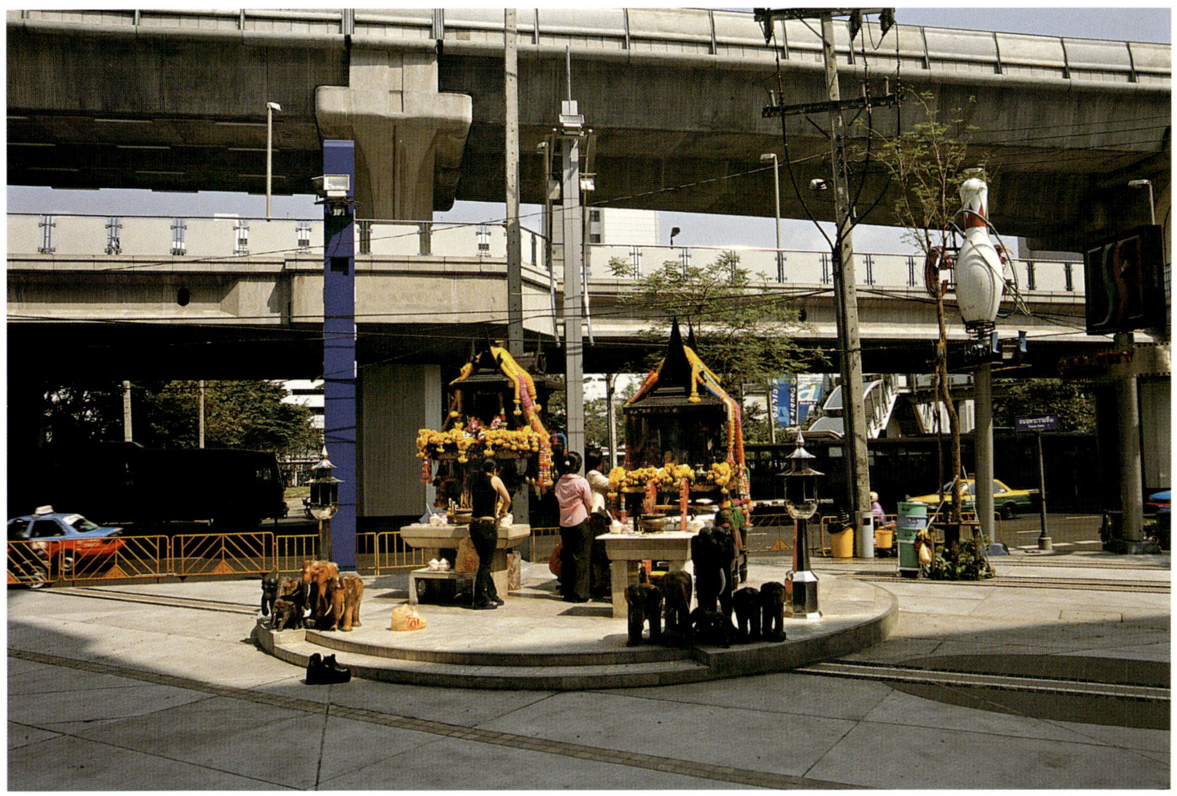

might appear antithetical to the city's Buddhist foundations. Yet they render the connection between personal and abstract order urbanistically legible. This change in scale, though still based in image, leads to more imaginative possibilities. The city and its celebratory symbols provide the intermediate link that makes the abstract ideals of Buddhist transcendence more approachable.

In Bangkok the important aspects of life that can be rendered or symbolized are given loving form. Images, mythical memories, journeys. Those conditions that should remain mysterious are alluded to or pointed at rather than illustrated. Yet their presence is recognized by these preparatory narrative foundations.

The importance of ritual. An early concern, an enduring reality. Bangkok has historically separated the world of commerce, typically associated with its Chinese merchants, from its places of symbolic expression. The precincts of practical work are situated just outside the city's walls. The more important activities within are rendered symbolically valuable by their location, ethnicity and striking forms. Observed in 1910, it is 'scarcely an exaggeration to say they [the Chinese] perform all the drudgery of the country while the Siamese exist in a state of blissful repose'.[2] For an American observer in the early twentieth century, the difficult and necessary work of maintaining ritual order is obscured by its apparent function as leisure.

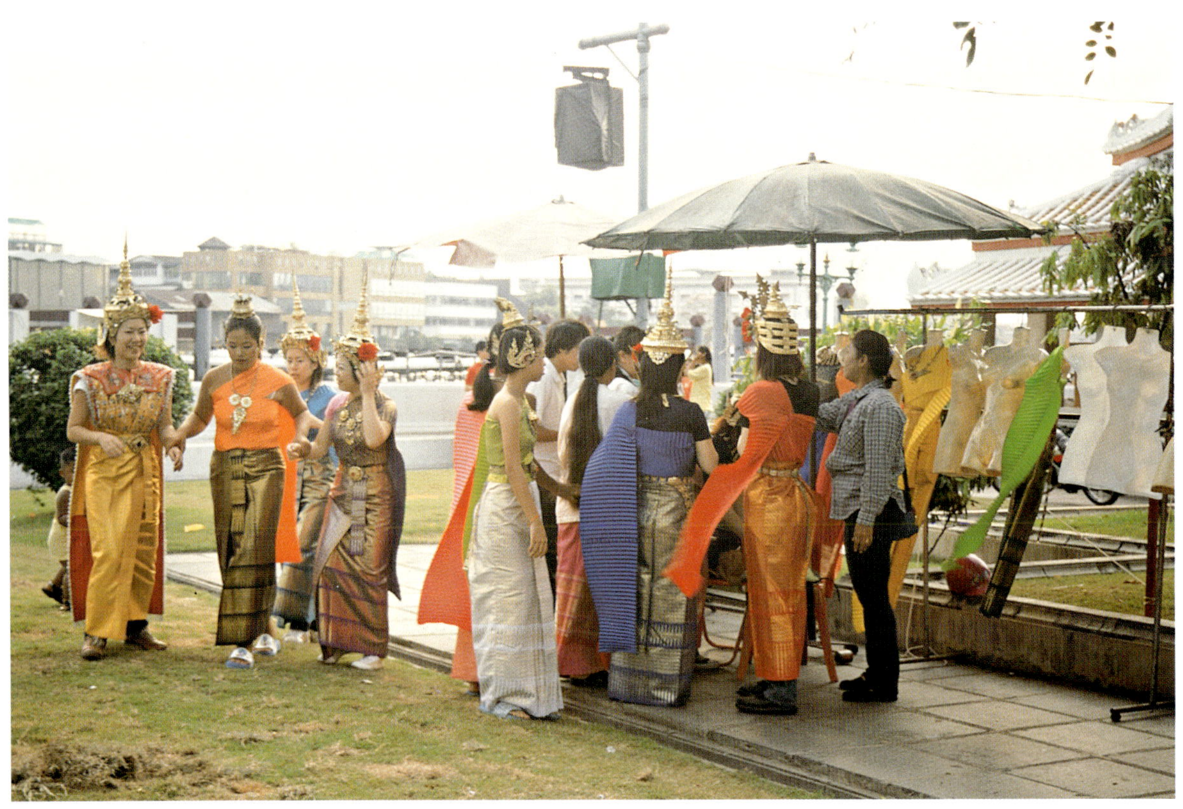

A question of focus and perceived significance.
Like all major cities, Bangkok faces many challenges.
For some observers this presents a seemingly
insurmountable condition. Yet, historically Bangkok
has solved its problems rather well. It just waits
longer than most, reacting only when the difficulties
become impossible to ignore. Until then these merely
practical issues do not appear to loom large in the
local consciousness. The new Sky Train works very
well, soon to be complemented by a subway. The
infrastructure helps to ameliorate the city's
horrendous traffic, and refocus its attention on
its environment. Late perhaps, arguably a decade
(or two) overdue, but just in time. Also in 1910:

Under the present system just enough of the
energy of the nation is devoted to necessary work
to enable the country to keep within measurable
distance of the times, but on the least excuse
serious work is suspended and all this energy
flows back into its natural channel, the
preparation of gorgeous pageants and shows.[3]

A city that inverts the importance of assumed
stabilities, issues of pressing practicality and the
value of its more significant ritual orders.

Celebration of instability, transient constructions.
Work or play? Perhaps versions of both. Bangkok
honours life's ephemera while also recognizing their
fate. Yet Bangkok, unlike Pattaya on the Gulf, is not

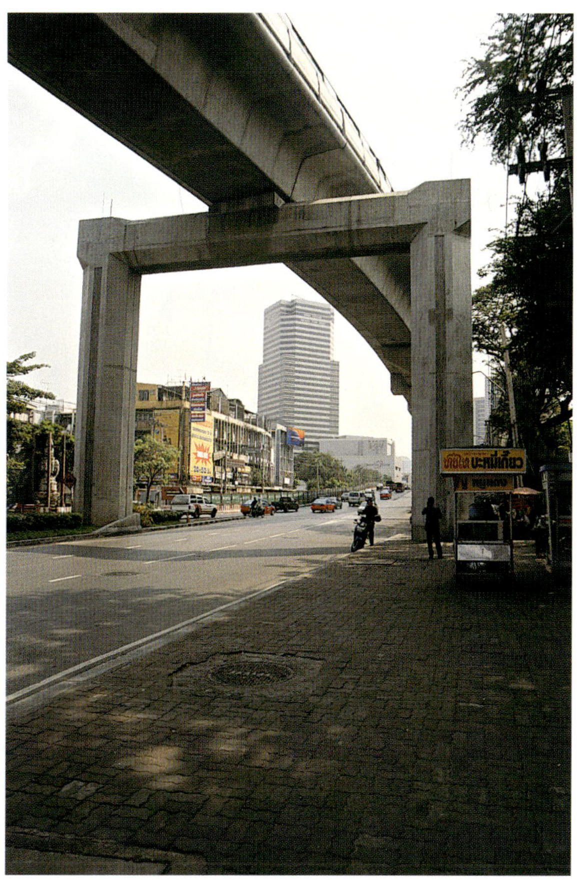

solely dedicated to the pleasures of surface. It highlights their qualities through exposure to an opposite, the metaphors of distant permanence embodied in the city's temples and landscapes. The city is a celebration of urban, and even existential, conversations.

Life in Balance

Order and ritual. Surface and transcendence. A city that renders a state of flux in variations of form and degree. The result is a perceptual unsteadiness, a challenging state. A reflection of necessary decisions:

hard work hiding under the illusions of lazy chaos and sensual freedom.

Bangkok manifests continued processes of constructed contradiction and tenuous balance. The qualities of light and dark, underworld and view, originally present in the *soi*–avenue pairing are vividly exaggerated in the experience of the Sky Train. An acceptance of the future is understood in terms that celebrate a mythical past. References to Mount Meru appear in a landscape devoid of topography. Land and water, the mountains and the sea. A city that is symbolically structured around ideal absence, but articulated in glittering form. Bangkok's contemporary constructions accentuate these contrasts. The relentless traffic adds to the tenuous instability of the ground. Sets of perplexing relations outline a dense field for possible interpretations.

Ordered contrasts? Articulated paths. The notion of path implies beginnings and ends, a sense of progression and some perception of development along the way. In Bangkok certain progressions are clear. From city to landscape, from outside to inside, and back. From the space of the image (the *bot*) to the *chedi*. The more abstract versions of passage and destination are articulated in the *chedis*' geometric progression, referential landscape and implied content (the relics of the Buddha). The path from the Golden Mount to the Grand Palace, Bangkok's most legible ceremonial route. A focused view is constructed towards the distant destination. Yet on arrival, Wat Phra Kaeo disappears behind its walls, to be represented by a small *chedi* floating above the boundary. Within, this symbol is dwarfed by the towers of the *wat*, their profusion of forms and colours accentuating the difference between the interior and the modest exterior image. No direct link

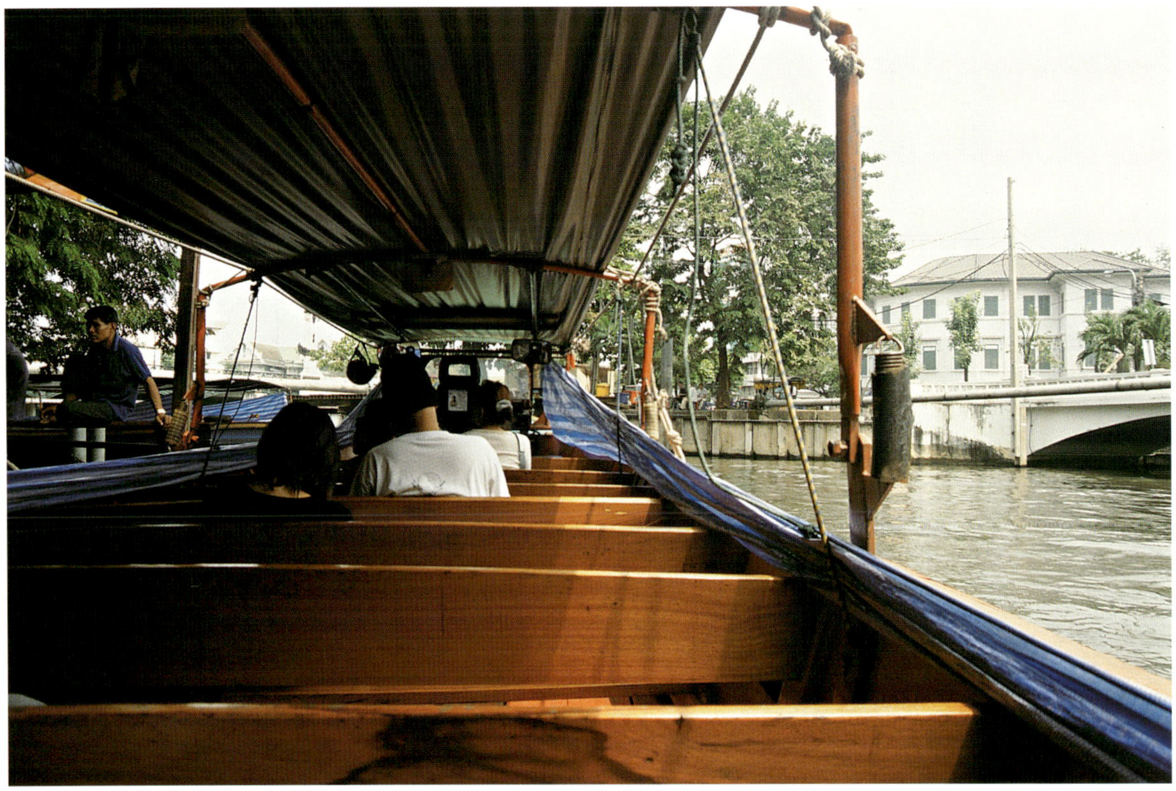

connects the route to the interior, the entry off-axis. Movement is displaced, requiring new orientations. Once inside, equally ambiguous travels. Distant orders presented, accomplishment always delayed. Glimpses, tantalizing beacons. Path as sequential education, yet never secure.

The broken journey. A crucial balance is constructed between these paths and their negation. Each journey must be visually enticing, but their physical resolution remains incomplete. Repeated dead-ends; cycles of metaphoric identity and rejection. The ground is unstable, the voyage difficult. And ultimately, each path is extended, each temporary achievement replaced. The *chedis'* points, the landscape's disappearance; the submersion into the mysterious depths of gold. An ascent to non-being.

The articulation of a powerful route without the support of a coherent ending is a difficult architectural challenge. Each path is articulated in form, yet each ultimately must reject form. Beauty is used to attract the participant, while it is also sacrificed as an illusory phenomenon. The ultimate pleasure of the path can only be mental, compelling in its impossible elegance and crystalline difficulty. In resolution, beauty as tool and trap, guide and distraction. Each angelic message is presented to be replaced and discarded.

Arguably these paths are intentionally constructed to reveal an objective truth. The city, a pedagogic

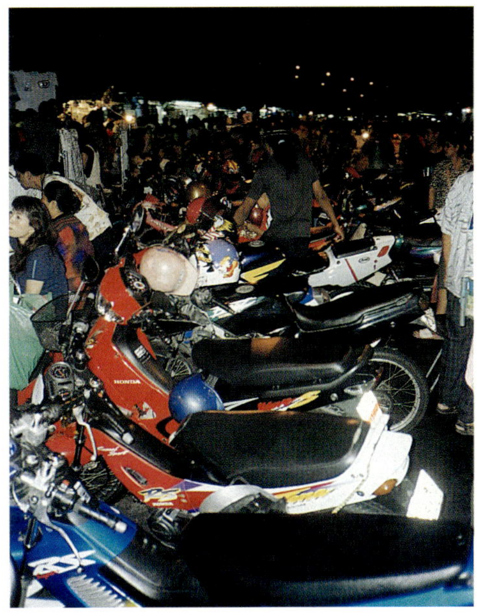

tool. But they are troubling lessons, resisting easy acceptance. Yet a sense of potential discovery is always present, whether in the partly defined axis, the fragments of light or the enigmatic smiles of the statues. Tantalizing, occasionally frustrating, always mysterious. This sense of incompletion, analogous to Bangkok's social humour and tolerance, reminds one of the necessary fluidity of earthly life, and the necessity of accepting its challenging realities.

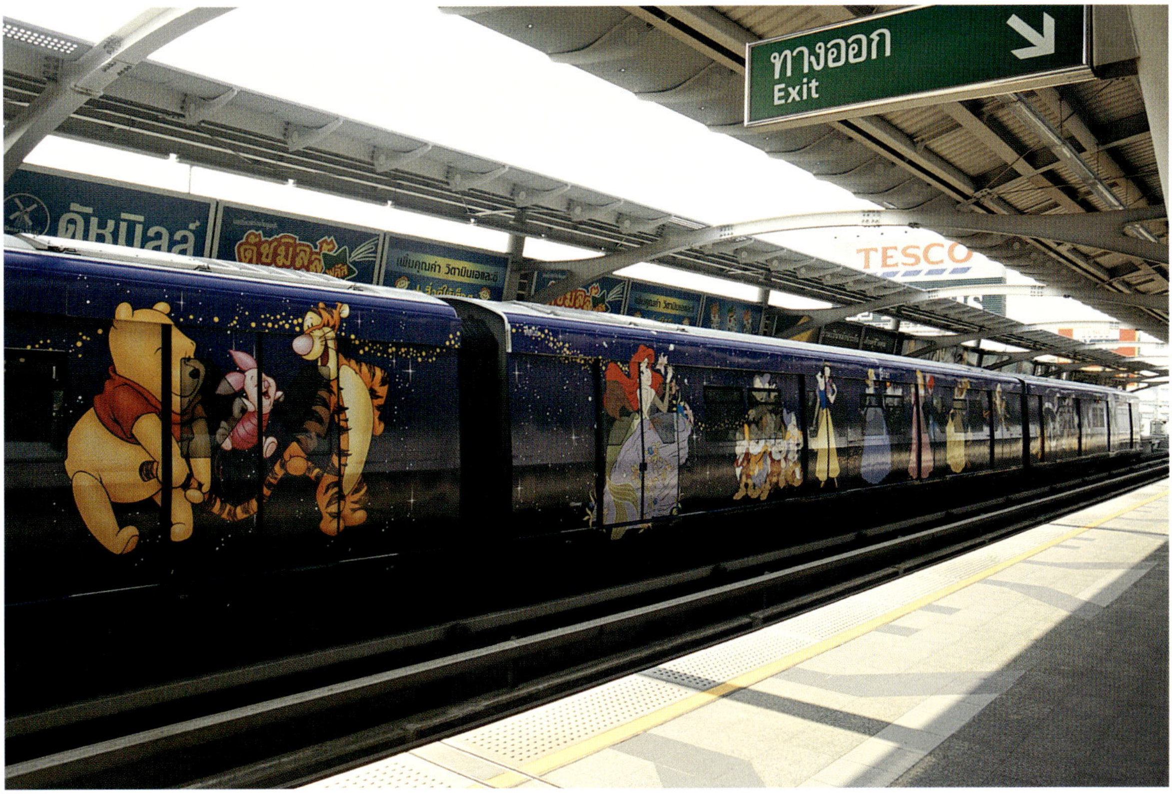

Bangkok internalizes and accentuates its own polemical dialectics. The means, a centred island carved from the marsh. A vision of royal eternity paralleled with a Buddhist dream of ultimate disappearance. Contradictory desires, built into a single urban phenomenon. Its lineaments: sculpted water. And which dream is victorious? What takes precedence in Bangkok's definition? A shared coexistence or a state of contented confusion? Ambiguous grounding as urban intent? This mental condition bears a challenging relation to the greater city, and perhaps the idea of the city in general. Bangkok, originally so perplexing, gradually coheres around its own attitudes. An urban narrative is experienced as a synthetic revelation. Possible lessons. Perhaps Bangkok is becoming increasingly coherent as narrative, some parts made almost uninhabitable to clarify the sense of the invisible other. A city that knows its own earthly destiny, and strives to articulate its opposite.

These conditions would seem to argue against a strong architectural culture. Yet so much of the place conspires to make the senses come alive. Consciously contradictory; a seeming paradox. Bangkok is an island, a refuge from artificial clarity. The celebration of life itself, structured through its conversation with its symbolic images of enduring form, animates the city in a rich architectural pageant.

Seasonal flooding foreshadowing the final descent into the sea. Bangkok, a new Atlantis under construction? A city of varied destinies and varied lessons. A city of myth with a more general urban message. The role of form today.

Form as Function

Bangkok is a challenge, demanding constant reassessment. A city in motion whose physical instabilities require continuous mental recon-struction. The role of urban form? A question for the city in general. Bangkok's metaphoric foundations are obscured by its contemporary flux. Fragments of imaginary landscape hidden within the celebration of rapid growth. The city's traffic: part of the journey. The froth of illusory movement, articulating the ground as the boats animate the river. Without stability, its floating condition is a challenge to expectation. Within this demanding context Bangkok's forms create vivid moments, rendering generic conditions specific. The city doesn't propose to control its landscape through formal order, but rather to highlight its distinct parts and heighten their conversation. To sharpen contrasts and articulate differences. Its purpose, the creation of vital, if subtle, frictions. The city is a place of architectural dualities. An existential state rather than a fixed image.

Bangkok presents no clearly resolved structure, or any coherent cosmological image. The city is the realm of the terrestrial and the transformative. And what can be transformed will eventually pass away. Resolved civic form is ultimately pointless. Symbolic nature applied as part of a metaphoric passage is, however, another issue. Contrasting images and sensibilities are brought to urban experience for a transformative purpose. The articulation of possible journeys. The sky, the mountains, the sea: all participate in Bangkok's landscape through image and suggested intent. Each articulates a distant destination, supported by its own architectural analogues. The more extreme the better. The result, a dense field of overlapping provocations and reminders.

The lack of formal closure central to Bangkok's experience helps to explain why the city is so little appreciated in world architectural culture. The coherent mountainous constructions of Angkor and Borobudur present clear images. They are remarkable in their scale and articulated craft, and comprehensible in their total symbolic order. These works are easily consumed within the perspectival imagination of the post-Renaissance West. Bangkok and its *wats* are much less final, less presentably complete. They cannot be quickly understood through any single metaphor of ideal order, or simply represented. Their embodied sensations of oscillation and ambiguity remain more symbolically perplexing. An architecture of discourse, difficult to encapsulate.

Yet this lack of historical finality is also a virtue. Bangkok is difficult to dismiss through allegorical summaries. The city reflects on its challenges, without relying on a comfortable submission to historic order. The greater formal clarity of an ideal past may be appreciated as a foil, remembered in part, but it cannot provide the answers for the more complex present. Bangkok's state is more strikingly contemporary, active and vivid. Indeed, Bangkok has arguably intuited the conditions of the modern world, and accepted the challenges of their future extrapolation. The city recognizes the pleasures of form and their limitations as bearers of contemporary symbolic coherence, and strives to articulate this relation. It refuses to accept the redundancy of form, a lazy conclusion prevalent elsewhere. Nor does it revert to a totalizing historicism. The fractious debate is held open, lively, dramatic and even humorous within the city's experimental culture.

Urban Message

On the delta plain, resting partly below sea level, Bangkok is subject to regular flooding. Areas of the city temporarily disappear every year. The city's plan becomes barely legible, visible in historic traces and built superstructure alone. This disordered condition seems to manifest a lazy acceptance of chaos. Yet the opposite may also be true. Bangkok, in its negation of land-based formal value, may be flowing to its true future, towards a shimmering aqueous state that directly challenges the limitations of terrestrial existence. Bangkok – its lessons complex – manifests a curious desire to explain. Its mission: to make tangible an ineffable coexistence. The physical landscape: a preparatory arena, a place to escape from. The city, a construction floating between. Blending or sharpening the differences.

Bangkok, city as mirror. To an extent all cities, in varying degrees, reflect their inhabitants back to them. A form of stability, this reflection may also be a challenge. Bangkok's less secure images are here especially poignant. In its flickering reflections the

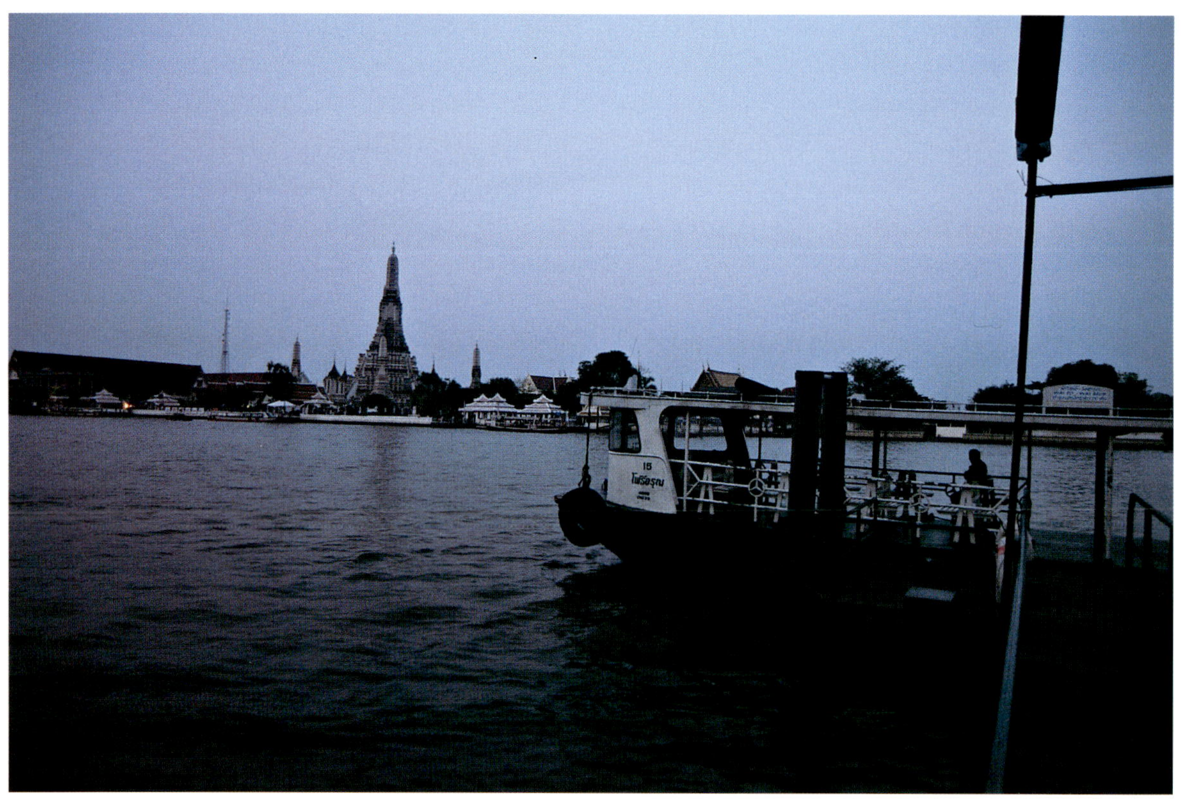

city appears more as an illusion or mirage than as a picture of comfortable reinforcement. But which? Illusion implies an intentional deception, its images constructed to create mistaken interpretations. Fraud. An intentional deception or simply the result of perceptual errors? Illusions, however temporarily solid, are eventually rejected once the truth is known, their life limited by their artificiality. The mirage? Equally intangible, perhaps even more so, yet a mirage is more a receptacle of desires and dreams than an intentional deception. A mirage is never taken at face value, except at times of delusion or delirium (the times when it is most likely to appear). One may wish clear answers on it, but the difficult responsibilities of perception lie with the viewer.

Delphic inscrutability; hidden truths. Deceptive or cryptic forms may still exist, but they are less intentional, less controllable. Indeed, mirages have a more natural connotation, conditions created from the dangerous combinations of heat, landscape and desire. They require a particular mental state for their full effect to be legible: their interpretation ever more challenging.

The more accurate metaphor of Bangkok? The mirage. Its mysterious forms, less consciously manipulated for personal gain. The city has its illusory aspects, but as a whole it doesn't maintain the formal consistency necessary to a convincing illusion. Bangkok is less imagistically focused. Indeed, its subtle ambiguities are a major part of its experience.

At times of mental clarity its sensibilities serve to break down illusion, since they create doubts, surfacing alongside the brilliant and seductive images. The city resists easy answers and interpretations, and confronts preconceptions. Its allusions to formal order provide only partial, if critical, clues. A compelling challenge.

To follow these clues without self-destructing. To maintain balance on its fine edge. Bangkok articulates a cognitive precipice, sharpened by its vivid open questions. The city remains an existential provocation, a condition long since lost in the comfortable familiarity of Fifth Avenue or the Rue St Honoré. City as challenge rather than as sheltered historic refuge from the encroaching contemporary world. Bangkok's form, while perhaps pointless in itself, is crucial in maintaining this urban conversation. Forms as contrast, as partial journey pointing to different understandings. Form, not as an image of arbitrary or historical order, but as symbol in the classic sense.

Bangkok slowly sinks into the sea, the strange flickering city returning to its ineffable state. An urban anti-myth? The original Atlantis disappeared through natural cataclysm. The disappearance of this new Atlantis, practically underwater already, is assisted by the calamity of modernity. Progress assisting process. With the expressways and Sky Train turning the city upside down, Bangkok appears to be accelerating towards its doom. The city's circumstance during the rainy season illustrates its tenuous hold on reality. Its rapid submersion a desired end. Perhaps it is only through this submersion that Bangkok can return to its ideal state. Daily life carried out below, in a strange and introspective world of its own, its visions of clarity floating above. Roofs and water. A self-conscious urge to make the ideal city real, to render its symbolic messages actual, even if it involves a large degree of self-destruction? A desired disappearance? A longed-for myth fulfilled, for taking the city's intangible ideals to be their logical conclusion?

Universal Lessons

It is difficult to balance an urban sensibility based on a barely tangible attitude with a desire for its experiential legibility. This quality can't be inferred through fixed formal orders. Its ambiguous images must remain in a tensile relationship to their urban function. Formal power is crucial, yet is never randomly applied. One is placed within a greater mass, understood, at best, only through metaphor. A delicate balance, rendered even more difficult by rapid growth. In the contemporary metropolis, size is at least partly responsible for the disappearance of legible urban order. In Bangkok, as elsewhere, progress is the unspoken historic protagonist of formlessness. Bangkok may be an angelic construction, but it is not one easily or fully understood. As a result, Bangkok is a version of the modern city, rendered extreme.

Bangkok: the revelation of an existential state. It maintains few illusions, but, rather, it manifests an honest and exuberant celebration of human limits and desires. A celebration with no simple answers. It is not based on a clear articulation of political authority. Its social orders are most evident in the urban precincts rather than in the city as a whole, each participating in the collective revelation of intent. The city reflects an open process of conversation, involving its different characters and

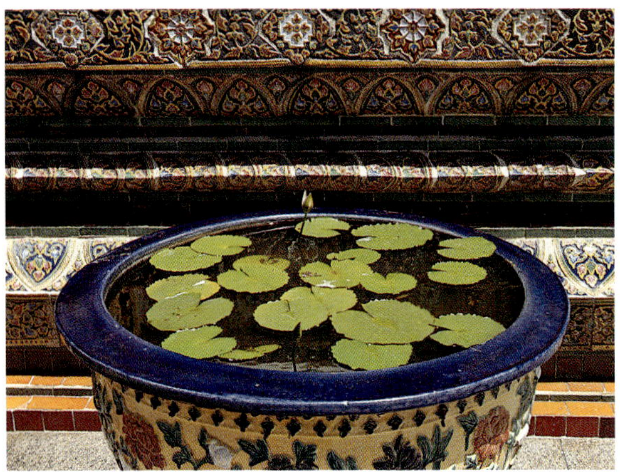

their possibilities simultaneously. Symbols are required, but are not relied on for an easy formal or historical clarity. Indeed, an avoidance of artificial closure or an illusory formal conclusion becomes a working principle within the city's experience.

This is a condition to be recognized and even celebrated. Bangkok narrates a quality or concern, not a single story. This revelation of a contemporary state of affairs is particularly relevant to the city today. Bangkok accepts the challenges that other cities avoid. An extreme version of a more general state. A more honest city, aware of its necessary incom-pletion, which thereby avoids any presumptuous finality. Bangkok leaves the questions of urban purpose provocatively open. Angelic message, foundation of the mythical city? It is an open and largely optimistic vision of the future, accepting of human frailties while pointing towards their possible transcendence. But with an awareness of the risk that such openness implies. Risk as an embodied urban condition. Balance between order and social flexibility, between a belief in symbolic history and an acceptance of daily reality.

Bangkok's ultimate message: an acceptance of change and seeming chaos in the desire to maintain an open relation to the future. A rejection of easy formal solutions. Architecture and urban form are special, but there is little presumption that they can provide any permanent answers on their own. Form exists to point the way, as do the festivals. A synthetic attitude, expressed in its various parts. Any final completion is the responsibility of the individual, a mental condition implicit in the urban challenge. In Bangkok, a challenge with provocative distractions highlighted along the way. The city points towards a greater understanding, and makes the journey as difficult as possible.

This all sounds rather grand. Perhaps getting carried away. Bangkok is, after all, a messy place, full of debris and social inequity. But its mysterious sensibilities continue to captivate and perplex. In a world so often more insidiously polluted by faceless historicism or official form masking mind-numbing social banality, being placed on a more explicitly uncomfortable edge might have value in itself. Messy, dense, chaotic, but symbolically rich. And honest. Bangkok: a difficult place to live; a good place to be alive.

Maps

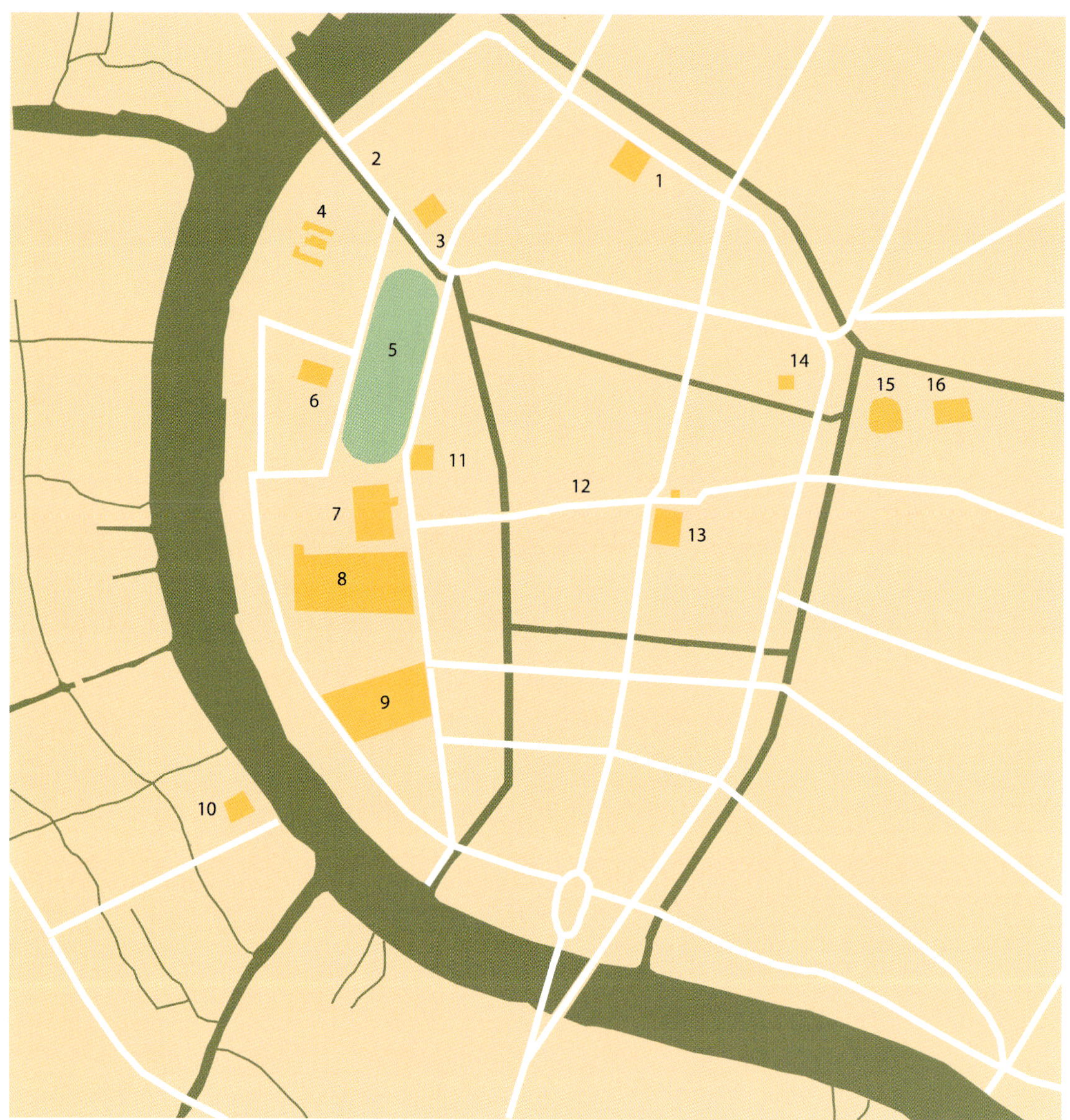

Central Bangkok		
1	Wat Bowenniwet	9 Wat Po
2	Phrapinklao Bridge Road	10 Wat Arun
3	National Gallery	11 Lak Muang
4	National Museum	12 Thanon Bamrung Muang
5	Sanam Luang	13 Wat Suthat
6	Wat Mahathat	14 Rachanadaram/Loha Prasat
7	Grand Palace: Wat Phra Kaeo	15 The Golden Mount
8	Grand Palace	16 Wat Saket

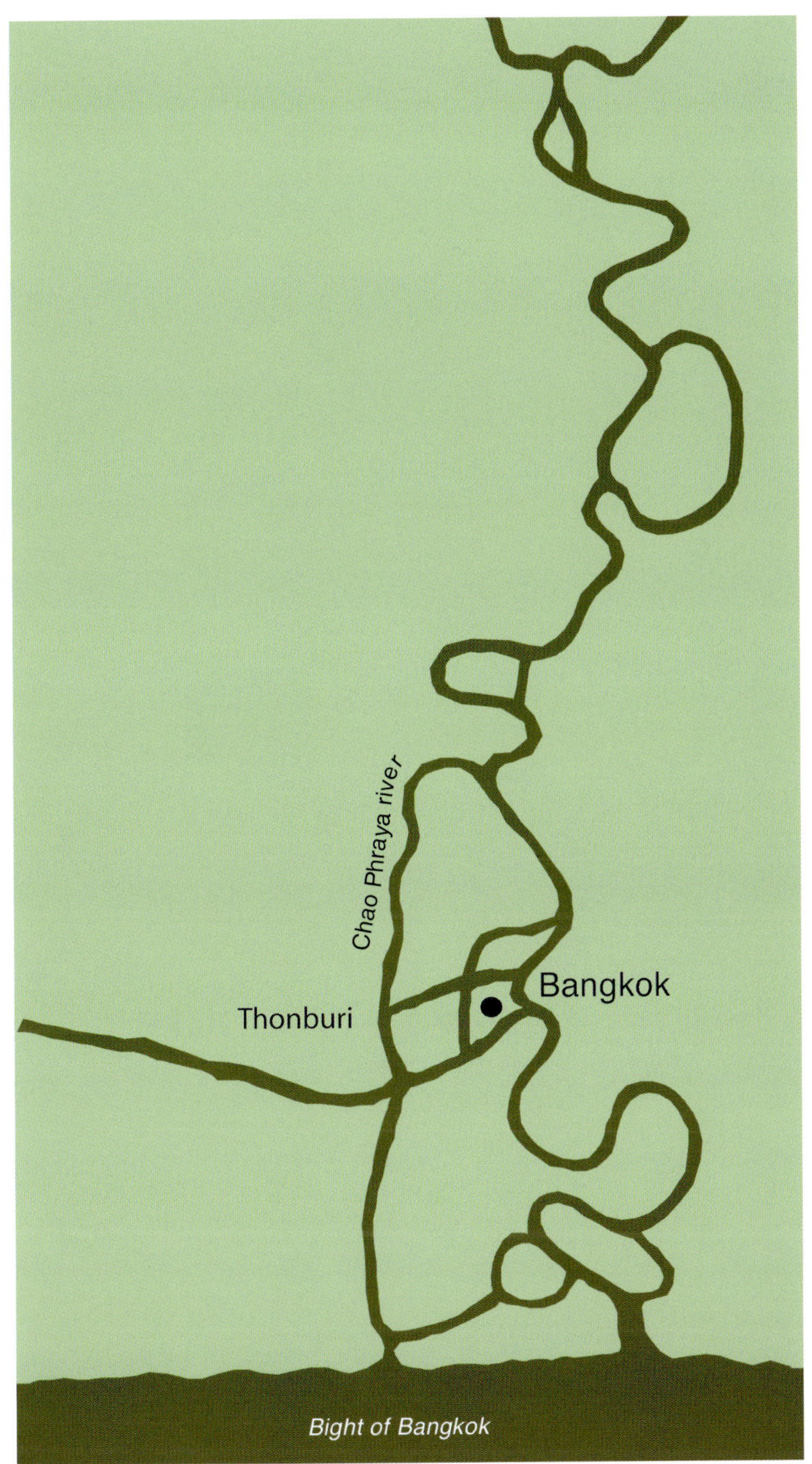

Chao Phraya river
Thonburi
Bangkok
Bight of Bangkok

References

ONE

1 Anna Harriet Leonowens, *Anna and the King of Siam: The English Governess at the Siamese Court (Being Recollections of Six Years in the Royal Palace at Bangkok)* (London, 1870).
2 *The Dhammapada* (Harmondsworth, 1973), 4.46.

TWO

1 This ideal of horizon is protected in Bangkok's building practices. No tall buildings are allowed within the core district / Grand Palace area to protect the predominant image of the royal centre. Immediately at its edges, now marked by bridges, large condominium towers appear, the first markers of the newer commercial city surrounding the symbolic. As a result Bangkok's general skyline is more like a bowl than a mountain, an inverted city.
2 Leon Battista Alberti, *On Painting* (Harmondsworth, 1991).
3 Karl Dohring, *The Country and People of Siam* (Bangkok, 1999), note to plate 74.

THREE

1 Gavin Pattison and John Villiers, *The Blue Guide: Thailand* (London, 1997).

FOUR

1 David K. Wyatt, *Thailand: A Short History* (New Haven and London, 1984), p. 56.
2 See Karl Dohring, *Buddhist Temples of Thailand* (Bangkok, 2000).
3 Jumet Jumsai, *Naga* (Bangkok, 1997), pp. 88–92.
4 Dohring, *Buddhist Temples*, pp. 31–3.

FIVE

1 Wyatt, *Thailand: A Short History*, p. 147.
2 Ayutthaya was itself a referential transposition of Ayodhya, Rama's textual home.
3 Wyatt, *Thailand: A Short History*, p. 146.
4 *Ibid.*, pp. 134–44.
5 Naga Jumet Jimsai, *Cultural Origins in Siam and the West Pacific* (Bangkok, 1977), p. 72.
6 *Ramakien: The Thai Ramayana*, ed. Meechai Thongthip (Bangkok, 1993), cf Ch. 9, note 1.

SIX

1 Engelbert Kaempfer, *A Description of the Kingdom of Siam, 1690* (Bangkok, 1996), p. 68.
2 P. A. Thompson, *Siam: An Account of the Country and the People* (Bangkok, 1987).
3 Jumsai, *Naga*, p. 33.

SEVEN

1 Thompson, *Siam*, p. 45.
2 Kaempfer, *Kingdom of Siam, 1690*, p. 26.
3 The present construction was completed under the reign of Rama III, enlarging an earlier figure. In 1780 King Taksin, the founder of Thonburi and immediate predecessor to Rama I, brought the Emerald Buddha to the site, bringing additional value to its new temporary home.

EIGHT

1 *The Dhammapada*, trans. Juan Mascaro (London, 1973), 4.46 (p. 42).

NINE

1 *Ramakien*, ed. Meechai Thongthip, p. 62.
2 Thompson, *Siam*, p. 57.
3 Thompson, *Siam*, p. 57.

List of Illustrations